William Scott

of
Fairfield County
South Carolina

and

His Descendents

O'Levia Neil Wilson Wiese

HERITAGE BOOKS
2018

HERITAGE BOOKS

AN IMPRINT OF HERITAGE BOOKS, INC.

Books, CDs, and more—Worldwide

For our listing of thousands of titles see our website
at
www.HeritageBooks.com

A Facsimile Reprint
Published 2018 by
HERITAGE BOOKS, INC.
Publishing Division
5810 Ruatan Street
Berwyn Heights, Md. 20740

Heritage Books by the author:

Cemetery Records of Greene County, Alabama, and Related Areas

A. F. Carl Wiese Descendants

William Scott of Fairfield County, South Carolina and His Descendents

The Woodville Republican: *Mississippi's Oldest Existing Newspaper:*

Volume 1: December 18, 1823–December 17, 1839

Volume 2: January 4, 1840–October 30, 1847

Volume 3: January 8, 1848–January 9, 1855

Volume 4: June 22, 1878–December 25, 1880

Volume 5: January 1, 1881–December 22, 1883

Volume 6: January 5, 1884–December 26, 1891

Volume 7: January 5, 1892–December 28, 1895

CD: *The Woodville Republican, Volumes 1-5*

— Publisher's Notice —

International Standard Book Number
Paperbound: 978-0-7884-5768-5

CONTENTS

INTRODUCTION

The initial concept for this book on the history of the SCOTT family began eleven years ago as my mother,Mittie Scott Wilson,and I were reminiscing about the separation of her parents,Vivi Ione Deloach and Samuel Scott,of Doloroso, Mississippi,a community approximately fifteen miles south of Natchez on Highway #61.After a stormy,but prolific marriage,the two had parted,each taking several children.

Living with her father,a logger in Mound,Louisiana,Mama spent her school years boarding with various families in order to receive an education. As these lonely years proved painful,very little was ever mentioned about her early years except she lovingly talked about her father and his youngest brother,Walter,who still lived in Doloroso. The memories of Uncle Walter and his wife Mary's,love and kindness during her brief visits to Doloroso had remained with Mama throughout her life.

One day I casually asked her about Aunt Annis Deloach Dooley,an aunt whom we had met in New Orleans at my grandmother's funeral. A simple phone call was the initial contact with Mama's family. The ensuing visits with Aunt Annis and Uncle Walter's daughter, Sherry Johnson and her husband Joe,provided me with data on both the DELOACH and the SCOTT families.Also,the SCOTT brothers from Fairfield,County,South Carolina, had married women from Wilkinson County; therefore,additional information was available in Woodville,the county seat of Wilkinson County.It was a simple step to document,to some degree,the lateral lines of these women.Thus,the JETER/GETER and the HOLMES lines are added in hope that someday,someone will continue rsearching these lines.The compilation of the DELOACH line must wait a short while.

Since that day in 1974,"kissing cousins" or descendents of these SCOTT brothers who immigrated into Wilkinson County from South Carolina,can be found not only in the states of Louisiana,Texas, Mississippi,Georgia and South Carolina, but scattered throughout the United States.

The reader must take into consideration that if time and age have distorted facts and truths,these memories are better than knowing nothing.

ACKNOWLEDGMENTS

This book could not have been written without the assistance and interest of many people. Not only have the relatives given strong support, but strangers were kind enough to give information concerning the family history as well as the family connections.

My sincere gratitude must go to JOE and SHERRY JOHNSON of Doloroso, Mississippi for their patience and fortitude in answering numerous questions. HERBERT (Pappy) JENSEN's colorful accounts of his younger days created pictures in my mind.

To my first cousins, CLARA TOWER HODGE, ROSE SCOTT MOORE and EDWARD SCOTT, I appreciate your belief in what I was attempting to do. To DORIS CARTER, ADRIAN GETER and DELLA COPELAND who shared the Holmes and Geter families with me. I thank you all.

The visit to Fairfield County, South Carolina was enhanced by the friendly people in Winnsboro. MR. GARY BASS, SR., MR. W.W. LEWIS, and MRS. RUTH STEVENSON gave much of their valuable time to help strangers from Texas. MRS. ISABEL HOY DUNLOP and her cousin, MRS. ALEX BALLENTINE, both descendents of Elisha and Jeminia Gibson Scott of Fairfield, County, are still working with me on a positive family connection.

FRANK JERNIGAN of Sumter, South Carolina must be recognized as the prime source in locating the WILLIAM and ANN SCOTT land. His letters throughout these years have been a source of delight and inspiration.

In Monterey, Louisana live two ladies that did not know exactly how they were related until the compilation of this information was begun. Both THELMA ENLOW GIRLINGHOUSE and MARVIN TRISLER PAUL, retired schoolteachers, have shared their homes and hours of correspondance with me in gathering information on the SCOTT brothers who eventually settled in Concordia and Catahoula Parishes. In 1985, Thelma, Marvin, and Thelma's sister, MELBA WHITE, joined FRANCES SCOTT THORNBURG and me in locating the WILLIAM SCOTT, JR.'s homeplace in Catahoula Parish.

Frances, who lives in my home town, was an added bonus when I discovered her father's line in the Central Texas Genealogical quarterly. Although we were both members, we did not know each other. She is a direct descendent of Thomas Francis Scott, the "lost brother" of my ancestor, Henry Scott. Since then, she has been another support to me while writing this book.

To RACHEL SCOTT MCGEE REEVES, a sincere thank you for sharing Judge McGee's notes on the Scott family.

To my husband, Ernest Ray Wiese, I extend my greatest appreciation for his support and forebearance in these last nine years. He has lived through interruptions that no normal man (who loves sports) should live through.

DEDICATION

THIS BOOK IS LOVINGLY DEDICATED TO MY MOTHER,MITTIE SCOTT WILSON

PASSAGE

"Come for the weekend Mom," I said.
(She is quite lonely now that dad is dead.)
"You know I'm writing our family history,
And you can be a reference aid for me."

I have a desk,and I computerize my book.
My mother stood behind me for a careful look.
She would smile and nod at the flickering screen,
The heart produced people,not words,that we've seen.

Ah,time meets time,and heart meets heart.
Through books and love our family will never part.
The room was still;yet a slight breeze stirred.
"No," I thought." 'Twas a movement,a whisper,I heard."

'Twas a flutter,a soft touch,a kiss on my face,
And I know that my father had given me grace.
Our love had torn the time curtains apart
And we met,momentarily,heart-to heart.

                              Lenora A. Gates

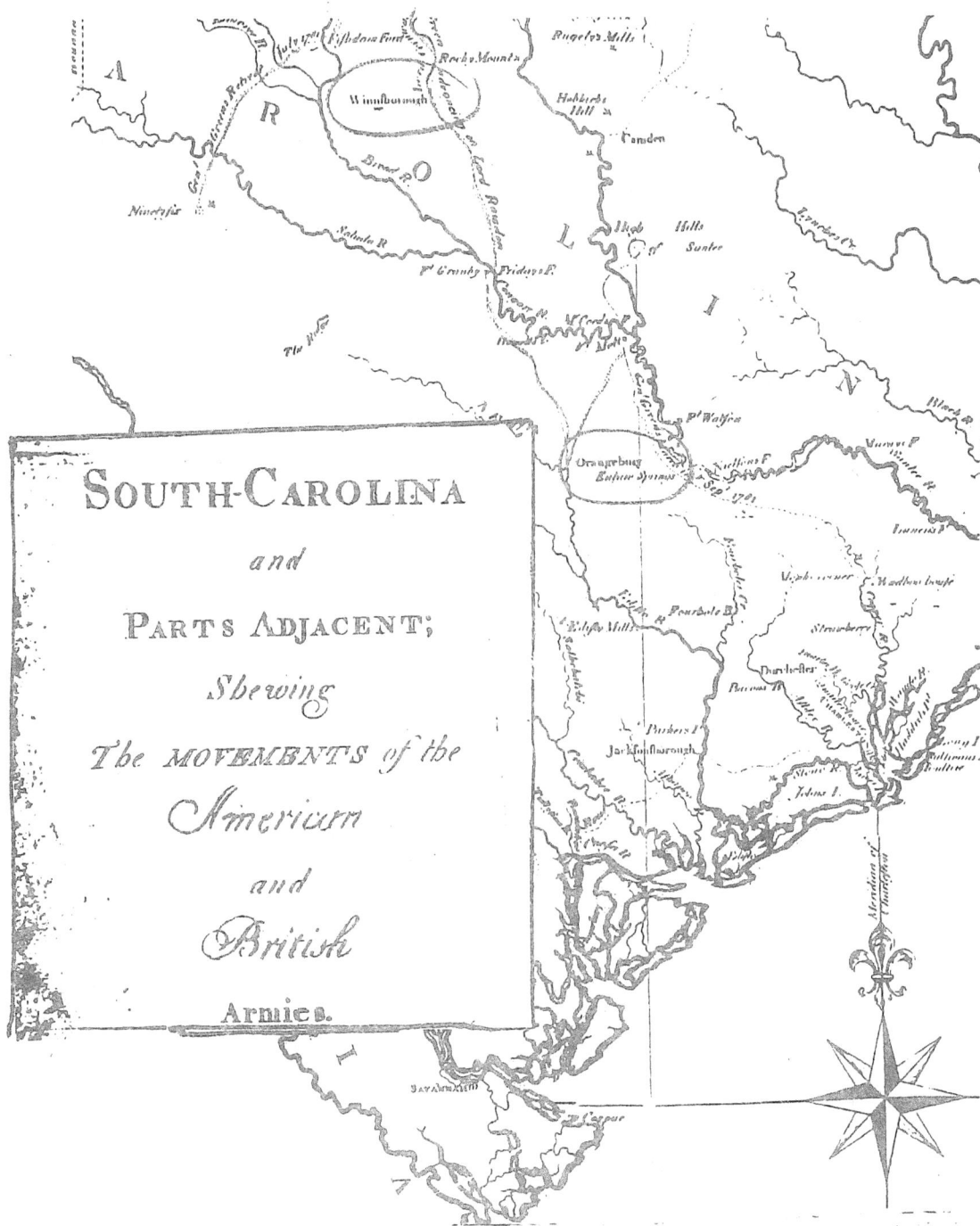

SOUTH-CAROLINA

and

PARTS ADJACENT;

Shewing

The MOVEMENTS of the

American

and

British

Armies.

V

WINNSBORO

S.C. Highway Dept
1984

LEGEND

1 - Wm & Ann Scott's Home pla...
2 - Scott's Crossing + Cemetery
3 - Williams Scott's 193 Acres
Old O Horeb Church

FOREST COUNTY

BROAD RIVER

418 - Acres

20 Chd po Inchi

Pine 30 n

Pine 30 n

Pine 30 n

(Road to Hillsboro land)

567   25

The Est of
John Robertson

Wm Scott

William Scott
Land —

Joshua Player bought this 418 Acre plat joining William Scott's "Homeplace"
of 100 Acres, more or less. This plat was originally granted to James Andrews
for 300 Acres. James Andrews's son, John was a witness to George Scott's will
in 1790 as well as John Robertson who owned land adjoining William Scott
around 1800......
                    (Frank Jernagan 1980)

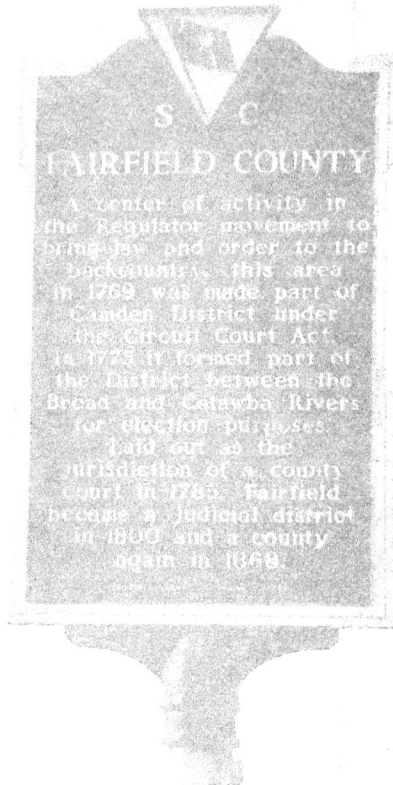

S C

FAIRFIELD COUNTY

A center of activity in the Regulator movement to bring law and order to the backcountry, this area in 1769 was made part of Camden District under the Circuit Court Act. In 1775 it formed part of the District between the Broad and Catawba Rivers for election purposes. Laid out as the jurisdiction of a county court in 1785, Fairfield became a judicial district in 1800 and a county again in 1868.

FAIRFIELD COUNTY
HISTORICAL
MUSEUM

The simple elegance of Federal architecture was chosen by Richard Cathcart when he built this home for his family in 1830. Located on Congress Street in Winnsboro, County Seat of Fairfield County, South Carolina, it has been a landmark in the area for over one hundred forty-seven years and now houses the Fairfield County Historical Museum.

Winnsboro, settled in the mid 18th Century, was chartered as a town in 1784.

On March 15, 1976, the beautifully restored Cathcart-Ketchin house in Winnsboro, opened its doors as the Fairfield County Museum with a collection of over 2000 items of historical interest. A special event is held every fourth Sunday in each month.

OLDEST CONTINUOUSLY RUNNING TOWN CLOCK IN THE UNITED
STATES. ERECTED 1833. Winnsboro,S.C.

FAIRFIELD COUNTY COURT HOUSE (1823)
WINNSBORO,SOUTH CAROLINA

Mr.Glen Bass Sr. and Ray at "SCOTTS CROSSING"
Mr.Bass was instrumental in cutting this road during
the years that he was county supervisor.

Granite quarry

Card 1 (top left)

S. | 3 | S.C.

George Scott

Prt, { Captain Joseph Warley's Co. in the 3d South Carolina Reg't of Continental Troops commanded by Col. William Thomson.

(Revolutionary War.)

Appears on

Company Pay Roll

of the organization named above for the month
of .... to July 1 ...., 1779 .
Commencement of pay .... Febry 7, 17 .
Commencement of subsistence .... , 17 .
To what time .... , 17 .
Amt. of time for pay .... 4mo. 24 days
Amt. of time for subsistence ....
Pay per month ....
Subsistence per month ....
Amt. of pay .... 32 dollars
Amt. of subsistence ....

Amt. of Continental and State pay:

Days ....
Pay per day ....
Amount .... $96 - - -

Card 2 (top middle)

S. | 3 | S.C.

George Scott

Prt, { Captain Joseph Warley's Co. in the 3d South Carolina Reg't of Continental Troops commanded by Col. William Thomson.

(Revolutionary War.)

Appears on

Company Pay Roll

of the organization named above for the month
of .... to August 1, 1779 .
Commencement of pay .... , 17 .
Commencement of subsistence .... , 17 .
To what time .... , 17 .
Amt. of time for pay ....
Amt. of time for subsistence ....
Pay per month .... 6 60 dollars
Subsistence per month .... 6 60 dollars
Amt. of pay .... 6 60 dollars
Amt. of subsistence ....

Amt. of Continental and State pay:

Days ....
Pay per day ....
Amount .... $20 - - -

Card 3 (top right)

S. | 3 | S.C.

George Scott

Appears with the rank of .... Prt .... on

Pay Roll

of Capt. Joseph Warley's Co., in the 3d Reg't commanded by Col. William Thomson, for the additional pay allowed by the State of South Carolina

(Revolutionary War,)

for the month of .... August ...., 1779 .
Amt. of time for Continental pay ....
Amt. of Continental pay .... 6 60 dollars
Amt. of time for State pay ....
Pay per day in currency ....
Pay per month in currency ....
Amt. of Continental and State pay .... $20 - -
Additional pay .... 9 . 3 . 4

Remarks: ....

Card 4 (bottom left)

S. | 3 | S.C.

George Scott

Prt, { Captain Joseph Warley's Co. in the 3d South Carolina Reg't of Continental Troops commanded by Col. William Thomson.

(Revolutionary War.)

Appears on

Company Pay Roll

of the organization named above for the month
of .... to August 1, 1779 .
Commencement of pay .... , 17 .
Commencement of subsistence .... , 17 .
To what time .... , 17 .
Amt. of time for pay ....
Amt. of time for subsistence ....
Pay per month .... 6 60 dollars
Subsistence per month .... 6 60 dollars
Amt. of pay .... 6 60 dollars
Amt. of subsistence ....

Amt. of Continental and State pay:

Days ....
Pay per day ....
Amount .... $20 - - -

Casualties ....

Remarks: ....

Card 5 (bottom middle)

| 3 | S.C.

George Scott

Appears with the rank of .... Prt .... on a

Pay Roll

of Capt. Joseph Warley's Co., in the 3d Reg't commanded by Col. William Thomson, for the additional pay allowed by the State of South Carolina,

(Revolutionary War,)

for the month of .... August ...., 1779 .
Amt. of time for Continental pay ....
Amt. of Continental pay .... 6 60 dollars
Amt. of time for State pay ....
Pay per day in currency ....
Pay per month in currency ....
Amt. of Continental and State pay .... $20 - - -
Additional pay .... 9 . 3 . 4

Remarks: ....

Card 6 (bottom right)

S. | 3 | S.C.

George Scott

Prt, { Capt. Joseph Warley's Company in the 3d South Carolina Regiment of Continental Troops, commanded by Col. William Thomson.

(Revolutionary War.)

Appears on

Company Pay Roll

of the organization named above for the month
of .... from Aug 1 to Nov 1, 1779 .
Commencement of pay .... Aug 1, 17 .
Commencement of subsistence .... Aug 18, 17 .
To what time .... Nov 1, 17 .
Am't. of time for pay .... 3 mos.
Amt. of time for subsistence .... 2 mos. 14 days
Pay per month 6 2/3
Subsistence per month 10
Whole amt. of pay and subsistence .... 44 63 dollars
Casualties ....

Remarks: ....

In the Name of God Amen I George Scott of the State
South Carolina Fairfield County Planter being Sick an
Weak of Body but of Perfect mind & Memory do make an
Ordain this my Last Will and Testament and as touching
My Worldly Goods where with it hath pleased God to bless
me with I give & dispose of in Manner & form following
that is say

Item I ~~Land~~ to my Beloved Wife Elizabeth Scott one hundred
Acres of Land Whereon I Now Dwell During her Life
or Widowhood & after her Death or Marriage to fall
To my son William Scott to him and his Heirs
forever.

Item I also Lend my Wife Elizabeth Scott all the Remain
of my Estate Consisting of Stock Tools Household
Furniture &C and after her Death to fall to my
fall to my Daughter Margret Montgomery and her
Heirs Lasly I do make and ordain and Appoint
my Trusty Friends Hugh Montgomery and Charles
Montgomery my Lawfull Executors of this my Last
Will and Testament Dated this Sixth Day of
July In the Year of our Lord One Thousand Seven
Hundred & Ninety,

Sign'd and Seal'd
in Presence of   George Scott

John Robertson

John Andrews   xii

George Scott

GEORGE SCOTT:FAIRFIELD CO.S.C.

In 1790,when George Scott, Revolution Soldier, dictated his last will and testament leaving a widow Elizabeth,a daughter Margaret and a son William,little could he have realized that by 1987, hundreds of his descendents would be scattered all over the United States. According to his will,Margaret married either a Hugh Montgomery or a Charles Montgomery but only the lineage of William is presently known.

In the estate papers of George Scott FF Estates Bx.7,Pk.203,7-203-1a,South Carolina Archives,dated July 6,1790,the exact wording of his will reads as follows:

"IN THE NAME OF GOD,AMEN. I GEORGE SCOTT OF THE STATE OF SOUTH CAROLINA FAIRFIELD COUNTY PLANTER BEING SICK AND WEAK OF BODY BUT OF PERFECT MIND AND MEMORY DO MAKE AND ORDAIN THIS MY LAST WILL AND TESTAMENT AND AS TAKING MY WORLDLY GOODS WHERE WITH IT HATH PLEASED GOD TO BLESS ME WITH I GIVE AND DISPOSE OF IN MANNER OF FORM FOLLOWING THAT IS TO SAY.........

ITEM; I GIVE TO MY BELOVED WIFE ELIZABETH SCOTT ONE HUNDERED ACRES WHEREON I NOW DWELL DURING HER LIFE OR WIDDOWHOOD AND AFTER HER DEATH OR MARIAGE TO FALL TO MY SON WILLIAM SCOTT TO HIM AND HIS HEIRS FOREVER.........

ITEM:I ALSO LEND MY WIFE ELIZABETH SCOTT ALL THE REMAINS OF MY ESTATE CONSISTING OF STOCK TOOLS HOUSHOLD FURNITURE (Etc?)AND AFTER HER DEATH TO FALL TO MY DAUGHTER MARGARET MONTGOMERY AND HER HEIRS LASLY I DO MAKE AND ORDAIN AND APPOINT MY TRUSTY FRIENDS HUGH MONTGOMERY AND CHARLES MONTGOMERY MY LAWFULL EXECUTORS OF THIS MY LAST WILL AND TESTAMENT DATED THIS SIXTH DAY OF JULY IN THE YEAR OF OUR LORD ONE THOUSAND SEVEN HUNDRED AND NINETY;

 Signed:GEORGE SCOTT

SIGNED AND SEALED IN THE PRESENCE OF JOHN ROBERTSON AND JOHN ANDREWS

The military rcord of George Scott was accepted by the Daughters of the American Revolution (DAR) and published in their journal in March,1981,pg.198.This preceded the membership of my mother, Mittie Scott Wilson of Waco,Texas.

The premise of the connection (other than the will),was the naming of the ONE HUNDRED ACRES WHEREON I NOW DWELL in George's will which also is described in William's estate. Frank Jernigan of Sumter,S.C. has diligently searched for the grant of this plat of land,but as of this date,has not been successful.
However,this tract followed the CARMAN line (William's daughter m.John Carman).It is possible that this 100 acres stemmed from

the settlement of John Stallings(Stallions) estate on Feb.27,1784 whereas a George Scott purchased a tract of land as well as did several other men.(Apt.65 Pck.#2297 FF Co.SC.)This particular tract was located in the Morris Creek Area--- the same area where the "homeplace" of William was located.

In 1985,in summerizing the material he had compiled for several years of researching both the Fairfield Courthouse and the South Carolina State Archives,Frank Jernigan sent me the following thoughts:

"Some facts,theories and random thoughts re: William Scott of waters of Morris Creek,Fairfield Co.S.C.....All of this is based on the assumption that this William Scott is the son named in the will of George Scott of Fairfield County dated 6,July,1790 and recorded 13,Apr.1792.

I felt that this assumption would be easy to prove if I could only find George Scott in the possession of ,in 1790,the same 100 acre tract of land where William Scott lived (1)in 1802 and where William's wife,Ann,lived until the 1840's.I have spent many hours researching this but nothing definite thus far.

I know where the 100 A. tract is located,both from ref(1) and the 1984 Fairfield Co.Tax Map.p.195,tracts No.29,23 & 27.The last time that this property was undivided,it was owned by Mr.George B.Hagood ca.1956.(3)

The property adjoining Scott on the SW was granted to James Andrews for 300 A in 1765 (2) and was resurveyed in 1803 as 418 A (4). The property to the SE was granted to William Willingham in 1765 (5).On both of these plats the Scott property was "vacant land".

The property on the NW was noted on ref (4) as the Estate of John Robertson,who had married Elizabeth Simpton Woodward,widow of Thomas Woodward.(6) The plat of Isaac Porcher's 794 A (7),which was later sold to Thomas Woodward,shows that the property to the SE as "Thomas Woodward land" and James Andrews.
"Some random thoughts regarding George Scott:
George Scott,John Robertson and John Richey,witness to the deed of John Martin to John Ball (9). (note ref(4))

The sale of the Estate of John Stallings Jr.,(10),last page, 27 Feb.,1784,lists GEORGE and WILLIAM SCOTT along with he Andrews,Willingham,Mrs.Woodward and Aulston. All the close neighbors along Morris Creek.Demcy Winburn,Silas Stallings,James Hanna Sr.and James Stallings were in York Co.Census in 1790.
The signature of George Scott on the Administrators bond of John Scott Sr.(11) looks very much like that on the will of George Scott.
William Scott witnessed the will of Elizabeth Woodward (12) on 24,Nov.1802 along with John Bell.
2

William Scott was granted Letters of Administrator for the estate
of George Scott.
William Scott sued Augustine Williams(who then owned the Andrews
land to the SW of his) for trespass and won.(13)
A William Scott was witness for plantiff in Stornes vs Gibson
(16) (both Morris Creek people)

Our William Scott was discharged from Capt.Willis Whitaker's Co.,
Col.Thomas Taylors Regt.of Milita at Orangeburg,South Carolina on
25,Oct.,1782.

I have tried to get some information by researching the
Montgomery family but too many Hugh's,Charles's,and Mary's for me
to identify.They seem to have lived just to the west of the Scott
land.
George was married by 1765 and would have been granted 100 A for
himself,50 for his wife and 50 for each child. If William was
over 21,he may have claimed 100 A in his own name.Mary may have
been married or George may have claimed 50 A for her.
Anyway,George scott could have been granted more than 100 A.He
must have bought this tract.Where ever the grant for this 100 A
is,it should say,bounded by lands laid out to James Andrews and
Wm Willingham".

On Sept.28th of this year, (only ten days before this manuscript
was due in the publisher's office), Frank informed me that he had
received information that authenticated the land of GEORGE SCOTT
and his son,William.He wrote:

"I believe we have now proved that this assumption was true. With
the help of Tony Draine,a researcher of Columbia,S.C. we have
land records that show that this 100 Acre tract was in the name
of George Scott in 1789,and the heirs of William Scott in 1807.
By compairing the will of George Scott of July 6,1790,and these
plats and other records that I listed in my earlier notes,I feel
that this William was the son mentioned in George's will.

The plot of the 25 A.grant to Minor Winn shows it to be bounded
on the S.E. by George Scott and the plat of the John Robertson
Estate,shows the same 25 A.tract to be bounded on the S.E.by the
heirs of William Scott......"

At last,the puzzle has been solved ! Frank has to been commended
for his painstaking research that has lasted for several years.
However,he also wrote me that the research must go on until we
discover more about George's wife,Elizabeth ,William's wife Ann,
and William's sister,Margaret, who married a Montgomery.

The two plats that were mentioned are included for closer
examination.

Where ever the grant for this 100 A is, it should say bounded by lands laid out to James Andrews and Wm Willingham."

Without the cooperation of Frank Jernigan concerning the military discharge of WILLIAM SCOTT in Orangeburg, South Carolina in 1782, an important piece of history would have been lost. Frank discovered (while visiting a cousin, Annie Lee Sheed of Fairfield County) a copy of this document among the personal papers of her mother.

In my correspondance with Mrs. Lloyd (Thelma) Gurlinghouse of Monterey, Louisana, she recollected that her mother, Ramoth Cross Enlow, "... had mailed this military discharge to her cousin sometimes between the years of 1918 and the late 1920's. This cousin would have been Annie Lee Shedd's grandmother, I believe". Thelma also added that this discharge evidently had been carried to Louisana in the John P.Cross bible when he moved his family from Fairfield Co., South Carolina to Monterey, Louisana in 1851. John P.Cross's mother, Elizabeth, was the oldest daughter of William and Ann Scott. Thus, the military discharge was saved for the ensuing generations.

Copy Irlas Aug 1904

This is to sertify that Wlm Scott has done his tower of duty and got this discharge Willis Whitaker Capt Cot at Orengburg

October 25th 1782 OrangeBurg District S.C.

In attempting to understand William Scott's military activity more fully, I wrote the Orangeburg County Historical Society in Orangeburg, South Carolina. On January 20, 1981 I received an answer to my query from Mr. Hugo S. Ackerman, Curator of Orangeburg County Historical Society concerning the discharge. He explained that during the final days of the war, many army units gathered there for the last battle to be fought in the south--that of Eutaw

4

Springs on Sept.8,1781. After the war,the British retreated to Charleston,where they remained for the rest of the war.Also,he added,that he knew of no documents saying so,but that a number of units must have been discharged after Eutaw,as they were no longer needed and the men were surely impatient to return home.
By the time of William's discharge from the army,he either was already married to Ann or did marry shortly afterwards as the first child, John W.Scott was born in 1785. Using census records,death records and bible records,the chronological order of eight of the nine children's births can be verified.Only James who died in 1844 cannot be placed,however,he was an adult when his estate was settled.There was one set of twins and possibly two more...it would depend on the dates when the various census records were taken.As a sequel to this observation,twins have been born in each generation of the Scott lineage.The last set documented are the births of twin sons in 1974 to my youngest sister,Marie.

WILLIAM SCOTT SR.

William Scott b.ca.1760 d.1805 Fairfield Co.S.C. m.Ann ? b.ca.1765 d.1848 Fairfield County ,S.C. (9 children)

1.JOHN W.SCOTT b. 1785 F.F.Co. d.Jan.28,1868 Concordia Parish,La.
2.ELIZABETH SCOTT b. 1790 FF.Co. d.Mar.1843 FF.Co. SC
3.GEORGE W. SCOTT b.1790 FF.Co. d.ca.1851 FF.Co.SC
4.MAJOR SCOTT b.1792 FF.Co.d.Apr.27,1843 FF.Co.SC
5.HENRY SCOTT b. 1796 FF.Co.,d.Feb.6,1860 Catahoula Parish,La.
6.WILLIAM SCOTT JR.b.1796 FF.Co.,d.1860-63 Catahoula Parish,La.
7.DANIEL SCOTT b.1800 FF.Co.,d.June 23,1878 FF,Co.SC
8.SARAH SCOTT b. 1800-1801 FF.Co.,d.1879-87 FF.Co.SC
9.JAMES SCOTT b. ? d.July 2,1844 (Possibly the youngest)

It could be assumed that William's death was unexpected as he had recently bought a tract of land in the Horeb Community.On Aug.2,1805,he bought 200 acres on Little River.His 100 acres on Morris Creek was referred to as the "homeplace"and after his death in 1805, Ann was left with nine children to rear.

Ann asked to be named adminintrator on July 10,1806 but on July 26,1807,both Ann and son John Scott were named joint administrators. By March 3,1809,the estate had been appraised by William Bell ,Edward Andrews,and Samuel Procter(.FF.Co.SC Estates Box 31,pkg.478,31-478-1,2,3,Front only ,4 Front and Back)
Some of the items appraised were as follows:

Pewter,crockery,cupboard and furniture,chest,jug,case and bottle,2 boxes,o cutting bone and knife,4 barrels,2 wheal heads,2 pails and buckets,churn,pot and oven,1 iron pot,1 oven,1 soothing iron tongues,1 table,books,4 chairs,1 beadstead,1 bead and furniture,4 beds and furniture,hinges,old iron ,wagon gear,

William Scott

bridles and bells,1 lott of iron,1 drawing knife,loom and harness
lott of hoes and axes,1 barrel and lott of old plows,1 small
cupboard, 1 waggon and log chain,2100 feet of pine plank,4 head
of horses,stock of hoggs,old plow pot and ?,stock of cattle,1
side saddle,4 bee hives,1 curry comb (?),stock of sheep,500 feet
of pine plank,1 cow hide,rifle ,Germand shot bag, 2 plows,cradle
and tools.
On March 5,1807,the estate sale was held and all the items were
sold,with Ann buying back many of these personal items which
today,we would assume would already belong to her.Elizabeth
bought several items as well as Capt.John Sims, William
Ashley,David Vandreax, Henry Jones,Jos. Woodard(Woodward),Joshua
Player ,John Dunkly,Cap.Andrews and George Scott--who bought a
"rifle gun". Total for the complete sale was $774.17.
Each heir received $41.83.6 each from the settlement.

In 1808,Elizabeth Scott married Samuel Cross.In reference to the
1810 census of Fairfield Co.,both Elizabeth and Samuel were
living with Ann and her children.By 1820,George,William,and
Daniel had established homes of their own but all three were
living next to their mother in Fairfield,County.

The 1829 local census found in the HISTORY OF FAIRFIELD COUNTY,
pgs.184-5,lists "Widow Scott as having 8 people in her household,
George Scott with 7, Major Scott with 3,and William Scott with a
grand total of 9 members in his household." Since William already
had 6 childrn by 1829 and one to be born in 1835,there left 1
extra person living with him that cannot be identified.

John W.Scott and Henry Scott were noticeably absent during 1829
as they were on their move to Wilkinson County,Mississippi.It is
not known why the Scott men decided to settle at that particular
location,however,by 1830,John W.,William and Henry were in
Wilkinson,County.Ms.Later these three Scott brothers would all
settle across the Mississippi River in both Concordia and
Catahoula Parishes in Louisana.

Elizabeth,Major,George W.,James,Daniel and Sarah remained in
Fairfield County,South Carolina. As years passed,only Daniel made
appearances in both South Carolina and Louisiana.Apparently he
kept in touch with both facets of the family as he constantly
traveled back and forth ,buying and selling land,slaves and
goods.Throughout his activities,he continued to calm the
discontented and appeared to hold the family in a harmonious
relationship.

The estate of their father,William would not be divided until the
death of thier mother in 1848.This fact was instrumental in the
cause of much infighting among the two groups. The final division
of the estate of William and Ann is better illustrated by
including the final legal decision of 1851.(FF Co.Equity Bill
1851 #6)

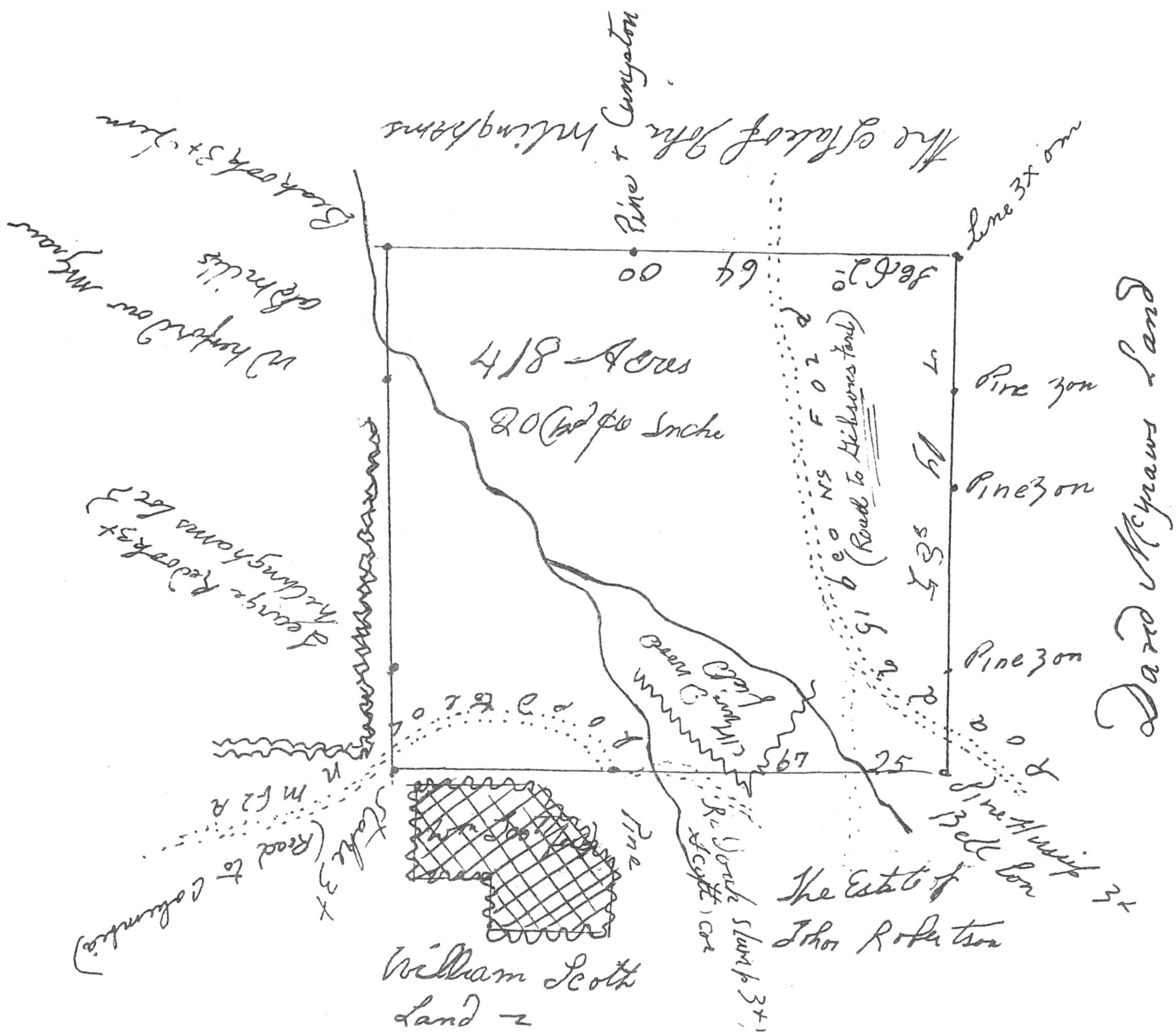

Joshua Player bought this 418 Acre plat joining William Scott's "Homeplace" of 100 Acres, more or less. This plat was originally granted to James Andrews for 300 Acres. James Andrews's son, John was a witness to George Scott's will in 1790 as well as John Robertson who owned land adjoining William Scott around 1800.....

(Frank Jernagan 1980)

6-1

Frank Jernigan and Frances Scott Thornburg

Frances at the location of the William Scott land

A Bill of Sale of the Goods and Chattels
and personal Estate of William Scott
Late of Fairfield Deceased March 1790

Names	articles	£		
	1 Lott of pewter	4		6
Ditto do	1 Lott of Crockery			9
Ditto do	1 Cuttenee & Chunk Bottles	15		
Do do	1 Chest			
Bill do	1 Jug 1 Case 2 Drawers Linen Stockings			
Capt Jno Lain	1 Cutting Box & Knife and Box & Jug			
x Ann Scott	5 Barrels			
Do Do	2 wheels and 1 pair of Cards			
Do Do	2 pails and 1 Bucket			
x William Betty	1 Churn 1 Bristle Breadtray & Sifter			
x Ann Scott	1 Iron pot and 2 ovens			
Do Do	1 Iron pot			
Do Do	oven lid Iron Trammel shovel candlestick	5	8	
Do Do	1 Table & box and Lott of books			
Do Do	4 Chairs and keg		1	
x Elizabeth Scott	1 Bed and Bedstead	1	27	
x Ann Scott	1 Bedstead & Bed and furniture	4		
Do Do	1 do do			15

Ann Scott	1 Lott ... Iron	
Do Do	1 Waggon Gear Buckles in 2 Bells	
Do Do	Lott of old Iron	
Do Do	Drawing Knife	
Do Do	Irons and Harness	
Do Do	Lott of hoes and axes	
Do Do	1 Barrel and Lott of old files	
David Andrews	Small Cupboard	
Capt Jo Sims	Log Chain & by ...	
Henry Jones	1 Waggon ... by Scott	
Ann Scott	a parcel of pine plank ...	
Ditto Do	a parcel of pine plank ...	
John Scott	1 horse	
Eliza Scott	1 ... horse	
Ann Scott	1 Bay horse	
Do Do	1 Sorrel horse	
Do Do	Stock of hogs	
Do Do	Stock of cattle	
Do	1 broad axe	
Do	plow and tubs	

		amt Brot over		19	
x	Jos Woddio	Curry Comb &c		1	7
x	Geroge Scott	1 Rifle Gun & Bayonet		11	
	Joshua player	1 head of sheep		16	2
	Capt Perkins	500 feett of pine plank 2 1/61		3	5
	John Dunkly	1 Cow hide C& By Abele		1	
		2 please		1	
		Cradle			26
Do	Do	Lott of tools —			8
Cap Andew		Rent of land £7 — —		11	13

I certify that the above is a just and
true Account of the sale of W_m Scott
Deceased March 5_th 1807 —
for
Anne B Scott } Admrs
Exrs

2d Sale

Sale Bill of the Estate of Ann Scott 20 January ___
made at the residence of Daniel Scott, on a credit of ___
months. Interest from day of Sale.

Daniel Scott	1 Cupboard	2.0_
Louisa Scott	1 Bed	__
Geo Mathews	1 " & Bedstead	9._
Dan. Scott	1 Empty Bbl & Candy Stand	._
Dan. Scott	1 Bed & Bedstead (out of doors)	2.2_
Dan. Scott	1 Lot _____ & irons of _____ & _____	2.00
Dan. Scott	3 Hackley 2 Chairs & 2 Churns	.2_
Dan. Scott	1 Trunk & Basket	2.8_
Dan. Scott	1 pot, 1 oven & frying pan	2._
Dan. Scott	1 Pail & Tub	._
Dan. Scott	7 Bee Gums	8.7_
Dan. Scott	1 Negro Woman Grace & 2 Children	730.__
Dan. Scott	1 Lot plank	.2_
		763.6_

J. S. Stewart
O. F. S.

The State of South Carolina.

Know all men by these Presents, that *I John P. Cross of Fairfield District of the aforesaid State, and intending to Move to the State of Louisiana and for a valuable consideration* do make, constitute and appoint *and by these presents do irrevocably constitute and appoint John A. Martin of the District of Fairfield and of the aforesaid State my* TRUE AND LAWFUL ATTORNEY for *me* and in *my* name *to demand and receive of and from James S. Stewart Ordinary for Fairfield District or his successor or successors in office such amount, money, as may be due and allotted to me as my distributive share of the Estate Ann Scott deceased and for one and my name to give receipts and other sufficient discharges with full power if necessary to sue and prosecute* with power also, an Attorney, or Attorneys, under *him* for that purpose, to make and substitute, and to do all lawful acts for effecting the Premises, hereby ratifying and confirming all that *my* said Attorney or *his* Substitute or Substitutes, shall do therein, by virtue thereof.

IN WITNESS WHEREOF, *I* have hereunto set *my* Hand and Seal this *fifteenth* day of *October* in the year of our Lord one thousand eight hundred and *forty-nine*.

Sealed and Delivered in the presence of—

O. V. Thompson

Daniel Scott

John P. Cross (SEAL)

BE IT KNOWN, That on the *20th* day of *October* one thousand eight hundred and *forty five* and in the *74th* year of the Independence of the United States of America, before me, *H. A. Glenn* Notary Public, by Letters Patent, under the Great Seal of the State, duly commissioned and sworn, came *John P. Cross* above named, and acknowledged the foregoing Power of Attorney, to be *his* act and deed.

In Testimony Whereof, I have hereunto set my Hand, and affixed my Seal of Office, at *my residence* in the State of South Carolina, the day and year last mentioned.

H. A. Glenn (SEAL)
N. P.

91-295-8

Mrs. Ann Scott [?]
To Sarah Carman Dr.

For Service rendered as Midwife
To Hannah & Children $9.00
To do. Grace & ....
                                    $18.00

State of South Carolina }
Fairfield Dist. } Personally
appeared Sarah Carman and
maketh oath that the above account
of Eighteen Dollars is justly due
her from the above, and that no part
has been received & sworn to before
me this August 24 1849.

Robert Hawthorne }   Sarah Carman
        Mag   }
        I. C. D.

Recd. 31 Aug. 1849. Eighteen dollars
in full of the above account
as for order. Judgt secured.
                        John Carman

91-295-9

Daniel 1848
12 Slaves

1

State of South Carolina }
Fairfield District }

Know all men by these presents
That we Daniel Scott and Spe I. Owens are
holden and firmly bound unto I.S. Stewart, Ord
-inary for the district of Fairfield, or to his succ
-essors in office, in the full and just sum of
Five thousand dollars. good and lawful Mon
-ey of this state. to be paid to the said J.S.
Stewart. Ordinary. or to his Successors. Ordinarys
of the said district. or to their certain attorneys
or assigns. to which payment well and truly
to be made we bind ourselves and every of us
our and every of our heirs. Executors. and
and Administrators. for the whole and in the
whole jointly and severally firmly by these
presents. Sealed with our seals and dated
the twenty third day of December, in the year
of our Lord One thousand eight hundred
and forty Eight.

The Condition of the above obligation is such
That whereas. Daniel Scott. hath hired from
I.S. Stewart, Ordinary. as aforsaid. and acting
as Administrator, by virtue of the Statute of the
State of South Carolina in such cases made
and provided, Twelve Negroes. named. Peggy. Grace
and her four children Tom Dick John & Lean, Daniel
and her three children Isaac Jacob & Sego; Give Esther
and boy Joe. for the sum of Five dollars. Untill the
fifteenth day of January, now next ensuing. Now
if the said Daniel Scott shall deliver unto the said
I. S. Stewart. Ordinary as aforsaid in the town of
Winnsborough on the fifteenth day of January now
next ensuing the said twelve Negroes as aforsaid
and pay the said Five dollars then this obligation
to be void. Else to remain in full force

Signed Sealed & delivered in presence
of   R. C. Woodward

91-295-2a

Daniel Scott
Jno T Owens

To the Honorable the Chancellors of the Said State.
Humbly complaining Show unto your Honor,your oratory,George
Scott,Daniel Scott, John Cross and Joseph E.Staton,and Susannah
P.H.Stanton,infants under the age of twenty one years,by their
Guardian and ? of this District and State aforesaid.

That your orators and oratorixes lately,towit,on the twenth day
of May in the year of our Lord one thousand eight hundred and
forty five, exibited and filed in this Honorable Court at
Fairfield Court House in the District and State aforesaid the
bill of Complaint against Ann Scott,John Scott,Henry
Scott,William Scott,John Carman and Sarah his wife,setting
fortwith,that WILLIAM SCOTT THE ELDER,the father of your orators
George Scott and Daniel scott,grandfather of your orator John
Cross and great-grandfather of your oratorixes,Margaret
M.Stanton,Sarah Caroline Stanton and Susanah P.H.Stanton,departed
this life intestate,in the year of our Lord one thousand eight
hundred and five,seize and possessed at the time of his death,in
fee simple,of two tracts of land,towit,a tract of land containing
one hundred acres, more or less,situated in the District and
State aforesaid,on Morris's Creek,joining land belonging to
Samuel Cork(Cook?) Zacheriah Wirick,and the Estate of Col.William
Kincaid,on which the said William Scott,the elder resided ever
since;and a tract of land containing two hundred acres,more or
less,sold and conveyed to the said William Scott,the elder,by one
said John Brown,on the second day of August S.D. 1805;situated in
the district and State aforesaid,on a branch of Little River,and
more fully described in said original bill;that said William
Scott the elder,left a widow,Ann Scott,and nine children,namely
ELIZABETH SCOTT,JOHN SCOTT,GEORGE SCOTT,MAJOR SCOTT,HENRY
SCOTT,WILLIAM SCOTT,DANIEL SCOTT,SARAH SCOTT.and JAMES SCOTT,his
heirs at law.

That your orator,David (Daniel) Scott has since purchased at
Sheriff sale,the undivided interest and share of Henry Scott,in
the aforesaid two tracts of land.That the aforesaid Elizabeth
Scott intermarried with one Samuel Cross.that said Samuel Cross
died many years ago leaving the Said Elizabeth him surviving.That
said Elizabeth Cross died intestate on the____day of March
A.D.1843 seized and possessed of the undivided one ninth of two
thirds of said tracts of land,and left two children,namely John
Cross,and Susannah who had intermarried with Joseph E.Stanton,her
heirs at law,entitled each to one half of her interest and share
in said lands.that said Susahah Stanton lately dec'd towit;on the
____day of ___A.D.1844,leaving her husband,viz,your orator Joseph
E.Stanton entitled to one third of her share of said land,and
three children,viz,your oratorixes Margaret m.Stanton,Sarah
Caroline Stanton,and Susannah P.H.Stanton,entitled each to one
third of two thirds of her interest in said land.

7

That the aforesaid Major Scott died intestate,on the ___day of September A.D.1843,seized and possessed in fee simple of the undivided one ninth of two thirds of the aforesaid tracts of land,leaving neither wife,nor lawful (?children?),but leaving his mother,Ann Scott,and his aforesaid brothers,John Scott,George Scott,Henry Scott,William Scott,Daniel Scott,his sister Sarah who has intermarried with John Carman,his brother James scott and the above named legal representation of his dceased sister,Elizabeth Cross,his heirs at law and who now hold his interest in and share lands or tenants in common.

That the aforesaid James Scott,died intestate on the ___day of ___,A.D.1844 (before the death of said Susanah Stanton) siezed and possessed fee simple,of his undivided one ninth of two thirds of said lands or one of the heirs at law of his father William Scott,the elder,and also of his undivided share of the interest of his aforesaid brother Major Scott deceased,that said James Scott was never married,but left his mother Ann Scott,and his aforesaid brothers,John Scott,George Scott,Henry Scott,William Scott the younger,Daniel Scott,his sister Sarah Carman and the above named heirs and representatives of his deceased sister Elizabeth Cross,his heirs at law,and who now hold his share of said land or tenents in common.That no partition or division has been made of either of the aforesaid tracts of land among the heirs of the said William Scott the elder,or the time of said Major Scott deceased,or the heirs of said James Scott deceased.

The said Ann Scott or widow of William Scott the elder is entitled to one third of the aforesaid tracts of land,and or one have cultivated the same.

And your orators and oratorixes by their said original bill prayed for partition or sale of said lands and for such relief at from the nature of the case,to his Honorable Court should same meet--that such proceedings were had upon said original bill, that an order was entered against the aforsaid defendants, Ann scott,John Scott,Henry Scott,William Scott,John Carman and Sarah his wife.All of which will more fully appear by reference to said bill,on file in the office of the commissioner in Equity for the District of Fairfield,aforesaid.

That before any further proceedings were had upc.. said original bill,towit,on the __day of __A.D. 1848,the said Ann Scott died intestate,whereby this said writ suit abated as to her,and all her interest and share in said tracts of land,described descended to her heirs at law,namely to the afforesaid George Scott,Daniel Scott,John Scott,Henry Scott,William Scott,and Sarah Carman, children of the said Ann Scott deceased,each one seventh;to the aforesaid John Cross,grandson of the said Ann Scott,one half of one seventh;and to the said Margaret M.Stanton,Sarah Caroline Stanton,and Susanah P.H.Stanton,great,grand daughters of the said Ann Scott,each one third of one half of one seventh.

That no partition has yet been made among any of the parties interestd in said lands but the same still remains in common,that your orator and oratorixes cannot enjoy their interest in said lands or tenants in common.

To the end therefore,that the said John Scott,Henry Scott,William Scott,John Carman and Sarah his wife,may full true and perfect answer make to all and singular the matter aforesaid or fully or is the same were here again repeated and they particularly interragated there to--that the said original bill may stand revised and be in the same plight,and condition or wherein the same abated.That a writ of partition may issue from this Honorable Court,directed to certain commissioners to be for that purpose appointed to make partition of the aforesaid two tracts of land among the several persons interested therein,according to their several and respective interest therein,whether such interest accrued to them at ___at law of the said William Scott the elder,Major scott,Jaqmes Scott,or otherwise and that you orators and oratorixes may have such others and further relief in the ___or from the nature of the case to your Honor shall have meet.

May it please your Honor to grant unto your orators and oratorixes a writ of subponea to be directed to the said John Scott,Henry Scott,William Scott,John Carman and Sarah his wife,of the time of his son,Major Scott deceased,he is further entitled to one ninth os one ninth of two thirds of aforsaid tracts of land.And as one of the heirs of her son James Scott decased,she is further entitled to one eighth of one ninth of two thirds and one eighth of one ninth of one ninth of two thirds thereof.

That John Scott,your orator George Scott,William Scott,your orator Daniel Scott,and Sarah Carman are each entitled to one ninth of two thirds of said__or part of the heirs at law of their father William Scott the elder and they are also each further entitled to one ninth of one ninth of two thirds thereof or part of the heirs at law of their brother Major Scott deceased and they are also each further entitled to one eighth of one ninth of one third and one eighth of one ninth of one ninth of two thirds thereof as part of the heirs at law of their brother James Scott,deceased;and your orator Daniel Scott is also entitled by purchase of the original share of his brother Henry Scott to one ninth of two thirds of said tracts of land.

That said Henry Scott is still entitled as one of the heirs of his brother,the Major Scott deceased ,to one ninth of one ninth of two thirds of said lands and he is also still entitled further as one of the heirs of his brother, James Scott deceased, to one eighth of one ninth of one ninth of two thirds of said lands.That the said John Cross is entitled as one of the heirs of said William Scott the elder, to one half of one ninth of two thirds of said tracts of land and as one of the heirs of said Major deceased he is further entitled to one half of one ninth of one ninth of two thirds of said land;and as one of the heirs of said James Scott,he is further entitled to one ninth of two thirds and one half of one eighth of one ninth of one ninth of two thirds of said tracts of land.

That your orator Joseph E.Stanton the husband of Susanah Stanton deceased,and your oratorixes Margaret M.Stanton,Sarah Caroline Stanton,and Susanah P.H.Stanton,children of said Susanah Stanton deceased who was a sister of said John Cross are together entitled to the same shares of said land as said John Cross above specified,that is to say;the said Joseph E.Stanton,to one third thereof and the said Margaret M.Stanton,Sarah Caroline Stanton and Susanah P.H.Stanton each to one third of the other two thereof.

That John Carman and wife have used and cultivated the plantation on Little River,or some portion thereof,for twelve years,or upwards and that they ought in justice and equity,to account your orators and oratorxies and their other as tenents for the rents and profits of said plantations during the time they thereby commanding them to on a certain day and under a certain pains to be therein invited to be and appear in this Honorable Court at Fairfield Court House;then and there to answer the premises and to abide and perform such order and __therein as to your Honor Shall meet---and your orators and oratorixes with we pray---
   D.M.Dowell

As mentioned before,the three Scott brothers who left South Carolina,first settled in Wilkinson County,Mississippi.In 1830, John W.Scott and Henry Scott paid taxes and four years later, William Scott joined them in paying his share.By the years of 1835,1836,1837,1838 Henry obviously had decided to relocate to Louisiana as only John and William were still in Wilkinson Co.

In the 1840 census,pg.62,Henry was a resident of Catahoula Parish,Louisiana where he would stay for the remainder of his life.William operated a stage line (US mail contract) between Woodville,Wilkinson county,Mississippi,the rail head,to Bayou Sara on the Mississippi River near St.Francisville in Feliciana Parish,Louisana for several years. In April,1846,John W.did not pay his taxes when they were due and as a result,his land was sold. Nevertheless,it stayed "in the family" as his nephew Thomas Francis Scott (William's son) bought the 120 acres for $6.50. (Sec.1/4,T3,R3W) It seems evident that John W.Scott had moved to Concordia Parish to be near his son George W.Scott, who married Frances H.Fink in 1847.Meanwhile,Daniel Jackson Scott traveled back and forth from Mississippi,Louisiana and South Carolina.

10

John W. Scott

WILLIAM AND ANN SCOTT
CHILD #1:JOHN W.SCOTT b. 1785,Fairfield Co.S.C.,d.Jan.28,1868
Concordia Parish,La.m. ?   in South Carolina.   (1 child)
     a)GEORGE W.SCOTT b.1810 S.C.,d.March 15,1879 m.May 29,1847
        Concordia Parish La.to Frances A.Fink(1 child)
           1.JOHN F.SCOTT b. 1848 La.
             (Possibly m.Nettie Faulkinberry 1890)

     In the 1850 Concordia Parish,La.Census,John W.Scott had
     real estate valued at $3,000.,George W.and John F.Scott
     were listed along with George's father and the family of
     John W's nephew,Henry Swatts.(Henry Swatts was the son of
     Major Scott,John's brother)
     Henry Swatts was 24 b.S.C.,wife,Elizabeth 24 b.S.C.and
     child, Henry W.Swatts 2, b La.

The family of John W.Scott were neighbors to another
nephew... Major A.Scott (son of William Jr.)This younger
Major Scott would later donate land to begin the SCOTT
CEMETERY which is still in use today.

On Dec.18,1858 (Bk N,p.336 Concordia) George W.Scott
exchanged land with Gabriel B.Shields.
(W 1/2 S18,t6,R.8E South of Bayou Cross Cocodre in that
section 240 A. W 1/2 S18,South of Cross Concordre Bayou
$1360.80, $1270 cash. Balance $89.25 for all land NE 1/4
S13,T6N,R8E,north of Cross Cocodre Bayou containing 17
Acres.(Spelling same as document:Concodre/Concordre)
Family #210 in 1860 lists George W. Scott 50,and John F.
Scott 12.His value of real estate was $25,000 and personal
estate was $100.00.
Family #211 lists John P.Cross 47 with his wife and
children.(Refer to child #2,Elizabeth who m.Samuel Cross).
Real estate value $10,000 and personal estate $500.00.

At this point in time,John W.Scott was an ill man and had
acquired land,slaves and etc.to the point that his son
George W.Scott could not work the land properly.In 1848,an
offer was made to John P.Cross who still lived in Fairfield
County,S.C.to come to Louisiana and help his uncle and
cousin.The agreement was that in time ,the land would be
divided and shared equally.The co-partner agreement was
honored on Mar.27,1861. 40 acres north of Red River (SW 1/4
of SW 1/4 of S17,+6N,R8E. Patent #10082)

On Feb.21,1871,another exchange of land took place between
George W.Scott and John P.Cross.(Bk O,p.746-47 Concordia)
160 Acres of land SW 1/2 & NW 1/4 ,S18 which lies south of
Cross Cocodria Bayou taken off next to said Concodria Bayou
leaving Scott 80 Acres in South side of said 1/4 S18,T6,R8
East and 1/2 of SE 1/4,S13 ,T6,R? which is next to Cross
Cocodre Bayou and bounded N of said Bayou,.W. by Horseshoe

11

Lake and E.by township line between 7&8. NE 1/4,S19,T6,N of R8 160.60/100 acres.

When George W.Scott d.March 15,1879,T.W.Wall admininstrator wanted to sell the land to pay debts.This land of 400 acres,consisted of 80 acres cleared, with the balance in woodland adjoining John P.Cross. Wall stated that no heirs remained in the parish or state and the value of the estate was less than $500.00.Debts were due to Thomas J.Glasscock.

On Dec.5,1879,John F.Scott of Texas,stated that," George W.Scott was his father who had died March 15.He has just learned of his death and that John F. Scott is the only heir.(Sucession BK O,pg.54,59)He claimed that the estate value is worth more than $500.00 That the county clerk had no legal right to attempt to take charge of the estate. The son will pay the debts as soon as he reaches the state. Furthermore,the description of the land is wrong--thus a clear title could not be granted."THE SALE HAD BEEN SCHEDULED THE NEXT DAY!   Petition was granted.

The following entries are included in anticipation that some descendent of John F.Scott wishes to continue the research on the John W.Scott lineage.
   1.On May 23,1889 a John F.Scott in Concordia Parish
      received $55.00 from Karl Lehmann for 3/4 interest in
      land bounded N by Cross and Glasscock,S& W by
      Coleman,E&S by Swamp,W by Horseshoe Lake. 250 acres
      in Concordia bought by Lehmann on June 20,for
      taxes of 1886 (Deed Book S,p.343)

   2.On July 8,1890,a John F.Scott m.Nettie Faulkenberry

   3.On Mar.15,1905,(Concordia Bk X,p.125)John F.Scott
      bought 40 acres of land SE 1/4 of SE 1/4 of
      S31,T6,R7,E.

   4.In 1918,(BK AA pg.565 the marital status of George
      W.Scott was given by C.C. Campbell to Concordia Land
      and Timber Co.

   5.On Jan.9,1922 (Bk CC pg.430 Concordia) a statement
      was taken from William Adkins Cross Sr.(son of John
      P.Cross),concerning the status of John F.Scott being
      the son of George W.Scott.
      Wm.A.Cross stated that he knew George W.Scott who
      died in 1879. That at one time he was a partner of
      John P. Cross who was William's father. Also,George
      had only one child,John F. Scott.

George W. Scott &
Wm J. Clapcott Dr

Attention services & Board for
1st to Decr 4th 1878 for $1.30
$141.00

" " 10th " " " to 1879

$9.00 th day   120.00
Raying Dr Harnsly   30.00
                                         $291.00

G. B. Shields
&c, Exchange of lands
to W. Scott

State of Louisiana and Parish of Concordia.

Bk. K, p. 336
1879

Be it known to all whom it may concern, that on this eighth day of December, in the year Eighteen hundred and fifty Eight, Gabriel B. Shields and George W. Scott, of Concordia parish in the State of Louisiana, have made a sale and partial exchange of lands in the parish of Concordia, as follows, wit: the said Shields Conveys to the said Scott all that part of the West half Section Eighteen, in township Six North, of Range Eight East, in the land District North of Red River, Louisiana, being that which lies South of the Bayou Cross Cocodre in that Section, and estimated to contain two hundred and forty acres, more or less; to have and to hold, the said portion of the said West half of said section eighteen, lying South of said Cross Cocodre Bayou, to the said Scott, his heirs and legal representatives forever, with full warranty against all claims whatsoever.

The price ... hundred and Sixty xx/100 Doll ... and Seventy xx/100 Dollars, the ... being the sum of Eighty nin... the said Shields, all that par... ix North, of Range Eight, Ea... Seventeen acres, more or les... his heirs and legal represent... whatsoever.

In testimony ... private signature on the da...

Signed in presence of
H. B. Shaw
A. G. Tyler.

John H. Pitts & wife
To Conveyance & Mortgage

... the Sum of Thirt...
... sum of Twelve hun...
...ledged, and for the bal...
...reby sells and conveys...
Section Thirteen, in Tou...
...codre Bayou, contain...
...land into said Shiel...
...ranty against all c...

signed this act ...
...itten.
Gab. B. Shields.
G. W. Scott

Concordia.

SUCCESSION SALE.

State of Louisiana. Parish of Concordia.

Parish Court.

Succession of Geo. W. Scott, dec'd.

TAKE NOTICE, that by virtue of an order issued out of the honorable the Parish Court of Concordia parish, and State aforesaid, in the above styled succession, and directed to the Sheriff of Concordia parish, commanding and empowering him to sell at public auction, to the last and highest bidder all the property, real or personal, belonging to said succession. I, James Randall, sheriff of said parish of Concordia, will offer for sale at the Court house door, in the town of Vidalia, Concordia parish, La., on

Saturday, the 6th day of December, A. D. 1879,

between the hours of 11 o'clock a. m. and 4 o'clock p. m., the following described property, viz:

A certain tract of land fronting on Horse Shoe Lake and adjoining lands of John P. Ross, containing about four hundred (400) acres of land, eighty of which are cleared, the balance being woodland. All of which is situated in the Parish of Concordia.

Terms of Sale—Cash on spot at not less than the appraised value.

Sheriff's office, Vidalia, Concordia parish, Louisiana, October 8th, A. D. 1879.

JAMES RANDALL,

12-2   Sheriff.

Recorded 6th June 1842.

Attest James Dunlap
Parish Judge

240 acres.

1842. Land 5 mi. north of Vidalia and 12 miles west of Mis. River

N E¼, S10, T10, N R ?9E Land entered in Land Office in 1839

John F. Goodrich
To
John F. Scott

Conveyance

Parish of Concordia
State of Louisiana

Be it remembered that on this thirty first day of May in the year of Our Lord, One thousand, Eight hundred and forty two — Before me Ebenezer Miller a Notary Public duly Commissioned and qualified according to Law in and for this Parish, and in presence of the witnesses hereinafter mentioned and undersigned, personally came and appeared John F. Goodrich a resident Citizen of the Parish aforesaid, who declared and said, that for the consideration hereinafter mentioned and expressed, that he has this day, bargained sold, transferred, conveyed and delivered, and by these presents doth bargain sell, transfer convey and deliver unto John F. Scott — also a Resident Citizen of this Parish, & who is now present before me the said Notary and acquiescing in this act, all the following mentioned and described tract or parcel of land which is situate in this Parish which is situate five miles North of the Town of Vidalia, and about twelve miles west of the Mississippi River and particularly designated and known by the public Survey, as the North East quarter of Section Number Ten in Township number number ten, North of Range Number nine East, in the Land District North of Red River, containing two hundred and forty acres be the same more or less — Said Land having been entered at the Land Office at Ouachitta by the aforesaid Goodrich some time about the ninth of December, in the year of Our Lord, One thousand Eight hundred thirty nine, as will appear by reference to the receipt of M. Holmes, the Receiver at said Office — To have and to hold the said described land and premises, and every part and species or parcel thereof together with all and singular, the improvements appurtenances privileges and advantages thereunto belonging or in any manner appertaining, unto the aforesaid John F. Scott, purchaser as aforesaid, his heirs, Executors, Administrators or assigns, and to his and their only proper use benefit and behoof forever, free from the claim or claims of all persons whomsoever, claiming or to claim the same — Now the consideration of the aforegoing Sale is declared to be the sum of One dollar and twenty five cents per acre for the said land, which amounts to in the aggregate the sum of Three hundred dollars, and which sum is declared to be the full and entire amount of the price of purchase of the said Land and premises, and which sum of three hundred dollars, he the said Goodrich — Vendor as aforesaid, hereby acknowledges to have received, in cash to him in hand paid — And the said Scott — Vendee as aforesaid, his heirs, Executors and assigns are forever released and discharged therefrom, by these presents —

And the said John F. Scott, being present as aforesaid, declares and says that he accepts of this act with all its clauses and contents, and that he waives and dispenses with the production of the Certificate of the Recorder of Mortgages in and for this Parish, as to any Mortgage lien or incumbrance of any kind or nature whatsoever which may exist of Record in said Office, against all and every part of the land hereinbefore mentioned and described & that he exhonerate and holds harmless me the said Notary, from all liability or responsibility for the passing of this act without the production of the same — In testimony of all hereof, the said parties have hereunto subscribed their names in confirmation of this act, in presence of Elijah Smith & S. W. Cole — competent Witnesses who reside in this Parish & who have also hereunto subscribed their names, in attestation hereof, in presence of said parties, of each other and of me the said Notary, at my Dwelling House in said Parish on the day first aforesaid — In faith of which I the said Notary grant these presents under my signature and my proper Seal of Office at the time and place aforesaid —

John F. Goodrich
John F. Scott

Elijah Smith
S. W. Cole

[Seal]

Ebenᵉᶻ Miller
Not. Pub.

12-3

Recorded 6th June 1842

Attest James Dunlap
Parish Judge

Elizabeth Scott Cross

WILLIAM AND ANN SCOTT
2nd child:ELIZABETH SCOTT b.1790 FF Co.S.C. d.Mar.1843 FF Co.SC.m
Samuel Cross b.ca 1774-1780,d.ca Nov.15-Apr.1820.FF Co.S.C.(4
children)
A schematic diagram of the Cross lineage is included.For further
details of the family,refer to published book CROSS FAMILY RECORD
1774-1984 by Girlinghouse,Jernigan and Smith.Edited by Hansell
Flynn Cross Phd.

ALSO ADDITIONAL INFORMATION IS INCLUDED ON THE MEMBERS OF THE
CROSS FAMILY THAT HAVE ASSISTED ME IN THIS RESEARCH.

        a)Name cut from Bible.male.b.Nov.6,1810
        b)JOHN PRESBURY b. Oct.18,1812 FF Co.SC d.Apr.29,1907
          Concordia Parish ,La.m.1st Dec.1,1835 FF Co.SC Phoebe
          Belle Steele b.May 29,1815.(10 children)
            1.ANN CROSS b.FF Co. SC Nov.13,1836 m.1st Oct.10,1856
            Jesse Lanehart of Catahoula Parish,La.
            Ann m.2nd Jack Willie Brown (2 children)
                a)JACK WILLIE BROWN
                b)IDA BROWN
            Ann and Jack Brown moved to Bell Co.Texas

            2.MARTHA CROSS b. Nov.25,1838 FF Co.SC d.Aug.1932
            Concordia Parish La.m.Apr.24,1856 James Crayton Crane
            (7 children)

                a)SAMUEL PINKNEY CRANE,SR.

                b)ELIZABETH M.CRANE

                c)OLLIE CRANE b.Aug.2,1871 d.May 30,1938
                  m.Dec.9,1886 Louis Fulda Broussard,Jr.
                  Dec.7,1849 (8 children)

                  1.ALEX P.BROUSSARD
                  2.LOUIS V. BROUSSARD
                  3.MATTIE B. BROUSSARD

                  4.OLA OLEVIA BROUSSARD b.Feb.3,1897 m.Eugene T.
                    Sturgeon (See HOLMES CHAPTER)(1 child)
                    a)MILLARD STURGEON m.Maargie Calhoun
                      1.JOHN M. STURGEON
                      2.LINDA STURGEON

                  5.PAULINE BROUSSARD WHITE
                  6.JESSE BROUSSARD
                  7.JULIA BROUSSARD HALL
                  8.CLIFFORD BROUSSARD

d)EDNA EFFIE CRANE 1st m.Orelia M.Broussard Sr.
   (4 children)

   1.ORELIA M.(Dock)BROUSSARD JR.m.Nan Lanehart
     Broussard (5 children)

     a)ORELIA M.BROUSSARD III
     b)SHIRLEY BROUSSARD
     c)ELAINE BROUSSARD GULLEDGE
     d)DONELLY BROUSSARD
     e)J.P.BROUSSARD
     f)LOUISE BROUSSARD

   2.CHARLEY C.BROUSSARD m.Lizzie Herron
     Broussard

   3.HOWARD BROUSSARD

   4.ALMA BROUSSARD

Edna m.2nd to Hunter C.Smith (3 children)

   5.ALBERT H.SMITH m.Ethel White Smith
     (5 children)
     a)ALBERT HUNTER SMITH JR.
     b)EDNA SMITH MAXWELL
     c)CHARLOTTE SMITH WILEY
     d)CAROLYN SMITH WILSON
     e)WILLIAM BILLY SMITH (deceased)

   6.ESSIE HAZEL SMITH

   7.ROBERT SMITH

e)EDITH IDELL CRANE m.Albert Lewis Smith,Sr.
   1.Henry Clarence Smith,Sr.
   2.Samuel Dave Smith,Sr.m.Julia Ferrell Glasscock
      a)SAMUEL HOLICE SMITH SR.
      b.SAMUEL DAVE SMITH,JR.
      c.GLEN WALLACE SMITH b.May 8,1927 Harmon
        La.m.Ola Mae Edwards b.May 23,1928
        (4 children)
          1.JUDY GLYN SMITH
          2.EVA KAY SMITH
          3.PAMELA DALE SMITH
          4.DENNIS WAYNE SMITH

        Glen m.Linda Dianne Bloodworth b.Nov.10,
        1948

```
          f)P.D.CRANE
          g)C.C. CRANE
     Martha m.2nd Jeff D.Thompson


3.WILLIAM ADKINS CROSS b.Dec.15,1840 FF Co.SC.Civil War
  Veteran, Co.C. 25th La.Infantry d.Monterey,Concordia
  Parish Sept.27,1934 buried Scott Cemetery.
  m.Oct.24,1866 Theresa Ann Scott b.Dec.30,1844,d.
  May 13,1916.dau. of Major Adkins Scott and Nancy
  Adeline Lanehart.(Major was the son of Wm Scott Jr.)
  (8 children)
     1.HARVEY ESTELLE CROSS
     2.SIDNEY BELL CROSS
     3.WILLIAM ADKINS CROSS
     4.HANSELL PINKNEY CROSS b.Mar.2,1874
        Monterey,La.d.May 21,1932 Wilson,La.m.July
        30,1907 Clinton,La.Mary Virginia Dawson,
        b.Apr.3,1879 Gurley,La.d.Dec.18,1973
           Centreville,Ms.(3 children)
           a)LILLIAN BEATRICE CROSS
           b)HANSEL FLYNN CROSS PhD.b.Oct.30,1913 m.1st
              1934 Laplace,La. Marjorie Lee Edwards
              b.July 16,1913 d.Mar.3,1972 (1 child)
                 1.MARY BELLE CROSS
              m.2nd Mar.19,1943 Mary Lucille McDonald
              Woodville,Ms.b.June 21,1923 Pelehatchee,Ms.
                 2.JAMES FLYNN CROSS
                 3.PAMELA JOY CROSS
           c) WILLIAM WINSTON CROSS
     5.EULA CROSS b.1877,d.1902 Monterey.m.1895 to
        William Ernest Burley.Both b.SCOTT CEMETERY.
        (2 children )
           a)HANSEL ENOS BURLEY b. 1897
           b)WILLIAM FRANKLIN BURLEY b.1899,d.1982
              buried SCOTT CEMETERY m.1921 Gladys Phoebe
              Cross b.1900 --Both grandchildren of John
              P. Cross)(4 children)
                 1.HANSELL ERNEST BURLEY
                 2.DONALD P.BURLEY
                 3.ADELINE BURLEY
                 4.WILLIAM FRANKLIN BURLEY,JR.

     6.MARSALIN GILLIS CROSS
     7.TINNIE CROSS

4.SAMUEL CROSS
5.ELIZABETH CROSS b.May 26,1845 FF Co.SC d.1891
Monterey,La.buried in CROSS CEMETERY m.John William
Powell b.Atlanta Ga. Dec.18,1842 d.Gatesville,Tx.
Dec.30,1909 (10 children)
```

a)OLIVIA POWELL
b)CARRIE POWELL
c)JONATHAN ALMERYNE POWELL
d)WADE HAMPTON POWELL
e)WILEY S.POWELL
f)JAMES DOUGLAS POWELL
g)SAMUEL DAVIS POWELL

h)CLARA BELL POWELL b.Fredersburg,La.Apr.11,1890
   d.San Antonio,Tx.Dec.30,1980 m.July 27,1909
      Wiley Clinton Roberson,Waco,Tx.
      1.SCOTT HARRINGTON ROBERSON
      2.VEARL VIRGINIA ROBERSON b.Waco,Tx.m.Charles
        Carlton Cupp, Lorina,Tx.(5 children)
           a.LA DEANNE CUPP
           b)NORMA JUNE CUPP
           c)CHARLES STEPHENS CUPP
           d)VIRGINIA LYNN CUPP
           e)JANIS CAROL CUPP
i)JEANNIE POWELL
j)SCOTT POWELL

6.GEORGE WARREN CROSS b.Fairfield Co.S.C.May 8,1847
  d.April 28,1926m.Jan.15,1873 Mary Katherine
  Holmes.b.Aug.11,1853 d.Dec.22,1918 Natchez,Ms.buried
  Lismore,La.(6 children)
       a)HUGH IRA CROSS
       b)ANNIE REBECCA CROSS
       c)WARREN PRESBERRY CROSS
       d)MARY ETHEL CROSS
       e)ALBERTINA CORA CROSS
       f)MARION WILBURN CROSS

7.HARRIET CROSS b.Apr.22,1849 Monterey,La.d.Oct.22,1875
  d.Oct.22,1875 m.CHARLIE BURLEY b.Aug.19,1846 FF Co.SC
  (2 children)After Harriet died,Charlie m.Helen Scott.
       a)CYRUS B. BURLEY
       b)WALTER S.BURLEY

8.NANCY CROSS b.Concordia Parish,La.Sept.18,1851
  d.Oct.27,1907 m.Thomas Jonthan Glasscock Sr.b.Feb.1,
  1848.(7 children)
       a)JOSEPH CRAIG GLASSCOCK
       b)BENJAMIN FARRIS GLASSCOCK
       c)LINNIE ELIZABETH GLASSCOCK
       d)THOMAS JONATHAN GLASSCOCK,JR.
       e)FRED GILLARD GLASSCOCK
       f)WILLIAM EDWARD GLASSCOCK
       g)WALTER WARREN GLASSCOCK.

9.THOMAS CROSS d.as infant

10.JONATHAN SIMMS CROSS b. Monterey La.1856 m.
   Addie Lanehart b. Monterey,1861 d. 1920
   Both buried SCOTT CEMETERY
       a)OLIE CROSS
       b)ELLA CROSS
       c)MATTIE J.CROSS
       d)JONATHAN PEAL CROSS
       e)GLADYS PHOEBE CROSS (Refer to her husband,
         WILLIAM FRANK BURLEY,SR.(4 children)
             1.HANSELL BURLEY
             2.DONALD BURLEY
             3.ADELINE BURLEY BLOUNT
             4.WILLIAM"Billy" BAURLEY

AFTER THE DEATH OF JOHN PRESBERRY CROSS 'S FIRST WIFE PHOEBE DE
BELLE STELLE,JOHN ,AT THE AGE OF 61,MARRIED FOR THE SECOND TIME.

John P.Cross m.Sept.12,1878 to Martha Jane (Wiggins) Brown,
b.April 23,1851 in Summerville,La.Martha had a daughter,Stella
Brown b.Dec.23,1876 Summerville,La.d.Aug.12,1951 Monterey and is
buried in SCOTT CEMETERY.(6 children)
STELLA BROWN m.Jess I. Lanehart b.Dec.7,1867 ,d.Aug.13,1940.Also
buried SCOTT CEMETERY.This couple became"beloved foster-parents"
of Thelma Enlow Girlinghouse.

11.JOHN ALLEN CROSS,SR. b.June 27,1879 ,d.Sept.10,1925
   b.SCOTT CEMETERY, m.July 23,1909 Alice Merrena
   Ferrell b.Sept.20,1890 (4 children)
       a)VELMA LORENA CROSS b.June 7,1910 d.Jan.17,1911
       b)EUGENE PRENTISS CROSS b.June 22,1911 d.July
         4,1911
       c)JESSE BOATNER CROSS
       c)JOHN ALLEN CROSS JR.

12.LEVI SCOTT CROSS,SR.b.July 9,1880,d.Oct.,1984 m.June
   8,1909 Mary Ella Showlesb.Oct.28,1890,d.Dec.22,1966.
   Both buried SCOTT CEMETERY (5 children)
       a)PHALA CROSS
       b)VELA CROSS
       c)OMER CROSS
       d)LOLA CORINNE CROSS
       e)LEVI SCOTT CROSS,JR.

13.RAMOTH CROSS b.April 23,1882
   Monterey,La.d.Aug.8,1977 Ferriday,La.buried SCOTT
   CEMETERY m.Jan.3,1900 Jesse McCormick Enlow,in
   Monterey,La.,Jesse b.Wilkinson Co.Ms.
   Aug.21,1871,d.Ferriday,Oct.1951,son of Benjamin
   Franklin Enlow and Nancy Sarah Ann Dawson.
   (9 children)

a) THELMA ENLOW b.Monterey Aug.20,1902 m.May 4,
   1927.Alexandria,La.to Lloyd Ray Girlinghouse
   b. May 17,1904,d.July 22,1953.Buried SCOTT
   CEMETERY,Son of Newman and Lettie Banks
   Girlinghouse.(1 child)

   1. ETHEL DEBELLE GIRLINGHOUSE b.July 7,1929
      m.Dec.18,1948 Dallas,Tx.to Clayton Allen
      b.Dec.19,1926 Brazos,Tx.son of Octavius &
      Ruby Allen (2 children)
      a) CLAYTON LLOYD ALLEN b. Sept.19,1956
         m.1st Elaine Daly (1 child)
         1. JOSHUA SHANE ALLEN b. 1966

         m.2nd Sonya Slayton (2 children)
         2. LINDSY TRICHELLE ALLEN b.1980

      b) ANDREA ALLEN BRENTZ b.Apr.29,1955
         m.Hendrix E.Brentz,Jr.(1 child)
         1. BRANDY ANN BRENTZ

b) CLINTON LEMUEL ENLOW b.Feb.11,1904 d.Dec.18,1976

c) ALTHEA MELBA ENLOW b.Monterey,La.Sept.29,1906
   m.Nov.15,1940 James Marvin Gibbs b.Sept.1904
   d.Ferriday June 6,1951 b. Minden,La.(1 child)

   a) JOHN CLINTON GIBBS b.May 14,1944 m.1st 1969
      Ann Holland (2 children)
      1. JOHN LOUIS GIBBS b.June 25,1970
      2. KRISTI ANN GIBBS b.Mar.8,1972
      John m.2nd to Judy Case Merrell 1981

   Melba m.2nd 1956 to Louis C.White b.Jan.1909
   d. Oct.1983

d) KILLIAN SCOTT ENLOW (Twin to Kermes Dawson)
   b.May 25,1909 d.Monterey,1912

e) KERMES DAWSON ENLOW b.May 25,1909 d.Nov.11,1913

f) JAMES MCCORMICK ENLOW b.1914 m.1950 Else(Vogel)
   Wahl b.1918,d.1975 Else and Herr Wahl had one
   daughter,Ursula Wahl,b.Germany June 20,1940
   who m.Roger Williams of Natchitoches,La. One
   daughter,Renee Williams b.1965
   James and Else had 1 son.

   a) JAMES C.ENLOW b.Jan.10,1950 Bad Wildungen,
      Germany m.June 21,1974 Baton Rouge,La. to

18

Rose Mary Macalusa b.May 2,1950,dau.of
Vincent Macalusa and Carrie Marie
Caracci.(2 children)
 1.JASON MCCORMICK ENLOW b.Dec.30,1975
 2.JAMES MICHAEL ENLOW b.Aug.21,1978

g)HARLEY N.ENLOW b.Monterey Apr.2,1916 d.Oct.1918

h)MALCOLM D. ENLOW SR.b.Jan.21,1920 m.1948 Joyce
M. Rogers b.July 4,1930 Dau of Jake Leroy
Rodgers and Clara Moon.(2 children)
 a)MALCOLM D.ENLOW,JR. b.Sept.20,1949

 b)BRENDA JOYCE ENLOW b. Aug.18,1952
 m.Dec.25,1981 Jim Rainford

i)DARWIN SHAY ENLOW SR.b.Mar.10,1922 m.1949 Ruth
Valentine Cross b.Feb.14,1930 divorced 1982
(4 children)
 a)DARWIN SHAY ENLOW JR. b.July 10,1951
 b)ETHEL AUGUSTA ENLOW b.1953 m.1st,James
 Adams (2 children)
  1.BRYAN ADAMS
  2.BRAD ADAMS
 Ethel m.2nd to Curtis Lambright who had one
 daughter,Tiffany Lambright by his 1st
 marriage.
 c)RAMOTH ROSALIE ENLOW THOMPSON b.1959
 m.John Wayne Thompson (1 child)
  1.RICHARD THOMPSON
 d)DOLLY DEWANA ENLOW b. 1965

14.MARY JANE CROSS b.Concordia Parish Aug.26,1885
d.Oct.16 1887 Concordia Parish.

15.JAMES DANIEL CROSS b.Monterey,La.Feb.7,1887 d.1971
Natchez.m.Feb.8,1916 Leona Clark,Jonesville,La.b.Aug
31,1887 d.1972 Natchez.(1 child)
a)JAMES ELLIOTT CROSS

On November 8,1982,in response to an inquiry concerning the SCOTT
relatives living in the Monterey and Parham Community,I received
the following information from Mrs.(Lloyd)Thelma Girlinghouse,the
grandaughter of John Presbury Cross.

"My mother was not quite seven years old when her mother,Martha
Jane Cross died.I would imagine the shock of losing one's mother
at such an early age could leave very vague memories of ever
having had a real mother. In fact,I can recall having my mother
Ramoth Cross Enlow, tell me so. Her father,John P.Cross was 77

years old at the time his wife died in 1889 leaving him to care for their four small childdren.They had a very hard time,but they seemed to love each other and their elderly father very much.He provided them with the wholesome farm foods that were available in those days.

Most of all,he provided them with spiritual food.At evening, before their early bedtime,my grandfather,even in this golden age period of his life,sang hymns and read scripture from the Bible with and to his four young children. There,after the scripture reading,he knelt with them in prayer.

Fortunately,my mother remembered much more about the spiritual and moral training in her life than she remembered about anything else from her heritage.She felt that her father's guidance and training meant everything.

Sometimes,mama could tell a few incidents of my grandfather's childhood in Fairfield County,South Carolina.She knew that life was not too easy for him because his mother (Elizabeth Scott) was a widow.She did not recall very much that she had heard about her two grandfathers,Samuel Cross and William Scott. Her great, grandfather Cross was a merchant in Charleston,South Carolina,and her great grandfather William Scott was a farmer,she thought.

My mother always loved the farm and disliked living in the small towns where she was forced to live during years when the Mississippi and the Red and the Black Rivers flooded her farm. She must have inherited the love of farming from the Scotts.

Mama knew that she had Scott relatives,but knew very little about them.After all,she had her father for only twenty- four years of her life. She knew that he came to Louisana because he had Scott relatives who had come earlier. They had told him that the land was fertile, and especially good, for growing cotton. He was evidently very interested in producing a profitable cash crop,but the Civil War came along ,plus the floods. So,I have an idea that his dream was not fulfilled,agriculturally speaking.

Among the Scotts whom mama knew were "Cousin Lorena(Dood) Scott Steele.Cousin Dood,as we knew her,was the mother of Naomi Hale who lives at Monterey.Now she is in her late 80's.Theresa Scott Cross was an older sister of Cousin Dood's and was married to her own cousin,William A.Cross. He was Mama's oldest half-brother. Rachel Scott McGee Reeves is the daughter of Cass Scott,a brother of Theresa Cross.

Rachel never lived or grew up at Monterey,so I,actually,never saw her many times. Mama never saw her but she remembered having seen her father,Cass Scott. So far as I know,or remember,that is the list of the Scotts that mama knew other than a few descendents in Monterey whom you have met."

16.BOLLIVER CROSS died as a child

c)SAMUEL WILLIAM CROSS b.Jan.17 (year missing)

d)SUSANNAH CROSS b.May 10,1818 Fairfield Co.SC.d.Oct.6,1844 Fairfield Co. m.Dec.24,1838 Joseph Ebenezer Stanton b.Fairfield Co.Nov.11,1814 ,d.Feb.23,1900 Member of the CSA South Carolina State Troops, 3rd Sgt.Co.H.4 Regt. Both buried at Little River Baptist Church "Longrun", Fairfield Co.SC.(3 children)

    a)MARGARET ANN STANTON b.Oct.18,1839,d.Aug.14,1864 m. Dec.13,1860 John W.Robinson who was killed in the war soon afterwards.Margaret resumed her maiden name.

    b)SARAH CAROLINE STANTON b.May 2,1841,d.Dec.17,1864 buried at "Longrun" Fairfield Baptist Church.

    c)SUSANNAH EMBURY STANTON b.Aug.26,1844,d.Dec.7,1931 m.May 23,1869 to John Leslie Dixon Young b.Nov.8,1829 Antrim,North Ireland d.Aug.18,1907.Both buried at the Fairfield Baptist Church.Hickory Ridge. Susannah was first named MARTHA HESTER but after the death of her mother,her father renamed her for her mother.She used the name ANNA E.(7 children)

        1.JOSEPH STANTON YOUNG b.Apr 1,1870,d.May 29,1947 m.June 28,1899 Sallie Robinson b.Feb.1871,d.Dec.23, 1952.Both buried Fairfield Baptist Church

        2.ANN TWEED YOUNG b.Oct.27,1871,d.Oct.13,1954 m.Feb.2,1898 Archie Andrew Young b.Dec.16,1877 d.Dec.13,1953 son of Andrew Mathews Young and Emma Henrietta Park.Both buried in the Blackjack Cemetery Fairfield Co.S.C..

        3.LILLIE ESTELL YOUNG b.Sep.30,1873,d.Feb.22,1963 m.Apr.15,1891 Samuel Timms b.Oct.15,1858,d.July 25,1935 son of Charles and Sarah Young Timms.

        4.JOHN ANDREW YOUNG b.Nov.13,1875 d.Aug.3,1937 b.Fairfield Baptist Church

        5.MARGARET PRESBURY YOUNG b.Sept.9,1877 m.May 26,1903 m.Henry C.Dickinson

6.ROSE ALICE YOUNG b.Oct.28,1882 d.1917 buried in the
  OLD ARP Cemetery,Winnsboro,S.C.   U.S.Army Nurse Corps
  WW II.

7.SARA EVELYN YOUNG b.Oct.L0,1884 d.May 24,1971
  m.June 5,1913 Levi Franklin Jernigan b.Dec.16,1873
  Marion Co.SC d.Oct.5,1955,both buried in Sumter,S.C.

  Levi Franklin was the son of William Lewis and Mary
  Jones Jernigan.(1 child)

      a)FRANK BLAKELY JERNIGAN b.May 30,1920 Marion Co.
        S.C.,m.June 3,1943 Sumter,S.C. to Sara Margaret
        Baker B.July 23,1922 Sumter,S.C.(3 children)
          1.SARA FRANCES JERNIGAN b. Sumter,SC
            Jan.2,1944 m.Robert Plowden Abbott,
            Columbia,S.C. (3 children)
                a)ROBERT (Bobby)PLOWDEN ABBOTT JR.
                  b.1963
                b)FRANK PATRICK ABBOTT b.1967
                c)CATHERINE ANN (Kathy) ABBOTT b.1969

          2.MARGARET ANN JERNIGAN b. Sumter,SC Apr.2,
            1953 m.Michael Edward Ross of Charleston,SC

          3.WILLIAM BLAKELY (Billy)JERNIGAN b.
            Greenville,SC Mar.25,1956,m.Celia Miriam
            Parrott of Columbia,SC (1 child)
                a)AMANDA CELIA JERNIGAN b.May 9,1987

Descendants Of John Cross, Parish Pioneer, Hold First Annual Reunion

(Special To The Democrat)

Ferriday, La., Oct. 22 — Last Sunday, on the 14th birthday anniversary of the late John Presberry Cross, pioneer settler of Concordia parish, the first annual reunion of his descendants was held on the banks of Horseshoe Lake, not far from the place where he migrated in 1849.

His descendents number about 300 and are living in many parts of the world. Over 200, including in-laws and a few friends, congregated and registered for this first reunion.

Two of these were the only two living children, and are considered honorary members of this large family group. They are James D. Cross, Vidalia merchant, and Mrs. Ramoth Cross Enlow of Monterey. Mrs. Enlow, who with her late husband, J. M. Enlow, celebrated her golden wedding in 1950, still lives at the ancestral home on Cross Bayou.

John Presberry Cross was born in Winnsboro, S. C. in 1812, the son of James Cross of Ireland and Elizabeth Scott Cross of Scotland. His ancestors were loyal patriots of the American revolution. His grandfather, William Scott, held an honorable discharge from the army that fought in that war.

Descendents of William Scott have fought in every war since the Revolution. John Presberry Cross was a member of the non-denominational Christian church, and believed in family worship. Each evening before retiring for the night, he assembled his family together for prayer and for the reading of the Bible.

The oldest living descendent, who was present at the reunion, is ninety-two-year-old Samuel P. Crane, Sr., a grandson, and former school board member. Many grandchildren ranging in age from 70 to well past 80 were present. Included in this group were Cyrus B. Burley, one of Louisiana's first county agents. (His brother, Walter S. Burley, Sr. of Natchez was unable to attend because of ill health.) Others of the elderly group of grandchildren present were Mrs. Lizzie Crane Rice and Mrs. Edna Crane Smith of Monterey, Mrs. Ollie Cross Campbell and Mrs. Ella Cross Mount of Jonesville, Mrs. Warren Presberry Cross of Monterey.

Other olders, but not elderly grandchildren present were Mrs. Mattie Cross Wilson of Wildsville, Mrs. Ethel Cross Rabb of Ferriday, J. Peale Cross and Marion W. Cross of Monterey.

Mrs. Levi S. Cross and Mrs. Marcie Cross of Ferriday, and Mrs J. Dawson Cross Sanders of Wilson were three widows of Cross grandsons who were among the older ladies present. Mrs. Aanders' sister, Mrs. Alma Sandal, accompanied Mr. and Mrs. Sanders from Wilson.

These ladies voiced a feeling of strong ties to the family, partly because of their own Cross descendants. Dr. H. P. Cross, Jr. is the son of Mrs. Sanders, Sheriff Noah Cross and Mrs. Bill Archer are the children of Mrs. Marcie Cross, and Omer Cross, who helped "dream up" the reunion, is one of the children of Mrs. Levi Cross.

Others who helped Omer Cross to vision this large congregation of kinsmen were Phala Cross Kelley, Vela Cross, Daniel, Clinton, Malcolm and Darwin Enlow and Melba E. Gibbs.

Helping with the invitations were Augusta Cross Burley and Ula Cross Moreland.

"The Cross reunion was really not planned in detail," says Mrs. Thelma Girlinghouse of Monterey, one of the descendants. "It was more of a pot-luck affair which just happened to turn into a huge success because of the large number present, the fine fellowship of kinsmen, the pleasant setting and the delightful food, which was supplied by all.

"No well-planned banquet could have surpassed the food; no decor could have equalled Concordia's own moss-draped trees nor the native palmettos that bordered the bayou setting. This setting was appropriate for these descendants of hardy Americans.

"Though many of them have air conditioned homes today and all modern conveniences, all felt that the pleasant autumn breeze with its sprinkle of falling leaves was perfect."

A short business session was held during the afternoon. Clay Smith acted as temporary chairman, with Mrs. Phala Cross Kelley as temporary secretary. A permanent organization was formed with J. S. Cross, Monroe, as president; Mrs. Gladys Cross Burley, treasurer, and Mrs. Thelma Enlow Girlinghouse as secretary. Motions were unanimously passed to form the Cross Reunion association, and to make the reunion an annual affair.

Many of the Crosses still live not far from the original home of John Presberry Cross. Mrs. Girlinghouse said that one member of the younger set remarked:

"What we lack in 'quality' we make up in quantity. I bet there's not another family in these United States that can rake over 200 kinpeople together on this short notice."

Mrs. Girlinghouse thinks he has a point there.

Marriages.

J. P. Cross & P. Steel were marriade
Dec 1ᵗʰ   1835

J. P. Cross and Martha Jane Brown was
married September 12th 1877

John Allen Cross Born June 27th 1879

Levi Scott Cross July 9th   1880

Ruroth Cross April 23   1882

Mary Jane Cross August 26th   1885

James Daniel Cross February 7th 1887

Bolivar Moses Cross December 27th 1888

Martha Jane Cross died January
24th 1889 J. W. Enlow
April 15, 1914

Ethel Girlinghouse
July 7 1929

Births.

Harley Norrold Enlow born apr 2 1916

Malcolm Donovan Enlow Jan 29, 1920

Seymour Shay Enlow Mar. 10, 1922.

Joseph Craig Hapcick

     March 2nd 1874

Benj" Farrar Glabeck, Apl 1st 1876

Linna Elizabeth Glassock Dec 2nd 1878

Ann Brown Died Jun 27 1896

Walter Warron Glasscock born July 30 1894

Died Jan 14 1895

    William Edwin Glasscock

    born May 19 1890

    died Sep 2 — 91,

    Linna E Glassock died Sep 2, 18

    Lela T. Enlow was born.

    Wednesday. Aug 20th 7—20 a.m. 1902

Clinton Lemuel Enlow was born

    Thursday Feb, 11 — 1904

    Althia Melbas Enlow was.

    born Sat Sept 29 1906,

Rosmond Killian Enlow

Malcolm Donovan Enlow,
Born Jan [...] 1920.

Births

Darwin [...] Enlow,
Born Mar [...] 1922.

Family record of John & Phebe Cross

[...] Cross born Nov 13th 1836

Martha Cross born Nov 25th 1838

William A. Cross born Dec 13th 1840

Samuel Cross born Feb 15th 1843

Elizabeth B. Cross born May 21 1845

George W. Cross born May 3rd 1847

Harriet Cross born Apr 22nd 1849

Nancy Cross born Sept 15th 1851

Thomas F. Cross born Feb 21 1854

Jonathan P. Cross born July 26 1856

John P. Cross born Oct 18th 1812

Phebe B. Cross born May 29th 1815

Phebe B. Cross Died Oct 7th [...] 4 o'[...]
A. M. 1876

Deaths.

William H Cross died Sept 26 1935

Nancy Glasscock died Oct 27. 1907

Elizabeth Cross died March 18th 1842

James Scott died July 2nd 1844

George Scott died Aug 30th 1850

John W Scott senior died Aug 31st 1856

Major Scott died Apr 27th 1843

Nancy Scott died Dec 25th 1842

Susannah P Stanton died Oct 6th 1841

Samuel S Cross died May 15th 1845

Anna Scott died June 25th 1848

George W Sanders died Nov 24th 1848

Thomas F Cross died Aug 4th 1862

Harriet Busby Died Oct 22nd 1873

Joseph Craig Glasscock Nov 14th 1876

Benjamin F Glasscock July 7th 1878

Mary Jane Cross Oct 16th 1887

Bolivar Moses Cross May 18th 1890

Jno P Cross died Apr 29th 1917

10 John 3 Oclock

Marion Trisler Paul and Ola Broussard
[...] by the mill stone brought [...]
[...] Parish by John F. Cross [...] 1856.

[...] [...] Birlinghouse
[...] the famous "Cross" bread.

Frances,Melba,Marvyn,Thelma and Neil

Neil on the tree stump on William Scott's. land
Black River,Catahoula Parish,La.

CROSS CEMETERY
Concordia Parish, La.

SCOTT- BRUCE CEMETERY
Catahoula Parish, La.

MAJOR A. SCOTT CEMETERY, Concordia Parish, La.
Thelama Enlow Girlinghouse and Ola Broussard Sturgeon

John P.Cross and daughter,Martha

Melba,Frances,Marvyn,Thelma and David

Major Scott

WILLIAM AND ANN SCOTT
3rd child: MAJOR (MINOR) SCOTT b.1792 Fairfield County,South
Carolina,d.Apr.27,1843.

The estate papers of Major Scott (FF Est.Box.79,pkg.128 p.1-a,SC
Archives) includes his last will given orally as he lay dying.
Quote:

MY LAST WILL AND TESTAMENT

"In the name of God,Amen.I Major Scott of Fairfield District
being sick and weak in body but of a sound and disposing
mind,memory and understanding considering the Certainty of Death
and the uncertainty of the time there of and being desirious to
leave this world when it Shall God to Call me hence,do therefore
make and publish this my last will and testament in manner and
form following: That is to Say-First and principally,I commit my
soul into the hands of allmighty God and my body to the earth,to
be decently buried at the descression of my excecutor hearin
after named and after my debts and Funeral Charges are paid,I
give and bequeathe unto my Six Illigitemate Children,that is
George Welch who is my first Born by Polly Welch vs.Henry Swatts
who is my Second Son by Milletant Swatts,and Mary Ann Scott who
is my first daughter of Artelissa Richison and my three others by
the same.
William Scott, Jeminia Scott,and John Scott which is my youngest
Son. I wish my Property to be Eaqualy Divided between the above
named Children.
Given and Sanctioned in the presence of Robert Hawthorns,Lewis
Haygood and DANIEL SCOTT."

The next day after the above was said to have been written & the
day before MAJOR SCOTT died,he said to me that he wished his
property to be equally divided amoungst his children.

        John B.Thompson

p.1-b_____
Lewis Haygood and Major's brother,Daniel Scott swore that they
heard Major say that he wished his property to go to his
children.
p.3_____
On May 12,1843 Adm.R.Buchanan ,Ordinary of the district summoned
the legal heirs of Major Scott;Ann Scott, John W.Scott,George
Scott,Henry Scott,William Scott,Daniel Scott,John Carman and
Sarah his wife,James Scott ,John P.Cross,Joseph E.Stanton and
Susanna his wife,to show why this last will and testament should
not be admitted to probate.

Thus began a legal battle to deny the children their inheritance.
First,on Sept.1843,the attending physician of Major gave a
deposition to the effect that Mary Taylor (Artelissa Richardson

was first written in and then crossed out)suggested that Major prepare his will after the Doctor told Major that his "case was doubtful".Major told the Doctor that he wanted his children to have his estate.Major was under the influence of opium but when aroused,was capable of understanding the situation.He appeared to be drowsy when not talking but would answer to questions put to him.

Three days later,Daniel had changed his mind as to who should inherit his brother's estate.
p.5___
Daniel filed a paper on May 15,giving the following:" That Major Scott,his brother,departed this life on the 27th day of April last,having neither wife,nor legitimate children living.And the little personal property belonging to the estate is in imminent danger of being apprehended and lost to others having interest in the estate."
Daniel wanted to be named administrator of the estate so as it would be protected .Permission was granted.

The will of Major was denied and on May 20,1843 the legal heirs; his mother Ann Scott,brothers John W.Scott,George W.Scott,Henry Scott ,William Scott,Daniel Scott,and James Scott were named. Also,sister Sarah Carmen and husband John Carman,nephew John P.Cross,niece Susanna Stanton with husband Joseph E.Stanton were listed.

As stated before,John W.Scott,Henry Scott and William Scott were already citizens of Louisana,therefore, they were not present at the division. They usually gave a lawyer or their nephew power of attorney to represent them whenever there was a death of a member of the family.

The sale of Major's personal property listed several names of local people who lived in the area.These neighbors as well as the family who bought items include the following:John Mushato,Arch Boyd,Capt.Owens,JohnBoyd,Robt.Boyd,Robt.Quigley,Monroe Scott, Monroe Stote,Caot Iwebs,Henry Swats (Major's son), R.Nicholson, Artelissa Richardson,Jesse Owns,Harry Swats,Saml Owens,Lany Mickler,Jans W.Seal,Lewis Haigood,Robt.Hawthorn,John Bernahan, James Boyd,John B.Thompson James Alston and Larry(Lany) Mickler.

Total from the sale amounted to $214.17 1/4

Artelissa Richardson gave oath that she had bought a cow from Benjamin Harrison in June 1843 and this cow that was found on Major Scott's place at the time of his death was HERS.
James M.Robinson confirmed this purchase.

1845(Bk PP o.166)
John Carman and Wife vs Danl Scott
Demand that a return has not been given on Major's land.

The place was rented in 1844 to Margt.Taylor and Stolt.
The lower place was rentd in 1845 to Artelissa Richardson and the
upper place was rented in 1845 to Henry Robertson.
Daniel bought both tracts in 1845(Bk PP p.166) for $1,134.
108 A known as the"Homeplace"of Major Scott and also 84 A.Both on
Mill Creek.
By 1850,Major's son by Polly Welch was listed in the census:

```
Pg.205,line 76   Welch,George          29 planter b. Fairfield,SC
                      ,Mary             25
                      ,Mary              8
                      ,Margaret E.       5


In 1860,          Welch,George          35              $150.00
#401                   ,Mary            19.
#402                   , Polly          65   was living with the
                  J.W.Harrison family.
```

In 1850,
Major's second son Henry Swatts was living with his uncl. John W.
Scott in Concordia Parish,Louisiana.This move probably coincided
with his cousin John P.Cross's decision to join the John W.Scott
family in the same parish after his grandmother Ann Scott died in
1849.

```
p 154-w    line 20-23
                  Swatts,Henry          24 b. S.C.
                        ,Elizabeth       24 b. S.C.
                        ,John             2 b. S.C.
                        ,Henry W.         4 mo. b.La.
                  Scott,John W.          65    b.S.C.  $3,000
                       ,George W.        38    b.S.C.
                       ,John F.           2    b.La.
```

At the same time (1850),the remaining children of Major Scott
were still with their mother,Artelissa Richardson in Fairfield
County,S.C.using their mother's maiden name.

```
p.223 ,line 244
    Richardson,Artelissa              40
    (Scott)    ,Margaret E.           22
    (Scott)    ,Wm.                   13
    (Scott)    ,Harriett Jeminia      11
    (Scott)    ,John                   8
               ,Rebecca                6
               ,Jesse C.               3
               ,James E.               3
               ,Baby (female)          5 mo.
```

It is obvious that Major had small children in his home when he
verbalized his will leaving the estate to his children to share
equally.

1

June the 7th 1843

The Sale Bill of The personal property of Major Scott Deceased

		$	
Daniel Scott	1 Bull	5	00
John Muskate	Cow & Calf Proved off by A Richardson	0	50
Daniel Scott	1 Brindled Yearling Proved off by Do.	2	00
James Scott	Lot of Razors And Strap	2	50
Wm. Scott	1 Watch	2	00
Daniel Scott	1 Lot of Sundrys	1	56¼
Daniel Scott	1 Trunk	2	50
Archd. Boyd	Lot of Axes No. 1		62½
Capt. Owens	Lot of Axes No. 2		75
John Boyd	Lot of Axes No. 3	1	25
Daniel Scott	1 Axe	2	25
John Cross	hand Axe	1	75
Robt. Boyd	Broad Axe	1	62½
Robt. Dugley	Vice	2	12½
Monroe Scott	1 Lot of tools No. 1		56¼
John Cross	1 Lot of tools No. 2	1	25
Danl. Scott	1 Lot of Irons No. 1		43¾
Monroe Scott	1 Lot of Irons No. 2		50
Capt. Owens	1 Auger		37½
Danl. Scott	1 Lot of Sundrys		56¼
Robt. Boyd	1 Lot of Plains		62½
Henry Swats	1 Pair Stilyards		62½
Robt. Boyd	1 Lot of Sundrys		02
George Scott	Lot of tools	2	6¼
Daniel Scott	Shot Gun & Bag	4	62½
R. Nicholson	1 Carriage whip		50
James Scott	whip, Chain & Sundrys		25
George Scott	Whips		13
A Richardson	Halter Chain		6¼
Saml. Owens	Powder Horn		81¼
A Richardson	Shovel & Tongs	1	12½
George Scott	Andirons Proved off by W Cork	1	56¼
A Richardson	Spinning Wheel	4	00
	Carried forward $	57	12½

Buyer	Item	£	s/d
	Brought forward	57	12½
Jesse T Owens	1 Meat		37½
Harry Swats	1 Clock		6¼
Daniel Scott	1 Looking Glass		37½
A. Richardson	Bed & Cloths	10	6¼
M. Stots	Bed & Cloths	8	6¼
Danl. Scott	Bedstead and Cord	3	12½
John Boyd	Bedstead and Cord		50
Danl. Scott	8 Chairs	6	8
Danl Scott	Sword and Scabbard		25
Harry Swats	1 Iron Wedge		31¼
A Richardson	Tables		12½
Danl Scott	Table		12½
Henry Swats	Table		25
Harry Swats (Son)	1 Small table		56¼
A. Richardson	Lot of Straw baskets	1	6¼
Henry Swats	Clock Works		6¼
George Scott	1 Drawing Knife		50
Saml. Owens	Powder Horn	1	31¼
M. Stots	Shoe Brushes		25
M. Stots	Lot of Sundrys		31¼
G. Scott	Lot of Pewter		25
Saml. Owens	1 box Shoe tools	1	00
Wm. Scott	Sundrys in the Chest	1	56¼
James Scott	Chest and lock	1	00
Saml. Owens	1 Crosscut Saw	2	93¾
John Boyd	1 Tea Kettle	1	20
Danl. Scott	Kettle ladder and Chain	1	00
A Richardson	two Ovens and Spider		50
A Richardson	1 large Pot	1	00
G. Scott	1 Bucket		25
Lany Mickler	Churn Pale and Piggen		75
A. Quigley	half Peck & Plunder		32
A. Richardson	1 Pale		12½
Saml. Owens	1 pair Stillyards		52½
A. Richardson	1 Coffee Mill		25
John Boyd	Plough Gear		62½
		8 104	28¾

	Brought forward	104	28¾
John Boyd	1 Blind bridle	1	25
James Scott	Saddle bridle & Equipage	5	25
A Richardson	fire dogs	1	00
Dan Scott	1 Loom		50
A Richardson	1 fair Harness		6¼
A Richardson	1 Cupboard and Contents		6¼
Jas W Seal	1 Bale mare	17	50
G Scott	1 Colt and Bell	1	00
John Boyd	1 Lot of Bottles &c		25
Lewis Haigwood	1 Tureen		87½
A Richardson	1 Lot of Crockery & ware		25
A Richardson	1 tray & Sieve		25
M Stott	1 trunk & Contents		62½
Robt Hawthorn	1 Hone		56
Henry Swaths	1 Lot of Cloths	5	12½
Danl Scott	1 Lot of Scantling No 1	3	93¾
D Scott	No 2		75
John Carnahan	1 Jug and Vinnegar		68¾
Lany Mickler	1 Keg and Vinnegar		50
Danl Scott	3 Jugs		41
G Scott	1 Keg and Vinnegar	1	00
Henry Swato	1 iron bound Keg		50
A Richardson	1 Barrel		12½
Saml Owens	1 Barrel and fawsett		25
M Stott	1 Lot of Barrels		37½
John Boyd	1 Hogshead & Churn		25
John Boyd	1 Single tree		12½
R Boyd	1 Lot Chains & P hoes		31
R Quigley	1 waggon tire		75
D Scott	1 Cutting box		12½
A Richardson	24½ Bushels of Corn et 63 Ct	15	27
	pr Bushel	15	27½
Saml Owens	1 Side Pot	4	00
Robt Hawthorn	1 Cider trough		87
George Scott	1 Lot of Peas	3	00
Daniel Scott	1 Lot of Turnips & 3 Barrels		37
Daniel Scott	1 Lot of Turnips do table & box		12
Robt Quigley	1 Jug & Vinnegar	173	63 27

Name	Item		$	¢
	Brought forward		173	21
John Boyd	1 Jug & Vinnegar			37
Henery Swats	1 Jug & Vinnegar			43
George Scott	1 Jug & Vinnegar			40
Saml. Mundie	1 Sythe & Cradle			50
Daniel Scott	1 Basket & Bottles			25
John Boyd	1 lot of Baskets			12
James Boyd	1 Lot of hoes & spade			62
George Scott	1 lot of Ayes			40
John B Thompson	1 Sheep Bell			60
Daniel Scott	1 lot of Ploughs			50
Daniel Scott	1 Lot of Sundreys		1	00
Henery Swats	1 Lot of Sundrys			6¼
James Alston	1 Stack Fodder 1st Choice		7	31
Saml. Mundie	1 Stack Fodder 2d Choice		7	95
George Scott	1439 lb Cotton at $102, pr hundred		14	67
H. Richardson	5 pigs			
H. Richardson	5 Hogs at 50 ¢ pr head		2	50
Daniel Scott	Balance of hogs		1	50
G. Scott	3 Bee guns			6¼
G. Scott	1332 Boards at 12½ ¢ p Cot		1	66
R. Quigley	1 grinding stone & Crank			50
		$	214	17¾

Daniel Scott

(Deduct amount Swond off by Arthr. Ritchison $1260
(Deduct Amount Sworn off by B. Scott 1364
Su affidavit inclosed)

		14	06¼
		200	11¾

79
Account of Sales
7 June 1849
Major Scott est
128
Recorded in Book
B. pag. 344. 347
John Witherspoon
R. R. I.

25-4

We audit the legal service of the ... Summons

George + Scott
(his mark)

Daniel Scott
John Carman

Sarah E carman
Ann ... (her mark)
James → Samy Scott
John P Crass
Jas E Stanton

John P Crass witness

Major Scotts estate

Summons for the Next of kin to object to Probate of Will.

79 — 128

Summons for next of kin to object to probate of Major Scott's Will

State of South Carolina } Personaly appeard
Fairfield Dist } before me Artelefs
Richardson and made
Oath that She own the Black & white Cow
and Calf and Prichased the same from
Benjamin Harrison which Cow was
found On the place at the Death of
Major Scott See and also Personaly
appeard Jame M. Robinson and made
Oath that she purchased the Same
Sworn to before me this 7th of June
1843

Rott Hawthorn Mag }   Artelefs Richardson

                                       James Robertson

State of South Carolina } Person aly
Fairfield Dist }   Appeard before
me Martha Stott and Made Oath that
a Moily Cow and Calf and a yearling
was Her property which was found on
the place of Major Scotts Dec and also
Artelef Richardson and Made Oath that
the Said Cow was given to her by her self
before the death of Major Scotts Sworn
to before me this 7th day of June 1843

Rott Hawthorne Magest }   Martha Stott
                                  Artelifse Richardson

25-6

George Scott

WILIAM AND ANN SCOTT

4th child:GEORGE SCOTT b.1790 Fairfield Co.SC,d.after 1850 .The 1850 census lists him with a wife and two daughters.However, in the census of 1830,George is listed next to his mother Anne Scott.(pg.391,Lines 21 and 22 respectively.)He had a male child between 5 & 10,one between 10 & 15,one between 15 & 20.He was at that time,40 years old. The females listed were 2 under 5 yrs. of age,one between 5 & 10,1 between 20 & 30.This gave a total of children as 3 sons and 3 daughters.

The 1840 census lists 3 sons between 20 & 30, one between 30 & 40 and George between 50 & 60. The females listed were 1 under 5 yrs,1 between 5 & 10, 3 between 10 & 15 and his wife between 30 & 40 years of age. At this period of time,he and his brother Daniel Jackson Scott were living next to each other.(Page 169, Lines 21-25 and 26.)

March 5, 1849(Bk RR p.177)
In 1844,Robert Quigley paid George Scott $32.00 for 2 1/2 acres,the same being a part of land originally granted to Peter Staines on the 27th of August AD 1771 for 252 acres.The same being situated in the District and State and on Morris Creek waters of Little River. The same being situated and bounded as follows: Morris Creek on one end for boundary and(??)2 chains thence SW 71 degrees,6 chains 40L to stake near Road thence SW 51 by said road 36 L 50 L to stake near Rod and Branch Thence SW 11 near So.branch 4 chains to stump X thence N 47 E 13 chains 80 lengths to the Creek.The same bounded on all sides by land of the said George Scott,Robt.Quigley,and Robert Boyd containing 2 1/2 acres.

For the first time,the 1850 census named each person in the household. Page 223,line 339 named George Scott as 60 years of age,a planter and born in Fairfield,SC.

He had two daughters,Eliza Scott 30,and Sarah Scott 23 still living with him and his wife Nancy,who was 55 years of age. His brother Daniel Scott 50 years old was a close neighbor.

Perhaps someday in the future,additional research will uncover more information on this family.No other evidence is found in Fairfield County after 1850.

After careful deliberation,I have decided to include my supposition on the family of Elisha and Jeminia's connection to the family of William and Ann Scott. Without absolute proof that what I believe to be true,I cannot state that it is a "fact".

However,using the census,land location and the evidence of George Scott's constant inclusion in the legal affairs of the family,I believe that Elisha Scott was one of the sons of George Scott.

Jeminia Gibson was the widow of Minor Gibson who died in 1841.His will,dated May 13,1841 stated that he was an old man advanced in years with a severe illness and not expected to recover.

He wanted his administrators to sell the tract of land with 67 acres that was bounded by Robert Hawthore,Lewis Haigood and McGraw.However,They were not to sell the Negroes,but to sell the Gin Head,the Running Gear,and the Screw. They were to keep the "homeplace" for the negroes to cultivate the corn,cotton,wheat and etc. and the proceeds to go to support his wife JEMINIA JANE GIBSON annually.The money obtained was to be used to educate his two daughters,Sarah Ann and Mary Ann Frances.

Any surplus money was to be given to his wife as long as she remained unmarried,but if she should choose to marry,she would loose all rights to his estate. If the any of the childrn should die,the rights would go to the one left and should both die,the wife would inherit.

Minor's brother,Stephen Gibson and Edward Andrews were administrators of the estate. (Equity Decree 1845,Bill #7) Shortly after Minor's death,Jeminia delivered a son, Minor, who she named for his father.

By 1944,(Bill #15) ELISHA SCOTT had married Jeminia Jane,widow of Minor Gibson.Evidently,Sarah Ann had died by this time as only the two children,Mary Frances and Minor Gibson,quote,"who is about 4 years of age",unquote, were named. The children were entitled to a legacy under the will of their father ,consisting of both real and personal property. ELISHA wished to be named guardian of Minor.This was recommended by William Holmes.

Jeminia claimed dower rights as well as an interest in the land.It was stated that there was no reason to keep the "homeplace"as there was little woodland on the place or timber for making repairs and keeping up the place.Also,the negroes (one man and one boy) could not cultivate the land to an advantage. Therefore, the money obtained in selling the land was more than could be gained through holding on to the land.

In the interest of all concerned the land was sold to ELISHA and JEMINIA. Elisha paid the sum of $594.12.

The land was described as lying on the road leading from Bells Mill to Columbia.and bounded by lands of Robert Quigley,Samuel Mundle,Arthur McGraw and GEORGE SCOTT. (Recorded Mar.25,1845)

In the 1850 census,Fairfield,County,the family of Elisha Scott is listed as #337. He was 27 years old and a planter. Jeminia was 25 and this indicated that she had been quite young when she married Minor Gibson. Only one child of Minor was listed...Mary who would marry John W. Boyd.

Mary (Gibson) was 9 years of age,John (Y) Scott was 5,Franklin Scott was 3,and Nancy Scott was 1. The family lived next to GEORGE SCOTT and his wife,Nancy and their two daughters,Eliza 30 and Sarah 23.

In the 1860 census,#632,the children were listed as John 16, Jemina 7,William E. 5,and Daniel Scott,2. The father and son were very close and during the years of the Civil War,Elisha and his son John Y. served together as members of Co.B ,7th Bat. S.C.V.

Elisha died before 1870 as the census lists Family #300,page 38, Jeminia Scott 48 years of age. Her children living with her were James D.Scott 13,George E.(Elisha) 10,and Samuel (Major) Scott 5.

John Y.Scott, Family #291,page 37,lists him with his second wife. Mary C.. John's first wife was Lydia (?) with whom he had one child,Susannah born July 31,1866. Lydia died and John married her sister,Mary C.(?)b.1835.

With the death of Mary C.,John remarried for the 3rd time.Things were not too happy in the household so Susannah was reared by her grandmother,Jeminia.At the age of 18,Susannah moved to Columbia where she met and married William Benson Hoy .Their daughter, Isabelle, born Sept.3,1894 ,married W.M.Dunlap and lives in Winnsboro.

Mary (Gibson) married John W. Boyd and in the 1870 census,Family #187,p.22,he is listed as being 40 and a farmer. Mary was 29,Nancy J.Boyd 7,Melissa (K or R)Boyd 5,and Mary G.Boyd was 3.

Another child of Jeminia and Elisha,Nancy,b.1847,had married an Arnold.In 1870 she and her son,James T.Arnold 2,were living with her brother John Y.Scott.

With the death of Jeminia Scott,on May 15,1883,John Y. was appointed as the administrator of her small estate of $25.00. (Probate Records Return Book C,pg.16) Also Box 50,#22.

Her survivors were Mary Boyd,wife of John W.Boyd,John Y.Scott, James D.Scott,George E.Scott and Samuel M. Scott,an infant.(He was 18).

ELISHA SCOTT b. 1820 d.1865-1870 Member of Co.B,7th Bat. S.C.V. CSA m.Mrs. Jeminia Jane Gibson b.1822 d. May 15,1883,widow of Minor Gibson,who left three children,Sarah Ann Elizabeth, Mary Ann Frances,and a son,Minor Gibson who was born after the father had died.The first child named in the will could have been the daughter of his first wife,Sarah Ann as Jeminia was only 16 when Minor died.

Elisha and Jeminia had 7 children.

1. MARY ANN FRANCES GIBSON b.1841,m.John W.Boyd b.1830,
   In the 1870 census,the children were Nancy J. 7, Melissa(K.or R.)5,and Mary G. 3.

2. JOHN Y.SCOTT b.1844 d. Jan.25,1910 member of Co.B.7th Bat. S.C.V.CSA. Buried under the oak tree on the "Homeplace" along with the grave of Sarah Gibson,1st wife of Minor Gibson,(Sarah died at age of 16). Also eleven unmarked graves including the graves of two children. These were marked with field stones.

   John m.1st,Lydia (?) one child,Susannah b.July 31,1866.
      1. SUSANNAH b. July 31,1866 m.William Benson Hoy.
         a) ISABELLE HOY b.Sept.3,1894 m.W.M.Dunlap
   John was married 3 times.

3. FRANKLIN SCOTT b. 1847 d. before 1860

4. NANCY SCOTT b. 1849 d. pre 1883 m. (?) Arnold
      1. James T. Arnold b. 1868
5. JEMINIA b. 1853 m. (?) Carman who was a grandson of SARAH SCOTT who married John Carman.

6. WILLIAM E. SCOTT b. 1855 d. pre 1883

7. JAMES DANIEL b. 1858. Killed on the Railroad.

8. GEORGE ELISHA SCOTT b. 1860 d. 1931.Buried in Bethel Cemetery,Fairfield Co.S.C.
   m.1st to Hattie Miller (7 children)
   1. MINNIE SCOTT m.a Brown
   2. JUANITA ETHEL SCOTT m. a Glenn and a Jones
   3. PEARL IRENE SCOTT m. W.V. Bundrick
   4. CALVIN BRICE SCOTT
   5. BENJAMIN SCOTT (Died at 6 months)
   6. ZEDDIE (Ed) WILLIAM SCOTT moved to Yoakum,Tx.
   7. GEORGE ELISHA SCOTT JR.(Little George) moved to Yoakum,Tx.
      a) Ruth Scott
      b) Betty Scott
      c) Marion Scott
      d) George Scott
   George m.2nd to Margaret Matilda Rimer buried Oaklawn Cemetery Winnsboro. (5 children)

8.AGNES LUCILLE SCOTT m. Loggins

9.ISABELL HOY SCOTT b. Sept.26,1912 m.Alex Ballentine.Lives in Blytheville.
Isabell and Kitty told me that during the War,"Aunt Jeminia" cried and begged Shermon not to ruin her hat.So all he did was shoot a cannon through the house.Years later,this shell was still lodged in the top of the house when it was torn down by the Railroad crew.

10.KITTY BROWN b.Sept.26,1914 m.Mr. Godwin. Lives in N.C. (1 child)
a)Ina Godwin m. Larry Jones
11.MARION EUGENE SCOTT. Lives in Gastonia N.C.(5 sons)
a)Ace Scott
b)Ted Scott
c)Larry Scott
d)Randolph Scott
e)Steve scott
12.JAMIE LOUISE SCOTT

9.SAMUEL MAJOR (MAJOR SAMUEL) SCOTT b. 1865. Major was about 18 or 19 years old when his mother died. One petition was made for a guardian when he was 18 and asked for Thomas W. Scruggs,then when he was 19,he asked for James R. Harvey as his guardian. This was granted. (Filed Oct.5,1885,Probate Records Book C.p.139.)

Major settled in Columbia,S.C. and operated a store.

After Jeminia died,the land (Homeplace) was sold for debts.The 97 acres were bought by Robert P. Brown for $645.00. In 1890,Brown sold the land to Ulysse G. DesPortes who in 1900,sold it to the wife of George Elisha Scott.A little of the land was lost to the railroad that crossed the land.It was now described as land on "Bells Mill Rd." Recorded Book A.S. p. 471,Oct.12,1900.

Hattie died April 17,1908 and George received a share as her husband. He owed over $300.00 to the Winnsboro State Bank. The bank fored him to sell the land in order to clear the debt.The land was surveyed by Edgar Trapp.

Tract #1 contained 33 1/2 acres which was sold to clear the debt.
      #2   10   acres to Charles H. Scott.
      #3   10   acres to Ethel Glenn
      #4   10   acres to Minnie Brown
      #5   10   acres to Zettie William
      #6   10   acres to Pearl Bundrick
      #7   10   acres to Calvin Brice Scott
      #8   5   acres to "Little George" who allowed

his father to live in the house and use the five acres. In 1929, his father moved to town and in 1935,George Jr.sold the land to the Winnsboro Blue Granite Co.,as George Jr.and his brother Zeddie had moved to Yoakum ,Texas.

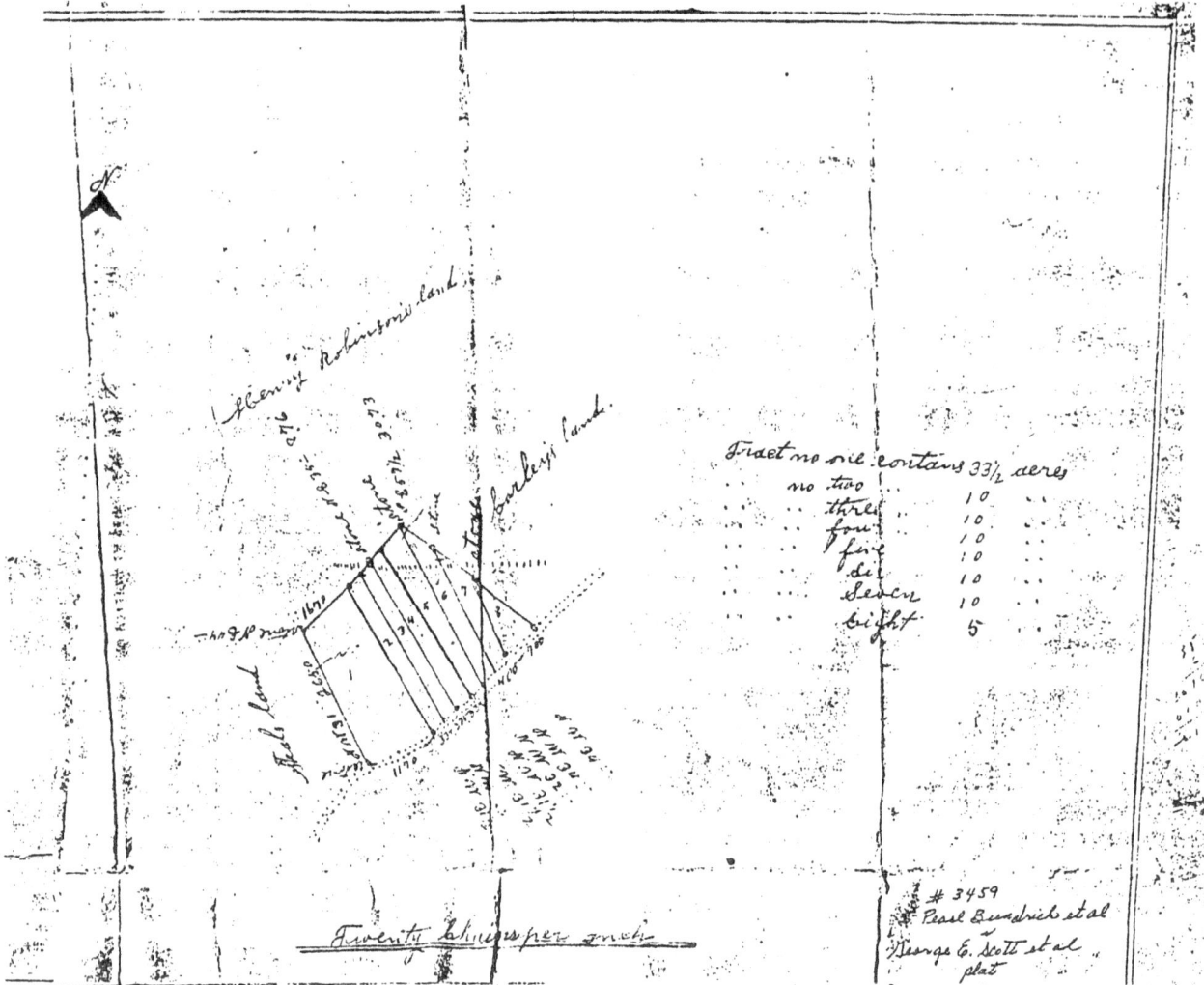

Tract no one contains 33½ acres
no two . . . 10
. . three . . 10
four . 10
five . 10
six . 10
seven 10
eight 5

Twenty chains per inch

#3459
Pearl Bundrick et al
George E. Scott et al
plat

South Carolina
By request of the Commissioners in the division of
George Scott place I have surveyed and divided up the
above delineated tract of land which I find to contain ninety eight
and one half acres situated in Fairfield County, having such
arms marks and boundaries as the above plat represents.
Surveyed Feb. 17. 1915.

Edgar Trapp
Surveyor

Gibson – Scott Cemetery
June 18, 1978

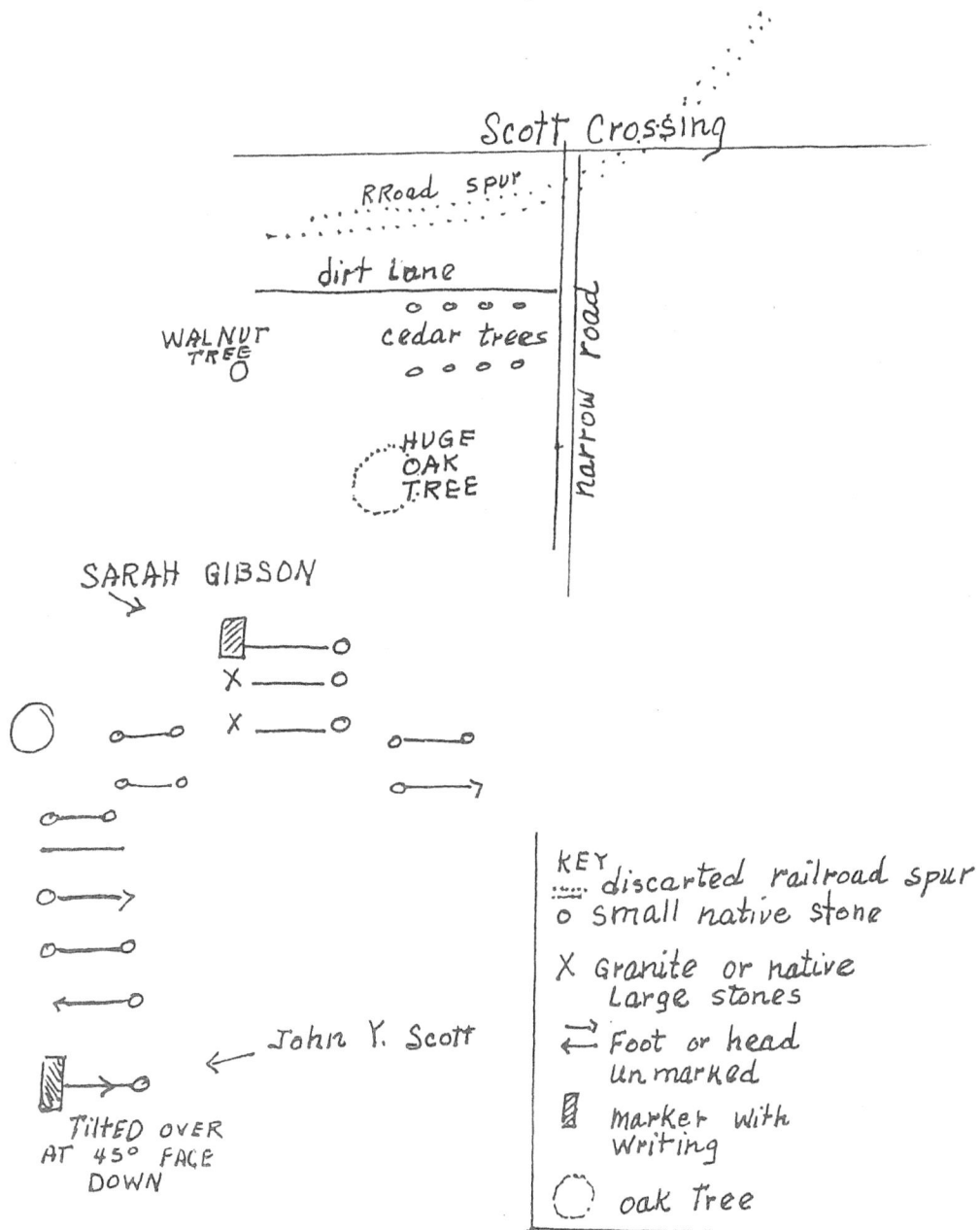

Scott Crossing

RRoad spur

dirt lane

WALNUT TREE

cedar trees

HUGE OAK TREE

narrow road

SARAH GIBSON

John Y. Scott

TiltED OVER AT 45° FACE DOWN

KEY
.::. discarded railroad spur
o small native stone
X Granite or native Large stones
⇄ Foot or head Un marked
▨ Marker with writing
◯ oak Tree

Henry Scott

HENRY SCOTT

5th Child of William Scott Sr.

HENRY SCOTT b.1796 Fairfield Co.SC.d.Feb.6,1860,Catahoula
    Parish,La.m. Jan.13,1822 Wilkinson Co.Ms.to Sarah
    Hennington.(6 known children)

Henry was a twin to William Scott Jr.who married
Lavinia (Atkins ?) in Fairfield County,South Carolina.
It is possible that Henry was a widower when he and
William,along with their brother,John W.Scott,immigrated
first to Wilkinson County.A few years later they made
their permanent homes in the Parham Community,Catahoula
Parish,Louisana,the Horse Shoe Lake area and the Monterey
Community in Concorda Parish,Louisana.

William lived for many years in Wilkinson Co.,paying
taxes until 1843.At this time,he and his wife Lavinia,
sold slaves to another brother,Daniel Jackson Scott,in
preparation for their move to Catahoula.Records show that
Daniel delt in slaves and land both in South Carolina,
Mississippi and Louisana but always kept his roots in
Fairfield County,South Carolina where he died in 1878.

Henry and William's oldest brother,John W.Scott,was a
resident in Wilkinson County from 1820 until 1847 when he
released his 120 acres of land for taxes.His nephew,Thomas
Francis Scott,the son of William,was the highest bidder.
As a result,Thomas acquired the land for the sum of $6.50.
Records also show that John W. was living in Concordia
Parish in January 1849,as his nephew,John P.Cross,son of
his sister Elizabeth,paid $500.00 for John's share of his
parents' estate in South Carolina.

After the settlement of William and Ann's estate,John P.
Cross prepared to move his family to Concordia to join
John W.Scott's son,George W.Scott in farming.The Catahoula
1850 census list John W.Scott as a farmer with land valued
at $3,000.00.

By 1860,John W.Scott,Henry and Sarah Scott was dead.Daniel
was back in South Carolina and only William was still in
Catahoula.His only companion was his son,Benjamin C.Scott,
as Lavinia had died before 1850.

WILLIAM SCOTT SR. Fairfield,Co,S.C.
CHILD #5:HENRY SCOTT b.1796 Fairfield County,South Carolina.
    d.Feb.6,1860 Parham Community,Catahoula Parish,Louisana.
    m.Jan.13,1822,Wilkinson County,Mississippi(Bk D,pg.181)
    to Sarah Hennington.(6 known children)

    1.MARY ANN SCOTT b. 1823 m.Jesse Holliman Jan.28,1838
      (Bk F,pg.217,Wilkinson County,Ms.) 2 children
      a)JESSE HOLLIMAN b. 1842
      b)NANCY HOLLIMAN b. 1844
      Mary Ann and Jesse died before 1850 as both children were
      wards of their grandparents,Henry and Sarah.

    2.JOHN MINOR SCOTT b. 1825,d.before 1853.m.Faithful (?)
      who later m.Arthur K.McDonald Nov.22,1853,Catahoula Parish
      Louisana.John and Faithful had one child.
      a)SARAH ANN SCOTT

    3.NANCY B. SCOTT b. 1830 m.July 25,1851 Concordia Parish,
      Louisana to William S. Steed.

    4.LEVISA SCOTT b.1832 m.Sept.16,1847 Catahoula Parish,Louis-
      ana to John F. Dye(1 child) In the 1850 census,Levisa and
      child were living with her parents.
      a)SARAH A.DYE b. 1848

    5.JAMES SCOTT b. 1834

    6.MATILDA CAROLINE SCOTT b.Mar. 13,1836 Wilkinson County,
      Mississippi. d.Mar.1,1926 Avoyelles Parish,Louisana.m.Feb.
      1850 to Henry Clay Trisler b.Feb.15,1816 in Ohio,d.Mayna,
      Louisana.Dec.23,1884.(1 child)

      a)JAMES SCOTT TRISLER b.Nov.15,1850 Mayna,La.d.Feb.26,
        1926,Mayna,La.m.Mary Virginia Walker,b.Oct.23,1853,d.
        Nov.8,1917.(8-10 children.Two died as infants--each a
        twin).
        1.JOE TRISLER m. Jenny Welch(4 children)
          a)JENNY TRISLER m.Dennis Furr
          b)JOE TRISLER(Toog) m.Ethel Girlinghouse
          c)CARRIE m.Orville McGuffie(1 child)
            1.GEORGE McGUFFIE
          d)ROSWELL TRISLER m. Geneva Hennigan
        2.TOM TRISLER
        3&4.JAMES SCOTT TRISLER JR. Never married.Twin died.
        5&6.HENRY TRISLER m.Bertha Lanias.No children but reared
          twin boys and perhaps adopted them.
          a)HARDY TRISLER
          b)HARVEY TRISLER

7.SAMUEL ALBERT TRISLER b.Jan.26,1884 Mayna,La.d.Mar.7,
   1876 Ferriday,La.m.Ruth Maude Dale Dec.22,1907.b.Sept
   9,1877 New Era,La.(3 children)

   a)MARY TRISLER b.Feb.7,1909 d.Jan.8,1972.m.1st
      1930 to Rayner Bell.(4 children)
      1.Son died when 3 days old.
      2.LARRY BELL b.July 1,1934 d.Apr.1962 m.1st June
         1957 to Carol(?) (2 children)
         a)JAN BELL b.1958 d. Apr.1962
         b)JEAN LORRAINE BELL b. Nov.1961
         Larry m.2nd 1963 to Beryl Bordelon(3 children)
         c)SUSAN BELL b. 1963
         d)LARRY NEIL BELL b. 1964
         e)MARY ELIZABETH BELL b. 1968
            Mary m.2nd 1939 to John Williams(2 children)

      3.LYNDA ANN WILLIAMS b.Aug.29,1940 m. 1962 Sammy
         Crane, b.1940 (2 children)
         a)LYNN CRANE b. 1963
         b)JULIE CRANE b. 1966

      4.JOHN W.(Dickie)WILLIAMS b. Oct.26,1941 m.Dec.25,
         1976 to Ruth Robertson.

   b)MARVYN MAUDE TRISLER b. Sept.29,1913 Mayna,La.m.Dec.
      30,1937 Carl Ussery Paul b. Aug.26,1903(2 children)

      1.CARLA RUTH PAUL b.Dec.25,1944 m.Ferriday,La.June
         1976 to Ray Mason b.Dec.1934.

      2.BRENDA KAY PAUL b. July 16,1951 m.Aug.26,1973 to
         Stephen Phillip Ellis b. Jan.1951.(2 children)
         a)LORI ANN ELLIS b. Sept.5,1979 West Monroe,La.
         b)DAVID PAUL ELLIS b.June 6,1982 Ft.Worth,Tx.

   c)SAMUEL ALBERT TRISLER JR.b.Dec.17,1917 m.1938 to
      Betty Burley (3 children)

      1.SAMMY MILLARD TRISLER b.July 2,1939 m.Feb.28,1966
         to Jennie Frost (3 children)
         a)BROOKS TRISLER
         b)CADE TRISLER
         c)ROGER TRISLER

      2.BETTY RUTH TRISLER b. Jan.8,1943 m.1961 to Warren
         Swingler(Butch) Cross Jr.(2 children)
         a)TRACE CROSS
         b)SHANE CROSS
         Betty m.2nd Mar.31,1975 to Elton Merck(1 child)
         c)ELBY DALE MERCK b.Dec.1979

3.CYNTHIA ANN TRISLER b.Jan.13,1953 m.Mar.31,1975 to
Robert Wooley(1 child)
a)DEREK WOOLEY b. 1977

7.ALEX TRISLER m.Jenny Sevaw (? children)
a)MILLARD TRISLER
b)LORENA TRISLER m.Elliot Magoun(1 child)
1.ALTHEA MAGOUN
c)MYRA TRISLER
d)LEONA TRISLER m.? Thornhill
e)NOAH TRISLER
f)JAMES TRISLER m."Cutie" Trisler(2 sons)
g)PHOEBE DELL TRISLER m.and lives in Alberquerque,NM.
h)COSBY TRISLER

8.MARY VIRGINIA(Mamie)TRISLER apr.30,1891,d.July 20,1982
m.Dec.20,1914 to John Alfred Gemar b.Nov.5,1883 d.Sept.
1,1960(3 children)

a)SAM COTTON GEMAR b.Feb.4,1916 m.Bama Holt 1940,Bama

b.Sept.1,1922 (1 child)
1.CRAIG ARNOLD GEMAR b&d Jan.7,1947

b)ANNA BELLE GEMAR b.June 5,1918, m.Feb.14,1941 Howard
Doyle Nixon b.June 1,1914 (1 child)

1.ANNA FRANCINE NIXON b.Jan.30,1947 m.1st.Aug.11,1967
Don Damon Bradley b.July 31,1947 (1 child)
a)DONYA DeSHAY BRADLEY b.Aug.4,1972
Anna m.2nd July 18,1980 Jay Robert Knierim b.Apr.13
1936.

c)ALFRED LLOYD GEMAR b.Apr.1,1925 m.Faith Lea Trisler,
June 12,1954.Faith b.Dec.3,1923(2 children)

1.ALFRED LLOYD GEMAR JR. b.Mar.22,1955 m.July 25,1975
to Teresa Paulette Parker b.Oct.23,1957(2 children)
a)JOHNNY DeLAND GEMAR b.Jan.18,1978
b)JERROD SCOTT GEMAR b.Oct.10,1980

2.CAROL MARIE GEMAR b. Sept.10,1957 m.Jan.7,1977
Winfred Wiley Jr.b.May 31,1955(2 children)
a)WILLIAM CRAIG WILEY b.May 14,1979
b)SARAH LEANN WILEY b.Nov.27,1982

9.LEONA TRISLER m.Charlie Beetz (2 children)
a)HENRY FORD BEETZ m.Merle Cross,dau. of Howard Cross
(2 sons,1 daughter)
b)OPAL MARY BEETZ m.Mr.Thornhill (large family)

Marvyn and Carl Paul, Concordia Parish, La.

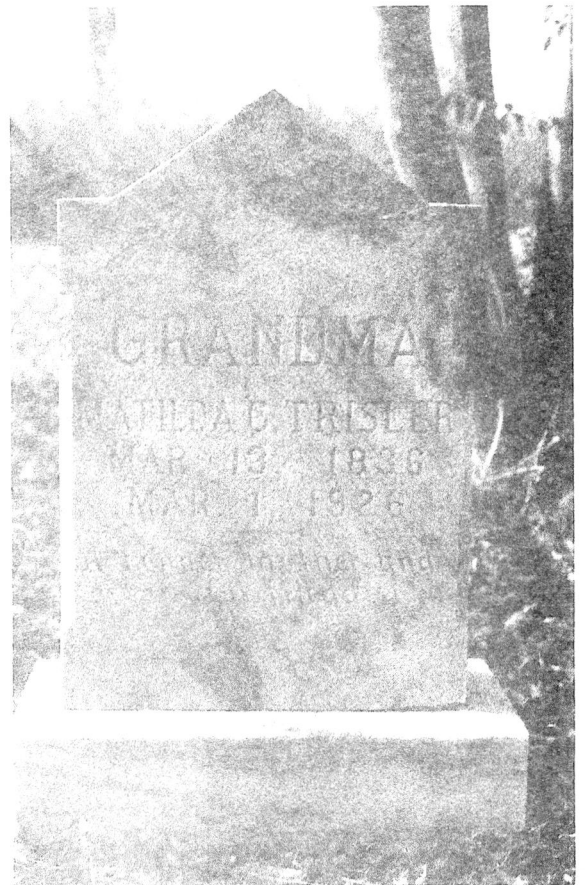

Henry and Matilda Scott Trisler, Catahoula Parish, La.

State of Louisiana } District Court 11th Judicial District
Parish of Catahoula }

To Henry Scott, William Scott, Dane
J. Scott, Henry Scott Jr & Samuel Scott. You and
each of you are hereby Summoned to attend at the
office of James G Taliaferro Esqr Recorder of the Parish
of Catahoula, on Saturday the 21st day of November
AD 1846, at 11 oClock in the Morning, to Compose
a family Meeting, as relatives of Nancy Holliman &
Jope Holliman, Minor Children of Jos. P Holliman
& Mary Ann Stewart decd, to take into Consider
the Application of James Stewart, to be appointed
tutor to said Minors, and herein fail not under
the penalties of the Law,

Given under my hand & the Seal of
Said Court this 7th day of November
AD 1846.

Wm M Few Clerk

I hereby acquire Service of this within Citation

                              her
                         Henry X Scott
                              mark
                         D J Scott
                         H N J Scott
                         Wm Scott
                         J B Scott

30-2

William Scott Jr.

WILLIAM SCOTT JR.

6th Child of William Scott Sr.

WILLIAM SCOTT JR. b.1796 Camden District,Fairfield County,South Carolina,the son of William Scott I and his wife,Ann. William,the father,died in 1805 leaving Ann with seven sons and two daughters to rear alone.John W.(21),Elizabeth (?16),Major (14),George W.(16 possibly twin to Elizabeth),Henry and William (10),Daniel Jackson (6),Sarah (5) and James who perhaps was the youngest of all the children as William died in 1805.

William Jr.m.LAVINIA (thought to be Atkins or Adkins as their first born was named Major Adkins), in South Carolina where all of their children were born except the youngest,John W. who was listed the 1850 Catahoula Parish,Louisana as being born in Alabama in 1835.In the 1860 census,John W. is listed as being born in Mississippi.This last entry would be correct as William and Lavinia were residing in Wilkinson County,Mississippi as early as 1831 when John W.Scott,William Scott and Henry Scott all paid taxes.

In 1841,William bought 38 1/2 acres on Beaver Creek in Wilkinson Co.(Bk M.) The same year,on Dec.6,he sold it to Daniel L.Flinn.(Bk N.p.6) Here,in Wilkinson County,the three brothers lived for several years. Henry married a local girl,Sarah Hemington,and in 1842,William operated a stage line for the US mail between Woodville,the rail head, to Bayou Sara on the Mississippi River near St.Francisville,Feliciana Parish. (Deed Book H,p.263,Catahoula Parish,Louisana).

A short time later,William and Lavinia were living in Concordia Parish,Louisana as he sold certain slaves to his brother Daniel Jackson.(DB H,p.319)This act of sale stated that William was a resident of Wilkinson County and apparently owned property in both states.It is evident that they moved freely from Concordia and Catahoula Parish ,Louisana and Wilkinson County,Mississippi as their children were living in all three areas.

Lavinia died before 1850 and William acquired his land in Catahoula Parish on July 1, 1859 (Bk M,pg.568,569 #813) and March 12,1861,(#814). This was known as the SCOTLAND PLANTATION on Black River,Catahoula Parish in what is now known as the PARHAM COMMUNITY. He also owned SOUTH BEND PLANTATION in Concordia Parish,across the Black River from the Scotland place.(This is not to be confused with the land known today as "Scottland")

In the CATAHOULA PARISH CEMETERIES,p.287,by Thelmarie Scott,the cemetery on the Black River land is listed as the "Fairbanks Place".Needless to say,the property was known as Scott property before it became known as Wm.(Billy)Bruce land and so forth...on down to today.

Numerious records are available concerning the distribution of Williams's estate.At his death in 1862,an oversight occurred. When the division was entered into the courthouse record book,two children were inadverently left out.Records show that neither Thomas Francis nor Henry Williamn's inheritence was continued to the next page in the book. This was an obvious oversight as both men did,indeed,receive their portion of their father's estate. (Probate Records Vol.E.p.368 Jan.12,1863,but no evidence having been filed.Rec.Jan.12,1866)

In the original division of 1863,Major Adkins Scott received the slaves Henry and Maria and their four children.All were appraised at $3900.00.

Samuel B.Scott received the slaves Jurny and Ellen and their two children,who were appraised at $3200.00 and one mule appraised at $250.00.

Benjamin C.Scott received the slaves Jerro,Phebe and Jerry as well as Julia and her child.All were appraised at $2,700.00. Also,one wagon,one clock and one jar.These items were appraised at $55.00.

John W.Scott received the slaves,Alford and Martha who were appraised at 2,000.00,one mule at $150.00,cattle at $255.00,hogs $192.00,corn $125.00 and all amounting to $2,792.00.

Ann Scott Bruce (twin to Benjamin) was represented by her husband,Wm.C.Bruce,(later to be known as Billy Bruce)who received 1/3 of the undivided land for the three children,Charles N.Bruce Aeolian N. Bruce and Benjamin L. Bruce.The land not yet divided was appraised at $135.00 per acre.This left 2/3 of the land unaccounted for and two sons,Henry W. and Thomas F.not listed in the Book of Succession.

With the onslaught of the Civil War,the legal proceedings were stilled until the war was over.By then nothing was left to divide except the 331.56 aacres of land on which William had lived when he died.(SE 1/4 Sec.30 NE 1/4 Sec.31,T6,NR 7E).

During the war years,Wm.Bruce and Ann moved onto William's homeplace.Here,Ann died in August,1864 and was buried close to the home in the family burying ground.According to her daughter Aeolian's diary,dated Saturday,November 11,1865,"Pa,Buddy,Walty and I went over to our old place and took the two little sweet children up and brought them over here and buried them by Ma and Oacar."(This suggests that the two children were twins--as twins have appeared in the Scott lineage each generation,up to 1973.)

This cemetery,located behind the present house,has deteriorated from years of high water,to a small knoll holding one marked grave...that of William J.Bruce's wife,SARA ELLEN b.Sept.20,1965, d.March 28,1906.

All of William and Ann's children had established their own homes by the time of their father's death.Major Adkins and John W.were living in Concordia Parish,Samuel B.,Benjamin C. and Wm.Bruce (Ann's husband) were in Catahoula Parish,and Henry William and Thomas Francis were living in Wilkinson Co.Ms.

In Aeolian's diary,written when she was 13 years of age,between 1865 and 1866,she mentions that "Uncle Ben"was using a cane,then later he would move over to "Uncle Sams".He was probably injured in the Civil War.Both he,John W.,Thomas Francis and Henry W. served their country well.

It is not known where William and Lavinia is buried.However,since William did not buy his land until Lavinia's death,they both could be buried in the SCOTT CEMETERY located across Black River in the parish of Concordia. This cemetery was located on William's eldest son,Major Scott's land and is still being used today.

Family records indicate that Major designated a portion of his land for a cemetery before 1858.Wives,children,parents and brothers as well as Major are believed to be buried here.In her diary,dated Friday,September 1,1865,Aeolian remarks,"It has been raining all day.We've just heard that Uncle Major lost his young child."(This would have been Ella Scott b. 1864).

Originally,the cemetery was much larger but throughout the years,high water obliterated many graves and washed away much of the area into Black River.

In 1978,Millard Sturgeon (who cared for the cemetery) explained how,after an overflow,he and his dad,Eugene Sturgeon would use poles to attempt to locate tombs through the crust of soil covering the cemetery.

Because of these natural occurances,few old markers exist today.This problem,coupled with the fact that the Civil War conditions prevented many from buying markers,left the graveyard without many stones.The only _Lavinia_ stone standing today is of he youngest child of WILLIAM AND ~~ANN~~ SCOTT, JOHN W.SCOTT who died on January 20,1868. Nevertheless,the cemetery is still in use today by the descendents of the people who are buried there.

A record of existing headstones in this cemetery was made in March 1984 and published in the Fall and Winter ,1985 issue of HART OF TEXAS RECORDS,pgs 80-86,and published by the Central

33

Texas Genealogical Society of Waco,Texas.Millard's wife,Margie
Calhoun Sturgeon ,Millard's wife,was most helpful in explaining
various areas where known people are buried without headstones.
These graves unfortunately,will never be recorded.

2874

John Lennex   No 93.
    vs   District Court Parish of Katahoula
William Scott   September Term 1847

By reason of the law and evidence in the
case being in favor of the Plaintiff and a trial duly had
it is ordered adjudged and decreed that plaintiff recover
of Defendant the sum of Three hundred and seventy ___
dollars sixty seven cents with five per cent interest per
annum from the 18th day of August 1847 and costs
suit to be taxed

Done Read & Signed in Open Court this 25th day of September 1847
                                    Edw J Barry
                                Judge 9th District

I hereby Certify the Above to be a true Copy of the original
Judgment on file and of Record in my Office
    In testimony whereof _____
and affix the Seal of the Said Court at Harrison burg
this 28th day of September AD 1847
                        Wm ___ Few Clerk
                    fr Carter J Beaman Jr
                        Dy Clerk C.

Sept 24th 1863 Catahoula Parish La

List of property appraised by Mr E Williams

and B Pool belonging to the heirs of William

Scott deceased   To wit

Land   383 acres Land at 35$ per acre   11.655

Slaves { Henry $1500
          Mariah   1200 }
          children 1200 $3900

        { Surry   1500
          Ellen   1200 }
          children   500   3200

          Alford   and   Martha   2000
          Julia   and   child   1500
          Jerry Phebe and child   1200
          Fox and Tiger 250 each   500
Mules   { Rock   150
          Beck   200

        17 head cattle 15$ 255
        24 do hogs 8   192
        500 bushels corn at 25=25th   225   125
        20 head goats 1$ 20
        1   waggon   40
        1   water jar   10
        1   clock   5
                                      2502.7

We have appraised the above property to the best of
our ability so help us God

                              Burrell Pool
                              Ebenezer Major

Original paper found in packet

34-2

Received of the Estate of William Scott the
slaves Henry and Mariah and their children
4 in number appraised at thirty nine hundred
dollars   M. A. Scott

Sept 24th 1863   Received of the Estate of
William Scott the slaves Livvy and Ellen and
their two children appraised at thirty two hundred
dollars and one mule appraised at 250$ S. B. Scott

Sept 24th 1863   Received of the Estate of William Scott
the slaves Jerry Phebe and Jerry jun and Julia and
child all appraised at twenty seven hundred dollars
and waggon clock and jar 56$ B. C. Scott

Sept. 24th 1863   Received of the Estate of William
Scott the slaves Alford and Martha appraised at
two thousand dollars one mule at 150$ cattle 255$
hogs ___ corn ___ ___ ___ amounting in all to ___
dollars   Jno. W. Scott

Sept 24th 1863
Received of the Estate of William Scott one third of
three hundred and thirty three acres of land valued
at thirty five dollars per acre the land not being yet divided
                                           Wm C Bruce
husband of Ann Scott Bruce daughter of William Scott

A true copy of the original
Rec'd the original from Wm Bruce to be Recorded
___ ___ ___ ___ the Estate of
the original Act now in my hand to be ___
___ to the ___
                                           M C Gardin
                                              Rec'd

Major Adkins Scott

WILLIAM AND LAVINIA SCOTT
Child #1:MAJOR ADKINS SCOTT b.1816,Fairfield Co.SC d.Feb.15,1875,
Concordia Parish La..Major was a plantation owner,a Justice of
the Peace and by 1853,he was tutoring children in his home.In
1863,the first school in the area was held in his home with Emma
Rountree as the first teacher.Mary later married his son,Wm.A.
Scott.Major was also a supporter of the church and the community.
Around 1853,Major donated land for a cemetery that bears his name
and is still in use today.The child that Aeolian mentions in her
diary was buried there in 1865.Major was married three times and
had 12 children.Major and all of his family are probably buried
in the cemetery.
1st marriage: Celia Ann Sapp b. 1824,d.Sept.3,1843.m.Dec.6,1840
(Marriage Book G.p.86,Wilkinson County,Mississippi.) 1 child
        a)WILLIAM ADKINS (ATKINS) SCOTT b. 1842 Ms. d.July
           30,1875.m.Dec.20,1865 Mary E.Rountree. He was a Capt.in
           the Confederate Army.(2 children)
              1.JOSIAH SCOTT b.,d. 1952 St.Joseph,La.Newspaper
                publisher of the THE TENSAS GAZETTE".
              2.MINOR A.SCOTT m.Annie Brady June 3, 1896 Concordia.

2nd marriage:Nancy Adaline (Lanehart) Comer b.1820,d.Aug.12,1861
Widow of Daniel Comer (m.May 4, 1838 MB F,p.229 Wilkinson Co.Ms.)
2 children from the Comer marriage.In 1850,"M" was 10, b.Ms.and
Benjamin Comer was 9, and born in Ky.

Major and Nancy were m.on Dec.24,1843 Wilkinson Co.Ms.(MB G.
p.253) 6 children.

1850 Census Concordis Parish ,La.p.154 Family #26

Scott,A	34	Farmer	$3,200	SC
,Nancy A.	24			Ms
,Wm.	9			Ms
Comer,M.	10			Ms
,Benj.	9			Ky.
Scott,T.	6			La.
,Z.	4			La.
,P.	1			La.

        b)THERESA SCOTT b.Dec.30,1844 d. May 16,1916 m.Oct.24,1866
        to William Adkins Cross,Concordia Parish,La.b.Dec.15,1840
        son of John Pressberry Cross b. 1813 and his wife,Pheebe.
        John P.Cross and Major A. Scott were first cousins.

        William Atkins Cross d.Sept.27,1934,Confederate soldier in
        Co.C,25th La.Inf.Buried in the SCOTT CEMETERY (7 children)

FOR FURTHUR INFORMATION ON THE CROSS LINE,REFER TO ELIZABETH
SCOTT,2nd child of William and Ann Scott.

1.HARVEY ESTELLE CROSS b.Nov.16,1867,d.June 11,1935
  Barstow,Tx. m.1st Elizabeth Wilson d.Jan.1903
  (7 children)
      a)MARION WILLIAM (Minor)CROSS,SR.
      b)MILTON SCOTT CROSS
      c)CHARLES BRUCE CROSS
      d)ORA CROSS
      e)JOSEPH ESTELL CROSS
      f)LOLA PAULINE CROSS
      g)AUGUSTA ELIZABETH CROSS

   Harvey m.2nd to Carrie Keller.(1 child)
      h)TINNIE MARIE CROSS

2. SIDNEY BELL CROSS b.Sept.27,1869 d.Nov.12,1951 m.
   Frances Vandilla Wilson b.Oct.20,1876,d.Aug.5,1953

3.WILLIAM ADKINS CROSS,JR. b.Apr.11,1871,d.June 13,1951
  m.Helen Olivia Cavin (6 children)
      a)HOWARD PUGH CROSS
      b)MYRTLE CROSS
      c)THERESA BELL CROSS
      d)HERMAN OBID CROSS
      e)UNA NETTERVILLE CROSS
      f)ULA SCOTT CROSS TWIN TO UNA

4.HANSELL PINKNEY CROSS b.Mar.2,1874,d.May 21,1932
  m.Mary Virginia Dawson on July 30,1907 b.Apr.3,1879
  d.Dec.18,1973.(3 children)
      a)LILLIAN BEATRICE CROSS
      b)HANSEL FLYNN CROSS PhD.b.Oct.30,1913 m.1st
        1934 Laplace,La.to Marjorie Lee Edwards
        b.July 16,1913 d.Mar.3,1972 (1 child)
          1.MARY BELLE CROSS
        m.2nd Mar.19,1943 Mary Lucille McDonald of
        Woodville,Ms.b.June 21,1923 Pelehatchee,Ms.
        (2 children)
          2.JAMES FLYNN CROSS
          3.PAMELA JOY CROSS
      c)WILLIAM WINSTON CROSS

 5.EULA CROSS b. 1877,d.1902 m. 1895 William Ernest
   Burley (2 children)
      a)HANSEL ENOS BURLEY b. 1897 d.1955
      b)WILLIAM FRANKLIN BURLEY b.1899,d.1982 m.1921
        Gladys Phoebe Cross b.1900

 6.MARSALIN GILLIS CROSS b.Feb.10,1879,d.Jan.1,1946 m.
   1901 Lydia Catherine Wilson b.Nov.20,1875,d.Nov.13,
   1957 (2 children)

```
                    a)LENA MAE CROSS
                    b)NOAH WEBSTER CROSS

          b)ZACHARIAS W. SCOTT b. 1847 m.June 1,187? to Alice A.Thomas

          c)PRISCILLA SCOTT b. 1849 m.July 9,1868 (Bk B.p.28 Concordia
            Parish) to John W.Butler

          d)PARYLEE SCOTT b.1851 m.Aug.26,1869 (Bk B.p.176 Concordia)
            to Levi B. Jackson (2 children)
                    a)CHARLEY DEAN JACKSON b. July 21,1873 d. Aug.25,1908
                      m.Jan.15,1903 (Bk L,p.316 Concordia) Isabella Eliz-
                      abeth Bairnsfather b. Aug.2,1882.dau.of Dr.Hartwell
                      Marion Bairnsfather (1857-1926.) 2 children)
                         1.SHELBY MARION JACKSON b. Nov.20,1903
                         2.CHARLEY DEAN JACKSON b. May 14,1909

          e)CATHERINE ANN SCOTT b. 1856 d. Oct.11,1865
          f)ELLEN SCOTT b. 1856,d.1858 TWIN TO CATHERINE

The third marriage of Major Scott was to Elizabeth Rachel(Burlew)
Criswell,a widow,on April 30,1862.Elizabeth had a son Milos
Criswell by her marriage with Criswell. She and Major had five
children.
          g)ELLA SCOTT b.1864,d.Sept.1,1865.(This was the baby
            mentioned in the diary of Aeolian Bruce.)

          h)LORENA SCOTT b. Aug.3,1866 d. Dec.1,1952.m.Jan.23,1883
            to Joseph Robert Steele in Concordia Parish.b.Nov.16,1862
            d.Oct.12,1940 son of Joseph Steele and Annie McClure
            Steele.(7 children)
                    1.FREDERICK F. STEELE b. Sept.20,1885

                    2.ANNIE ELIZABETH STEELE b. Oct.30,1890 d.Mar.7,197-

                    3.BESSIE BELLE STEELE b. May 3,1892 m.1st to David
                      Wolf who d. 1918.Bellie m.2nd to David L.Nelson.

                    4.NAOMI STEELE b. July 25,1894 m.May 18,1919 to Scott
                      Hale,who d.Feb.14,1920 (1 child)

                         a)LORENA SCOTT HALE b. July 24,1920 m.Bailey
                           Preston Northcott.(1 child)
                              1.RACHEL SCOTT NORTHCOTT m.John Swartz
                                (3 children)

                                   a)FREDRICK SWARTZ d.8 mo.
                                   b)SHANNON LEE SWARTZ
                                   c)JOSEPH ROBERT STEELE SWARTZ
                                   Rachel m.2nd to Darrel G.Kohn
```

5.LOUIS RAWLINGS STEELE b. Feb.9,1896 m.Sadie Smith who
    died in 1924.

6 WM. GASTON STEELE b. Jan.91901 m. Alva Campbell
    (1child).

        a)LESSLEY VANCE CROSS m. Gay Blount

7.PHOEBE STEELE b. Sept.3,1904 m.Aug.1927 to Shelby
    Marion Jackson (1 child)
        a)PATRICIA DIANA JACKSON b. Jan.30,1937

i)NAOMI SCOTT b.   d.Sept.29,1911 m.Feb.13,1878 Concordia
    Parish to James Foreman b. June 8,1858 d. Apr.12,1918
    (6 children)
        1.MAUDE FOREMAN b. Dec.9,1878 m.Nov.21,1896 Concordia
        Parish to William Cowser Brown b. Sug.24,1875
        d.Nov.28,1930
        2.MOODY ATKINS FOREMAN b.Dec.4,1890 d.Dec.4,1955 m.
        Beulah Steele.
        3.DAISY FOREMAN d.1960 m.Ben Keene
        4.FELIX FOREMAN   m.Lorena Steele
        5.MINERVA FOREMAN   m.Walter Trisler
        6.MARY S(Elizabeth N.) FOREMAN m.(Jack) Frank Schneider
        Jan.6,1873.

j)MINOR ATKINS SCOTT d. Jan.11,1889

k)CASSIUS MONROE SCOTT b.Dec.8,1875 m.Dec.24,1905 to Ada
    Mabel Wilson b. Aug.25,1873.dau.of Thomas Jefferson Wilson
    b.Apr.12,1852,d.May 17,1940 and wife,Catherine Elizabeth
    Dale Wilson b. Feb.4,1860.d.Nov.25,1951 dau of Geo W.Dale
    who was a confederate soldier and died at Monticello,Ark.
    while serving in the army in 1864.(3 children)

    1.WADE WILSON SCOTT b. Apr.26,1907 m.Beulah Levron in
        1929.He was a newspaper publisher and writer.d.Nov.
        17,1954 in Houma,La.

    2.MABEL ELIZABETH SCOTT b. Apr.23,1909 m.Raymond
        Lawrence Wright,son of Langston Preston Wright.

    3.RACHEL KATE SCOTT b. Feb.25,1915 m.Jan.23,1949Judge
        Jessie E. McGee b.Apr.12,1895 d. May 11,1969

        Rachel m.2nd March 12,1974 to W.D.Reeves
        b.Sept.24,1912,d. April 31,1980.

MAJOR A. SCOTT'S "Homeplace", Concordia Parish, La.

Gladys and William Burley

Naomi Steele

UNITED STATES OF AMERICA,

State of Louisiana.

BY JOSEPH WALKER.
GOVERNOR OF THE STATE OF LOUISIANA.

These are to Certify, THAT *Mo A. Scott.* whose name is subscribed to the instrument of writing herein annexed is and was, at the time of subscribing his name to said instrument, Justice of the peace in and for the parish of Concordia State aforesaid and that his attestation to the same is made in due form of law and by the proper officer ————

GIVEN at BATON ROUGE, under my Hand, and the Seal of the State, this *fifth* day of *August* one thousand eight h red and fifty *two* and of the Independence of the ed States the seventy *Seventh*.

By the Governor,

Charles Gayarre

Secretary of State.

Joseph Walker

J. Jachne, Stationer, 112 Chartres Street.

Order No. 9513	Description	Reference - S. C. Archives			
36/6 *	Estate Papers of Ann Scott	Fairfield Estates, Box 91, pk. 295, 91 295 2 front, 4 front, 6 7 8 9 20 21 FRONTS	295	4	4

38-2

The State of Louisiana }
Parish of Concordia }

        Know All men by these
presents that I William Scott of the Parish
and state aforesaid have made, constituted,
and appointed, and by these presents do make
constitute, and appoint and in my place and
stead put and depute John A. Martine of
the state of southcarolina fairfield district
my true and lawfull attorney for me and
in my name, and for my use to ask demand
sue for recover and receive all such sum
and sums of money, debts, goods, wares, dues,
accounts, and other demands whatsoever, which
are or may be due owing payable, and
belonging to me or detained from me by
any maner of ways or means whatsoever or
in whose hands soever the same may be found
in the above mentioned state of southcarolina
fairfield district, giving and granting unto my
said attorney, by these presents my full power
and authority in and about the premises
to have use and take all lawfull ways and
means in my name and for the purpose aforesaid
and upon the receipt of any such debts dues
or sums of money, acquitances or other suffi-
-cient discharges for me, and in my name
to make seal and deliver. And generally all
and every act or acts thing or things whatsoever
needfull and necessary to be done in and
about the premises for me and in my name
to do execute and perform as fully largely,

Hereby ratifying, allowing all and whatsoever my said attorney shall lawfully do in and about the premises aforesaid by virtue hereof.

In witness whereof I hereunto set my hand and seal in the presence of John P Gray and W. P. D. Coleman both Competent witnesses this the 30th day of July AD 1832

Wm N Scott

Witness,

Wm. P. D. Coleman,

John P Gray

personally appeared before me the undersigned Justice of the Peace William Scott who ~~acknowledges~~ acknowledges the above to be his act,

this the 30 day of July. AD 1832

M. A. Scott J. Peace

[This document written by Major Adkins Scott of Monterey. Louisiana.]

S. C. Scott
one Load of
Salt to $ 2998
M. A. Scott 98
one Load Salt
          3026
           600
          ————
          3626

BILL OF LADEN RECEIPT FROM

SAMUEL C. SCOTT TO MAJOR A.SCOTT

MONTEREY LANDING

38-5

Thomas Francis Scott

WILLIAM AND LAVINIA SCOTT
Child # 2:THOMAS FRANCIS SCOTT b.1818 Fairfield County,SC,
d.ca.1865 Catahoula Parish,La., m May 19,1838 Natchez,Ms.Adams
Co.(Bk 6 p.262)Elizabeth Callicoatte b.ca 1815 N.C.,d.1868
Upshur Co.(Camp) Texas,dau of Sarah and George W.Callicoatte Sr.
(6 children)

Thomas F.and Elizabeth lived in Wilkinson Co.Ms.where all six of
the children were born.He lived adjacent to WILEY DELOACH (my
great,great grandfather) in the Ft.Adams area,west of Woodville.
This was an area quite a few miles from his brother,HENRY W.SCOTT
of Doloroso which is approximately 15 miles south of Natchez.

On April 26,1855,Thomas sold his two tracts of land to his
brother Henry W.Scott for $1,000.(Land Deed Bk Q,p.515
Wilkinson,Co.Ms.)

One tract consisted of 160 25/100 acres and the other contained
82 and 12/100 acres.Also,he sold to Henry for $800,"a certain
negro man slave named Joe about forty five years of age and a
slave for life,and I hereby warrent said slave Joe to be sound in
body and mind."

In 1858,Thomas's wife Elizabeth moved to Upshur(Camp)County Texas
where she bought land from John Callicoatte near Pittsburg.There,
she lived with her children until her death in 1868.

In the 1860 census of Upshur Co.Tx.,Elizabeth is listed with her
five children.Evidently Thomas chose not to be listed in the
census record.

Thomas,as well as his brother Henry, traveled back and forth from
Catahoula and Concordia Parishes and Wilkinson County keeping in
close touch with his brothers,uncles,and brother -in-law,William
G.Bruce.

Thomas's brother Samuel B.Scott had married the widow of Bruce's
brother.Susannah and her baby,named Daniel, had died shortly
after the marriage. This threw the estate of Susannah into court
with constant litiagation between Bruce and Samuel with Bruce
trying to protect the inheritance of Susannah's childrn of her
first marriage. As a result of this on- going process,Thomas was
in the Catahoula court and made a deposition on March 30,1855.
Unfortunately,only the envelope which held the document exists
today.

On March 18,1862,Thomas F.Scott volunteered for the Confederate
Army at Monterey,La.(In A HISTORY OF CONCORDIA PARISH by Robert
Dabney Calhoun,pg.65,"We are informed by Mr.William A.Cross that
Samuel C. Scott,under whom he served in the Civil War, was a

Captain under General Zachary Taylor at the storming and capture
of Monterey,and that, on his return from Mexico,in commemoration
of that event,he gave his landing and plantation in Black Rver
the name of Monterey." This Samuel C.Scott was no relation to our
Scotts from Fairfield County,South Carolina)

Thomas Francis Scott was a Private,with Co.C. 25th Reg.
#46975760,5956 and 6028 and on May 11,1862,he was wounded at
Corinth,Ms.. In November and December he was home on sick leave.

In October or early November 1865,family records show that Thomas
was in Catahoula Parish taking care of cotton bales to be sold
from his father,William Scott's plantation .This was after his
father had died but the estate had not been settled.

Along with his son Francis Marion Scott,20,he was sitting on the
bank of Black River,waiting for the boat to arrive to load the
bales of cotton.Suddenly,a shot rang out,seemly from behind them
although there were soldiers across the river in Concordia.The
the son ran but Thomas did not move.When the family came back to
the location,Thomas's body was not to be found.No one knows who
shot Thomas nor what happened to his body.

On Nov.23,1865,his brother-in-law,Wm.G.Bruce,filed an order of an
inventory of the estate.He wished to be appointed administrator
No evidence has been found of this appointment nor the settlement
of his estate.
Thomas F. and Elizabeth had 6 children.
    a)SARAH A.SCOTT b. 1838 Wilkinson co.Ms.d. 1879 Upshur Co.
      (Camp) Co.Tx.m.1st to F.Monroe Callicoatte.(3 children)
        1.IDA CALLICOATTE
        2.FANNIE CALLICOATTE
        3.LAURA CALLICOATTE
      Sarah m.2nd to Jeff Lester (2 children)
        4.WILLIE LESTER
        5.JEFF LESTER JR.

    b)FRANCIS MARION SCOTT b.Aug.29,1845 Woodville,Ms.m.in
        1870 Upshur Co.,Tx. 1st to Martha (Mattie) Callicoatte
        b.Jan.1850 d.June 1874 Camp Co.Tx.(Upshur)(2 children)
        1.WINFIELD HUNTER SCOTT b. Sept.2,1872 d.Jan.28,1960
        Gatesville,Tx.m.July 15,1897 Dorcas D.Irvin.
        (3 sons)
        a)IRVIN MARION SCOTT b Mar.19,1899,d.Apr.29,1974
        m.Mar.27,1937 Frances Burnett b Dec.31,1910
        Martins Mills,Tx.d.Feb.24,1956 (1 child)
        1.TONYA ELIZABETH SCOTT m.1st Walter Eugene
        Cudmore(Children took the name of 2nd marrige)
        a)VALERIE ELIZABETH PRESCOTT b.Sept.20,1966
        Arcadia,Calif.
        b)BRADLEY(Brad)EUGENE PRESCOTT b.June 25,1969
        Tonya m.2nd to Fredrick Stephen Prescott MD
        b. May 4, 1936 Grand Rapids Mich.

b)I.O SCOTT b.Mar.3,1903 Coryell Co.Tx.d.Jan.10,1975
   m.1st.Mar.22,1926 Lubbock,Tx.Gladys Ruth Baker
   b.Jan.19,1907 (2 children)

   1.IRVIN KENT SCOTT b.Aug.1,1928 Gatesville,Tx.
      d.Aug.16,1967 Hobbs,NM m.1st Sept.28,1951
      Lovington,NM to Marguerite Louise Standish
      b.1928 Bartlesville,Okla.(1 child)
         a)CHRISTOPHER KENT SCOTT b. Feb.20,1956
            d.June 19,1960 Carlsbad,NM.
      Irvin m.2nd Mar.12,1966 Hobbs NM to Wanda Rae
      Linam b.Aug.7,1931 Tuscon,Ariz.

   2.DON BAKER SCOTT b.Nov.30,1930 Gatesville,Tx.
      m.1st Jan.27,1957 Hobbs NM to Goldena Mae Peters
      (1 child)
         a)STEVEN BAKER SCOTT b.Dec.5,1957 Hobbs,NM

      m.2nd Jan.15,1960 to Dolores Lee Maxey b.May 10,
      1929 Wink,Tx.(1 child)
         b)DAVID LYNN SCOTT b.Aug.21,1962 Hobbs,NM.

   I.O.m.2nd Peggy Burt from Pendleton,Tx. No
   children.

   I.O.m.3rd Dec.20,1947 Baton Rouge,La.Gwendolyn
   L. Casey from Moody,Tx.b.Oct.6,1922,d.Jan.7,1974
   Waco,Tx. (2 children)

   3.GARRY LYNN SCOTT b.Dec.4,1958 Waco m.1978
      Barbara Goetsch.(Divorced, 2 children)
         a)STEVEN RAY SCOTT b. Sept.25,1978 Waco.
         b)BILLY WAYNE SCOTT b.Jan.28,1980 Waco.

   4.TERI FAITH SCOTT b.July 1,1962 Waco ,m.June 5,
      1981 Michael K.Sharp.(Divorced,1 child)
         a)CHRYSTAL FAITH SHARP b.July 26,1982

c)FAY LOUIS SCOTT b. Oct.18,1906 d.Mar.2,1926
   Gatesville,Tx.

2.HENRY WILLIAM SCOTT b. 1874. Both baby and mother
   died when the baby was born.

Francis Marion Scott Sr. came to Central Texas at the end of 1875 to settle at the small town of Eagle Springs where he had acquired 219 acres. He and his little son,Winfield Hunter Scott, arrived in two wagons along with his widowed sister,Sarah and her three little girls who were to live with him .They planned to live in the wagons until a house could be built but these living conditions proved to be so hard that only Francis Marion and Winfield stayed to continue the work.When Francis M.left the farm to gather materials to continue working,Winfield stayed with an elderly couple that lived in the area until his father returned.All of the other nights and days were spent living in the wagons while the building continued.

Francis Marion's first house had two rooms and a dirt floor.In this house,5 children of the 12,would be born.Their 5th child,Francis Marion Jr.,was three weeks old when they moved into their second built house.It is still standing today (1987),and was occupied by the youngest child (Burl Scott),at his death in 1985. The land has been in the family for 111 years.

Francis Marion and Susan Rachel had 4 sons and 8 daughters.Only 2 sons and 2 daughters married,one daughter died at 3 years of age, while the remaining chose to stay single.

Francis m.2nd 1882 Coryell,Co.Tx. to Susan Rachel Franks b.Feb.10 1861 Bienville Parish,La. d. Apr.21,1937 Coryell County,Tx.,dau. of Dr.and Matilda Cummings Franks.Both Francis Marion and Susan are buried in the Eagle Springs Cemetery.(12 children)

> (12 children)
>   3.WALTER THOMAS SCOTT b. Sept.17,1883 Coryell Co.Tx.
>   d.Jan.6,1962 m.Aug.14,1914 Eva Estell Cash
>   (5 children)
>   a)HAZEL SCOTT b.July 13,1914 m.Charles Shubert
>   Morse b. Oct.2,1915.(2 children)
>   1.CAROLYN MORRIS
>   2.CHARLES SHUBERT MORSE JR.
>
>   b)ROY THOMAS SCOTT b.July 24,1915 m.Crystal Arleen
>   Richardson b. Jan.8,1922 (4 children)
>   1.VIRGINIA ARLEEN SCOTT b. May 12,1944
>   2.THOMAS LEE SCOTT b. Sept.10,1947
>   3.DAVID RAY SCOTT (Twin to Thomas)
>   4.SUE ANN b. Apr.9,1949
>
>   c)JAMES EDWIN SCOTT b.Mar.15,1917 m.Zelda Mae
>   Morris b.Mar.28,1919 (2 children)
>   1.MARTHA SCOTT m.Curtis Eugene Pryor
>   2.

        d)WILLIAM (Billy) DERWOOD SCOTT b.July 30,1920
          m.May 23,1945 to Joyce Winfred Organ b.Mar.26,
          1927 Gloucester (County) England (2 children)
              1.PAMELA RUTH SCOTT b. Jan.9,1960 m.
                Donald Vanderveer
              2.MICHAEL WILLIAM SCOTT b. Nov.21,1951

        e)MARY EUGENIA (Jean) SCOTT b. Aug.4,1925
          m.Raymond Edward Petty Jr. b. June 12,1925
          (1 child)
              1.CLYDE RAY PETTY b. Mar.5,1948
4.EMMA ELIZABETH SCOTT b. Nov.14,1884 d.June 21,1965

5.SARAH(Sallie)ESTELLE SCOTT b. Feb.25,1887 d.June 2,
  1962 m.Feb.14,1911 William L. Bowlin (2 children)
      a)HAROLD BOWLIN
      b)AZALIA BOWLIN.m.   Collins (2 sons)

6.IOLA SCOTT b.June 11,1888 d.Jan.12,1977

7.FRANCIS MARION SCOTT JR. b. July 15,1890 d. July
  20,1967 m.Apr.24,1914 Lena Ellen Cox b.Nov.11,1897,
  Bell Co.d.Sept.24,1980.Both buried in Rosemound
  Cemetery,Waco,Tex.(3 children)
      a)DONALD H. SCOTT b. Mar.2,1915 Coryell Co.
        d.Mar.22,1976 Rosemound Cemetery.m.April 12,
        Vivian Vaughn
              1.DONNA A. SCOTT (2 children)
              2.DANNIEL FRANCIS SCOTT (2 children)
              3.ELLEN MARIE SCOTT (3 children)

      b)EMILY LOUISE SCOTT b.June 5,1918 d. Nov.27,1954
        m. H.R. Willis. Rosemound Cemetery

      c)FRANCES ELLENOR SCOTT b. Dec.5,1919 m.1st
        Thelbert Bell (2 children)

          1.BOBBY EUGENE BELL b.Dec.24,1937 m.1958
            Temple,Tx.Claudia Jane Lewis b.Mar.2,1939
            (2 children)

            a)Theresa (Teri) Lei Bell b.July 5,1959
              m.1979 Steven Snider (1 child)
              1.CHRISTOPHER SCOTT SNIDER b.July 24,1983

            b)MICHAEL GLENN Bell b. May 30,1963
              m.Temple,Tx.July 1986 Debbie Williams
              from Pennsylvania.

        2.J.B. BELL b.July 22,1939 m.Bell Co.Tx.Nov.5,
          1960 to Marline Jane Bailey (2 children)
          a)MONICA JANE BELL b. Oct.5,1965
          b)JASON BRYAN BELL b. May 30,1967

        Frances m.2nd to Edward C.Thornburg b. Aug.25,1923
        Clinton Co.Ohio,son of Mary and Ramon B. Thornburg

    8.ANNIE MYRTLE SCOTT b. Oct.9,1892 d.Dec.5,1895

    9.WILLIAM SCOTT b. June 3, 1895 d. Nov.5,1918 Germany
      WW I veteran.

    10.MABEL CLAIR SCOTT b. Nov.13,1896 d. Feb.27,1982

    11.LILLIAN BESSIE SCOTT b. Aug.15,1898 d.

    12.ETHEL ALBERTA SCOTT b. Aug.7,1900 d. April 28,1966

    13.AZALIE LUCILE SCOTT b.Dec. 28,1903 d. Oct.4,1977 m.
       m.Aug.27,1931 Herman Wheat b.Aug.27,1898 d. June 23,
       1934.(2 children)
         a)JESSE MARION WHEAT b&d July 4,1932
         b)PATRICIA ANN WHEAT b. Mar 7,1934 m.Joe Ellis
           Martin b. Jan.18,1932 d.May 28,1975,son of
           Cora Bell Walden and James Ellis Martin.
           (3 children)
             1.JAMES ELLIS MARTIN b. Oct.20,1954 d. May 3,
               1977
             2.GARY LYNN MARTIN b.June 3,1956 m.Aug.30,
               1975 to Helen Diane Wade b. Dec.28,1959 dau
               of Mae Wade Schiller and David Wade
               (2 children)
                 a)DEBRA MICHEALE MARTᵀN b.June 11,1977
                 b)JAMES DAVID MARTIN b. Sept.25,1982
             3.JO ANNE MARTIN b. June 24,1965

    14.DANIEL BURL SCOTT b. Dec.16,1905 d.Aug.16,1985

c)THOMAS SCOTT JR.b.1846 Wilkinson Co.Ms.d.Dec.1859 Upshur

d)LAVINIA ELIZABETH SCOTT b.Mar.27,1848 Wilkinson Co.Ms.
  d.May 10,1911 Hill co.Tx. m.ca 1867 Robert Poer
  (At least 8 children but no further information.)

e)MARTHA SCOTT b. Feb.1850 Wilkinson Co.Ms.d.Upshur Co.Tx
  ca 1866

f)DAVIS WINFIELD SCOTT b.Sept.9,1851 Wilkinson Co. Ms.
  d.Sept.26,1925 Taylor Co.Tx m.ca 1890 Minnie Griffith
  (At least 10 children but no further information)

BIRTHS

J. M. Scott Bornd August 29 the	1845
S. R. Scott Bornd February 16 the	1861
W. A. Scott Bornd September 2 the	1872
H. W. Scott Bornd June 25 the	1874
W. J. Scott Bornd September 17 the	1883
Emma E. Scott Bornd November 14 the	1884
Sallie Scott Bornd Febuary 25 the	1887
Johla Scott Bornd June 11 the	1888
Francis M. Scott Bornd July 15 the	1890
Annie M. Scott Bornd October 9 the	1882
Will Scott Barned June 3 the	1895
Mabel E Scott Barnd Nov 13 the	1896
Bessie Lillian Scott Bornd August 15 the	1898
Ethel Alberta Scott Bornd August 7 the	1900
Azlee Lucile Scott Bornd December 28	1903
Daniel Burl Scott Brn Dec 16 - 1905 d.	
	Aug 16. 1985

44-1

MARRIAGES

F. M. Scott & S. R. Franks —
Married August 30th 1882

W. H. Scott & Dorcas Irvin Married July 15th 1897

Sallie E. Scott & W. L. Bowlin Married Feb. 14th. 1911

W. L. Scott & Eva E. Cash Married August 14, 1913

Francis M. Scott Jr. & Lena Cox Married April 26th 1914

STATE OF MISSISSIPPI, }
Adams County.

Know all Men by these Presents,

That we Thomas Scott and Stephen J. Waddius of said county, are held and firmly bound unto Alexander G. McNutt Governor of the state of Mississippi, aforesaid, or his successors in office, in the sum of *two hundred dollars*, lawful money of said state, to which payment well and truly to be made to the said governor for the time being, or his successors in office, we bind ourselves, our heirs, executors and administrators, each and every of us and them, jointly and severally, firmly by these presents. Sealed with our seals, and dated this nineteenth day of May eighteen hundred and thirty eight

THE CONDITION OF THIS OBLIGATION IS SUCH,

That whereas a marriage is shortly intended to be celebrated between the above bound Thomas Scott and Elizabeth Callicott now if there is no lawful cause to obstruct the said marriage, then this obligation to be void, otherwise to remain in full force and virtue.

Signed, sealed and delivered }
in presence of

Thomas F. Scott [Seal]

Stephen Waddius [Seal]

State of Mississippi, Adams County.

To any Judge, Minister, or Justice, lawfully authorized to celebrate the rites of Matrimony—You are hereby Licensed to celebrate the rites of Matrimony between Thomas Scott and Elizabeth Callicott

Given under my hand, and seal of my office, this nineteenth day of May one thousand eight hundred and thirty eight

44—2

DEATHS

Annie Myrtle died December 5th 1895

William Scott died November 5th. 1918

Francis Marion Scott died Dec 19, 1927

Susan Rachel Scott died April 21, 1937

Frances Scott Thornburg

Francis Marion Scott's family
Row 1, Lucille,F.M.Sott Sr. Ethel,Susan R.,Sallie,Johla,Burl
Row 2, Winfield,Francis M.Jr.,Bill,Lillian,Walter,Emma,Mable

Frank Jernigan and Frances Scott Thornbury
Sumter, S.C.

Melba ,Frances,Marvyn,Thelma and David

Henry Williams Scott

WILKINSON COUNTY COURTHOUSE

The Tax Collector held quite a levee in the Court House yard on Monday Tuesday and Wednesday over the sale of lands for delinquent taxes. In some instances the bidding was lively.

We regret to announce the death of Mr. H. W. Scott, one of our oldest and most esteemed citizens, of the Cold Springs neighborhood, who died at his residence on Saturday last.

Mr. S. E. McDonald, one of the oldest and most respected citizens of this county died at his residence 9 miles north of Woodville on Saturday of last week.

Judge Van Eaton, Capt. W. C. Cage, and Mr. Henry Johnson, returned from Brandon the latter part of last week. Business called them home before the trial commenced. It is the intention of some of the gentlemen to return, if possible, later in in the progress of the trial.

The Board of Supervisors met on Monday, all the members present, and adjourned after two days session.

The Farmers Alliance held a meeting here on Monday last, at which, we are informed, important business was transacted. It is hardly necessary for the REPUBLICAN to state, that, anything important to the members of the Alliance or to the public generally, would find a place in its columns very readily. Mr. T.

country, excepting those on the Pacific Coast. This trust represents $60,000,000. It controls the sugar market and the product—not of raw sugar of course, but no one uses raw sugar. Each refinery surrendered its property absolutely to a board of directors and received certificates in the stock of the trust. The committee at last accounts had not been able to get hold of the contract between these refiners.

Congress has been investigating the Standard oil and cotton seed oil trust, and we see that a bill has been introduced in the House declaring trusts to be unlawful. So sweeping a bill as that should not become a law; for certain purposes and within certain limits trusts should not be prohibited. It is the massing of a controlling interest of an industry in the hands of half a dozen directors, the monopoly in production, which should be declared unlawful.

The public has little idea how far trusts have extended; the further they are investigated the more their ramifications are seen. It is a mistake to suppose that only great enterprises are attempted; A trust in envelopes, for instance, was unearthed the other day. It was located in Connecticut, and had a capital of only $5,000 at the start, but it largely controls the product and price of envelopes in this country, and would no doubt raise the price 50 or 100 per cent. if the Government did not manufacture its own envelopes and also stamped envelopes. Legislation of the severest kind should be applied to trust by the States and

"WOODVILLE REPUBLICIAN"
Oldest newspaper in Mississippi.
Death notice of Henry William Scott
Woodville, Mississippi, March 10, 1888,

pg. 44-6

KNOW ALL MEN BY THESE PRESENTS, That we

Henry M Scott & Micajah M. Wammack

of said County, are held and firmly bound unto *A G McNutt* Governor of the State of Mississippi, aforesaid, or his successors in office, in the sum of two hundred dollars, lawful money of said state, to which payment well and truly to be made to the said Governor, for the time being or his successors in office, we bind ourselves, our heirs, executors and administrators, each and every of us, and them, jointly and severally, firmly by these presents; sealed with our seals, and dated this *4th* day of *March* one thousand eight hundred and *forty one*

THE CONDITION OF THIS OBLIGATION IS SUCH; That whereas a Marriage is shortly intended to be celebrated between the above bound *Henry M Scott & miss Elizabeth Geter*.

Now, if there is no lawful cause to obstruct the said marriage, then this obligation to be void, otherwise to remain in full force and virtue.

Signed, Sealed and Delivered, }
in Presence of }

Henry M Scott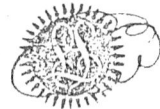

M H Womack

THE STATE OF MISSISSIPPI—WILKINSON COUNTY.

To any Judge, Minister, or Justice, lawfully authorized to Celebrate the Rites of matrimony.

YOU ARE HEREBY LICENSED, To Celebrate the RITES of MATRIMONY between

Henry M Scott and miss Elizabeth Geter

Card 1 (top left):

(Confederate)

S. | 38 Cav. | Miss.

H. W. Scott

Prt, | Capt. J. H. Jones' Company,
38 Reg't Mississippi Mtd. Inf.

Age 36 years.

Appears on

Company Muster Roll

of the organization named above,

for (Dated June 30, 1864

Joined for duty and enrolled:

When Apl 29, 1862
Where Woodville Miss
By whom Lieut Bullock
Period 3 yrs or War

Last paid:

By whom Maj Williams
To what time June 30, 1862

Present or absent Absent

Remarks Absent on Detach. service

Card 2 (top middle):

(Confederate)

S. | 38 Cav. | Miss.

H. W. Scott

Prt, Co. D., 38 Reg't Mississippi Vols.

Appears on

Company Muster Roll

of the organization named above,

for Nov & Dec, 1863

Enlisted:

When Apl 29, 1862
Where Woodville
By whom Lieut Bullock
Period 3 years

Last paid:

By whom Capt Shephard
To what time June 30, 1862

Present or absent Present

Remarks:

Card 3 (top right):

(Confederate)

S. | 38 Cav. | Miss.

H. W. Scott

Prt, Co. D., 38 Reg't Mississippi Vols.

Appears on

Company Muster Roll

of the organization named above,

for Apl 30 to Oct 31, 1863

Enlisted:

When Apl 29, 1862
Where Woodville
By whom Lieut Bullock
Period 3 years

Last paid:

By whom
To what time , 186

Present or absent Absent

Remarks En route for Enterprise

Card 4 (bottom left):

(Confederate)

S. | 38 Cav. | Miss.

H. W. Scott

Prt, Co. D., 38 Reg't Mississippi Vols.

Appears on

Company Muster Roll

of the organization named above,

for Nov & Dec, 1862

Enlisted:

When Apl 29, 186
Where Woodville
By whom Lieut Bullock
Period 3 years

Last paid:

By whom Cap. Shepard
To what time June 30, 186

Present or absent Absent

Remarks Sick sent to hospital

The 38th Regiment Mississippi Infantry was organized about
May 12, 1862. Early in 1864 the designation was changed to 38th
Regiment Mississippi Mounted Infantry, and in 1865 it was known
as the 38th Regiment Mississippi Cavalry. By S. O. No. —, Head-
quarters Dist. Miss., E. La., and W. Tenn., dated Columbus, Miss.,
March 2, 1865, the 38th Regiment Mississippi Cavalry, 14th Regiment Confederate Cavalry, and 3d Regiment Mississippi Cavalry
were consolidated into one regiment known as the 38th, 14th and
3d Regiments Consolidated, Mississippi Cavalry.

Book mark:

Card 5 (bottom middle):

(Confederate)

S. | 38 Cav. | Miss.

H. W. Scott

Prt, Co. D., 38 Reg't Mississippi Vols.

Appears on

Company Muster Roll

of the organization named above,

for Sept & Oct, 1862

Enlisted:

When Apl 29, 186
Where Woodville
By whom Lieut Bullock
Period 3 years

Last paid:

By whom Capt Shepoard
To what time June 30, 186

Present or absent Absent

Remarks Sick in Hospital

The 38th Regiment Mississippi Infantry was organized about
May 12, 1862. Early in 1864 the designation was changed to 38th
Regiment Mississippi Mounted Infantry, and in 1865 it was known
as the 38th Regiment Mississippi Cavalry. By S. O. No. —, Head-
quarters Dist. Miss., E. La., and W. Tenn., dated Columbus, Miss.,
March 2, 1865, the 38th Regiment Mississippi Cavalry, 14th Regiment Confederate Cavalry, and 3d Regiment Mississippi Cavalry
were consolidated into one regiment known as the 38th, 14th and
3d Regiments Consolidated, Mississippi Cavalry.

Book mark:

Card 6 (bottom right):

(Confederate)

S. | 38 Cav. | Miss.

H. W. Scott

Prt, Co. D., 38 Reg't Mississippi Vols.

Appears on

Company Muster Roll

of the organization named above,

for July & Aug, 1862

Enlisted:

When Apl 29, 186
Where Woodville
By whom Lieut R. F. Bullock
Period 3 yrs or War

Last paid:

By whom Capt Shippard
To what time June 30, 186

Present or absent Present

Remarks:

The 38th Regiment Mississippi Infantry was organized about
May 12, 1862. Early in 1864 the designation was changed to 38th
Regiment Mississippi Mounted Infantry, and in 1865 it was known
as the 38th Regiment Mississippi Cavalry. By S. O. No. —, Head-
quarters Dist. Miss., E. La., and W. Tenn., dated Columbus, Miss.,
March 2, 1865, the 38th Regiment Mississippi Cavalry, 14th Regiment Confederate Cavalry, and 3d Regiment Mississippi Cavalry
were consolidated into one regiment known as the 38th, 14th and
3d Regiments Consolidated, Mississippi Cavalry.

Book mark:

For and in consideration of my natural love and affection for **my son Arglas W. Scott**, and the further consideration that he is to manage the property herein conveyed free of charge and to care for and support me during my natural life, I hereby warrant and convey to said Arglas W. Scott the following lands towit the South part of Claim Section Twenty Six (26) Containing Three hundred and Twenty five Acres (325); Also Lot Four of Section Twenty Seven (27) Containing Fifty $\frac{35}{100}$ acres (50 $\frac{35}{100}$); Also Lots one Two and Twelve (1 2 & 12) and Thirty Eight acres in the north part of Lot Eight of Section Thirty Seven (37) Containing One hundred and Ninety one $\frac{67}{100}$ acres (191 $\frac{67}{100}$) reserving to myself during my natural life the use and Control of all the property herein Conveyed and hereby declaring that the design of this Conveyance is that the possession of the land herein described shall only vest in said Arglas W. Scott at my death.

Witness my signature this the 1st day of December 1890.

Elizabeth ^{her} x _{mark} Scott

State of Mississippi
Wilkinson County } Personally appeared before me B. W. Brabman a Justice of the Peace of said County Elizabeth Scott who acknowledged that she signed and delivered the foregoing instrument on the day and year therein mentioned.

Given under my hand this 1st day of December 1890.

B. W. Brabman J.P.

Filed for Record December 23rd 1890, at 12 oclock M.

D. H. Huff Clerk

44-9

On November 2,1895,Arglass Scott set aside 1 acre of land for the purpose of establishing a school for the children that lived in the Cold Springs Precinct (Doloroso).Quote:

"For in consideration of the regard I have for the welfare and education of the white children of Cold Springs Precinct of Wilkinson County,Mississippi and for the benefit of said educational purposes,I hereby transfer and convey to the county of Wilkinson,one acre of land situated in Wilkinson County, Mississippi,described as follows. The north east acre of land in Section 26,Township 4,Range 2 West and bounded on the north of lands of B.W.Brannan ,on the east by land of Wyatt Barnes and on the south and west by land of A.W.Scott." (BK LL,p.16)

The school house consisted of one room where the children in the neighborhood received their education .Although no one living today remembers just when the school ceased to be a school,Nelse Jensen does remember going to the school.However,during the ensuing years,the building was remodeled and became a home.

By 1933,the old school,now located on Arglass's grandson,Walter T.Scott's land,was at that time,empty.When Walter's nephew, Tom Scott married Wilna Flowers,Tom and Wilna moved into the "old school building"and lived there until 1941.

With the discontinuation the school,the land reverted back to the family.

It is evident that Arglass wanted his children to receive a quality education as he was a school trustee in Wilkinson County. In the fall term (December)1899,Arglass Scott,B.W.(Benjamin) Brannan and Rufus Geter,trustees of the school system, agreed to "sell and convey to J.E.Kellebien (for 10 years)all the timber and trees on the school Section 30,Township 4,Range 3 West for the amount of $955.00 for 10 years." (BK LL,p.16)

ATTORNEY	𝔇epartment of 𝔈ducation	SECRETARIES
RICHARD T. WATSON	𝔚ilkinson 𝔒ounty	MRS. LEONA D. IRWIN
BOOKKEEPER	CHARLES E. JOHNSON, SUPERINTENDENT	MISS AUDREY VEALS
MRS. EDNA S. KAIGLER	P. O. Box 785	
	WOODVILLE, MISSISSIPPI 39669	
	January 15, 1981	

Mrs. Ernest R. Wiese
3712 Charleston Ave.
Waco, Texas 76711

Dear Mrs. Wiese:

We have made another search of our List of Educable Children of Wilkinson
County, Mississippi and below is a list of our findings on the Scotts in the
Doloroso area from 1906 through 1927:

Year of Book	Name of Parent or Guardian	Name of Child	Age	Sex
1906	A. W. Scott	Mary	18	F
		Walter	14	M
	A. W. Scott	Howard	20	M
		Walter	15	M
1908	Sam Scott (Only one child shown)	Gladys	5	F (Page 162)
	Mrs. Sallie Scott	Walter Scott	17	M
		Willie Bunch	17	M
1912	David Scott	Tom	8	M
		Dorris	6	F
1916	Howard Scott	Harry	8	M
		Noland	7	M
1920	Howard Scott	Harry	12	M
		Nolan	11	M
		Rosalee	7	F
		Leroy	5	M
	Mrs. Sallie Scott	Tom	15	M
		Dorris	13	F
1923	W. T. Scott	Doris	15	F
		Tom	12	M
	Mary E. Scott	Harry	15	M
		Nolan	14	M
		Rosa Lee	10	F
		Leroy	8	M
		Juanita	6	F
	M. J. Scott	Grantham	7	M

44-11

Year of Book	Name of Parent or Guardian	Name of Child	Age	Sex
1925	H. W. Scott	Glenn	17	M
		Harry	16	M
		Nolan	11	M
		Rosa Lee	10	F
		LeRoy	8	M
		Juanita	5	F
	M. J. Scott	Grahm	8	M
		Willie	7	F
	Walter Scott	Tom	19	M
		Dorris	18	F
1927	Walter Scott	Doris	20	F
	H. W. Scott	Harry	19	M
		Noland	18	M
		Rosa Lee	13	F
		Leroy	12	M
		Juanita	10	F
		Glenn	6	M
	M. J. Scott	Grantham	10	M
		Willie Ray	9	F

These books were not prepared every year as you will notice. Usually every two years, but there are periods when there is a 4 year lapse between the books.

The 1908 book is the only one to show the family of Sam Scott with the one child shown. Probably the other children attended between 1908 and 1912 or between 1916 and 1920.

We are sorry to be unable to produce a proof of age for your mother Mittie Scott.

Sincerely,

Charles E. Johnson
Superintendent of Education
Wilkinson County

44-12

Sarah (Sallie) Rebecca Holmes Scott

Mittie Scott Wilson,grandaughter,holdin
Sallie's fan and locket.

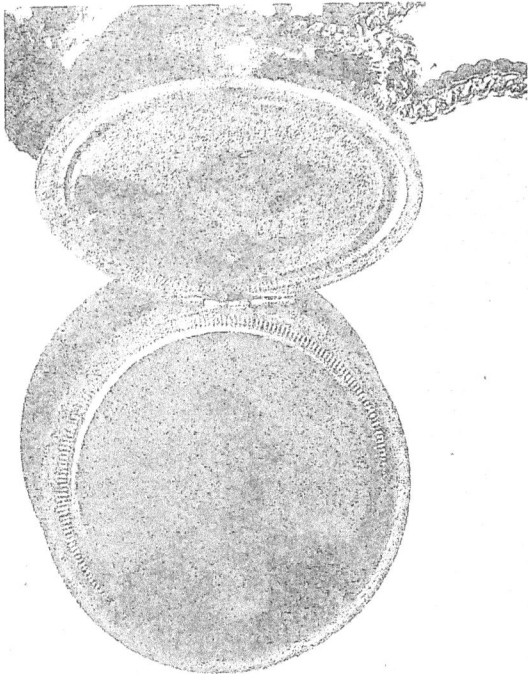
Argless Scott

Sallie Holmes Scott

Henry W. and Elizabeth Geter Scott's homeplace that
burned ca.1890's. Argiass and Sallie rebuilt on same site.

Sallie Holmes Scott with her four sons, Howard, Walter, Major & Sam.

SARAH HOLMES SCOTT

ARGLASS SCOTT

Joe D. and his dad,Joe Johnson,picking up shards of pottery
at SCOTT "homeplace".Wilkinson County,Ms.

SCOTT REUNION HELD JUNE 24

Sunday June 24, was the first annual reunion of the descendants of Henry Scott and Elizabeth Jeter Scott. The 51 descendants of the union were hosted by Joe and Sherry Scott Johnson of Doloroso.

Attending from Woodville were Lonnie and Linda Lipe, Willie Rae McCarstle, Mittie Lee Davis, Lonnie and Mamie Sturgeon, Holmes Sturgeon, Alonzo Sturgeon, Nelson Jensen, Viney and Jessica Pearson, Sarah Lipe, and Nelson Jensen, Jr.

Among those present from Natchez were Walter and Marie Scott, Patricia and Christopher W. Scott, J. L. and Nita Sesser, Nolan and Frances Sesser, Jim and David Sesser, Cliff McCarstle, Anna McCarstle, Glen and Gladys Scott, Tanya Sanders, and Rudy and Jennine Wilson.

Those present from Vicksburg were Leroy and Christine Scott and Harry and Jewell Scott.

Texas residents attending were Mrs. Mittie Scott Wilson and her daughters, Agnes Wilson Simmons and O'Levia Neil Wilson Wiese from Waco, Texas.

Vidalia was represented by Larry and Sue Scott.

Centreville is the home of Jo Ann Davis Koch and her two daughters, Leslie and Leanne. Also Larry and Diane Scott, and Amy, and Valerie and Lorie Scott were present.

Mrs. Olivia (Major) Johnson Scott of Woodville was recognized as the oldest member present and Davis Sesser of Natchez (6 months) the youngest. However all would agree Christopher W. Scott was the friendliest.

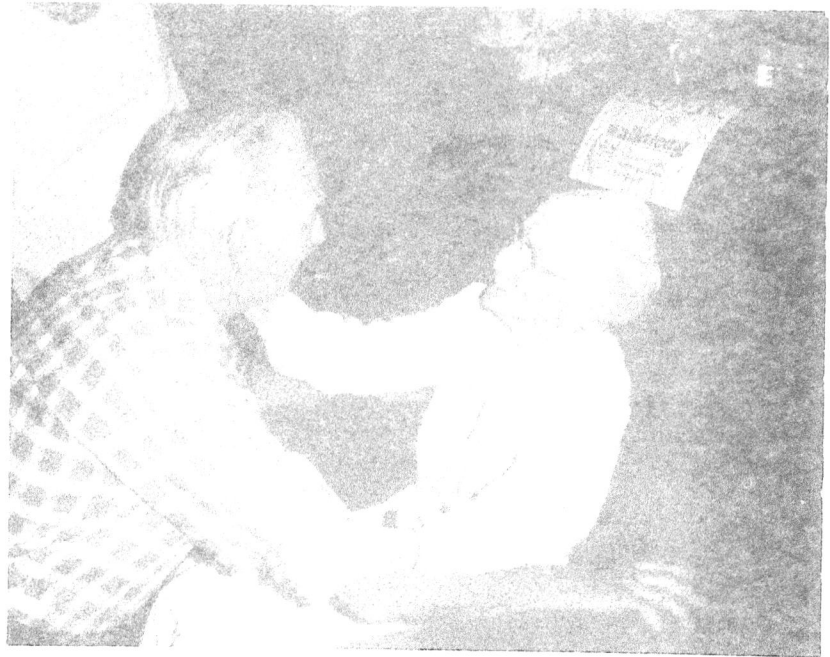

Leroy Scott and Aunt Levia Scott

1st row: Walter and Leroy
2nd row: Glen and Harry, Willie Ray and, Christine
3rd. Lonnie , Levia, and Mamie

Willie Ray,Christine,Jewel,Nita and Marie

Christine,Jewel and Nita

Neil and Holmes Sturgeon

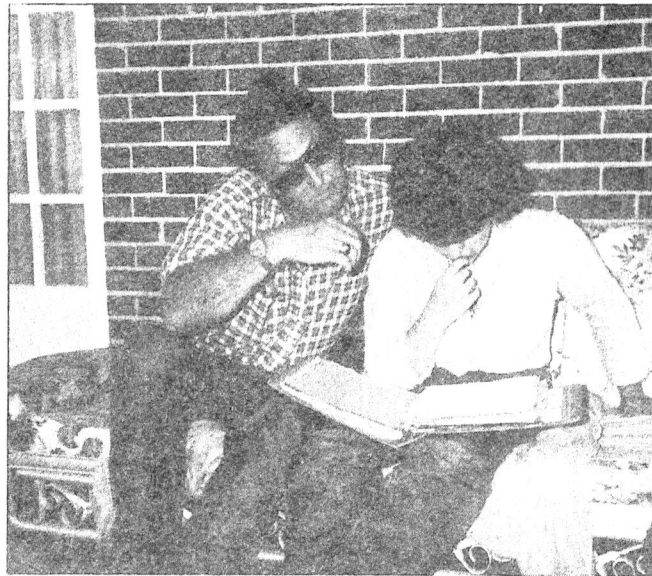

Patricia Scott and Clifford McCarstle

Agnes Simmons and her mother, Mittie

Glen, Gladys, and Harry Scott

REUNION '85

June 27, 1985

SCOTT REUNION
HELD AT DOLOROSO
SUNDAY, JUNE 23

Sunday, June 23, was the second reunion of the descendants of Henry William Scott and Elizabeth Geter Scott.

The 80 descendants were hosted by Joe and Sherry Scott Johnson of Doloroso.

Family members were present from Waycross and Dalton, Georgia; Columbia, Tennessee; Tallulah, Bossier City, Oak Grove, Lake Charles and Destrehan, Louisiana; Greenville, Vicksburg, Jackson, Natchez and Woodville, Mississippi; and Waco, Centerville, Austin, Crawford and McGregor, Texas.

Bricks from Arglass Scott's mill

Rev. Harry Scott

Walter Scott and Arglass Davis

Edward Scott from Resaca, Ga.

Greg,Beth and Sam Scott from Ga.and Fla.

Amye,George,William Avis Rose,Dave,Ann and John

Joe, Sherry, Jeanne and Rudy

Raymond, Chris and Patricia

Avis, Rose, Bob and John

Joe, Dave, Arglass, Bob, Roy and Rose

Harry Scott,Jewel Sesser,Herbert Jensen and Dave Moore

Ray Wiese and Joe Johnson

Nolan and David Sesser

Ray and Sherry

pg. 44-24

Sherry, Ann, Greg, Sam, Sherry

Rose,John,Roy,Ed,and Herbert

Lois,Bertha,Amye,Ann,John,Dave,Herbert,Roy and Rose

Herbert,Jewel,Ray,Lois,Bertha and Ed

Neil,Lois,and children,Bertha,Edward

Roy,Avis,Mittie,and Roger (Bernie)

Roy,Avis Mittie

Mittie,Roy, Herbert and Roger

Neil,marie,Roger,Sam, ,Agnes,Bob,Greg
Avis,Mittie, Pearl

Bertha,Sallie Vee,Marie,Mittie,Willie Ray and Roy

John,Ann,Greg,Sam,Bob and Sherry

Dot and Mittie

Dave,Rose,Brendi,Avis,Opal,Sherry Ann and Michelle

JOE AND SHERRY JOHNSON HOME,DOLOROSO,MS.
1986 Reunion

Weese,Burnell and Dot

Tessie,Jo Ann,Elizabeth,Mittie Lee,Leslie,Ruth,and Janet

Nolan,Francis,Nita,Jewel,Leta,Mimi,Jim and David

Anthony,Donnis,Anna,Willie Ray,Clifton and Katie

Walking to the Scott burying ground from Joe and Sherry's home

pg.44-35

Katherine and Sherry under the oak tree (1979)

This land was once the Thomas Brannon homesite.His wife,Jane Jeter, was a sister to Elizabeth Scott.It is believed that several Brannon relations are also buried here.Uncle Walter placed markers on some of the Scott graves.His mother,Mary,wrote that the three unmarked graves belonged to Henry and Elizabeth Jeter Scott and their son,Major J.Scott.

Ray,Glenn and Burnell

HARRY SCOTT

HARRY SCOTT b.1876 d.1897 of spinal meningitis in
Waco,Texas while visiting his Holmes relatives.

MOUND, LOUISANA   SAM SCOTT'S 2 TEAMS OF OXEN.
44-40

In 1981, Uncle John Scott of Mound, Louisana related to me a few memories of his life as a young boy growing up in Mound.

The family of Sam and Vivi Deloach Scott came to Louisana from Mississippi. They had been living and working on the Briars plantation where everyone became ill with maleria so they returned to Mississippi. Carol had died in Brier and Sammie had been born there the same year.

"When we finished (logging) work on Kings Point, we came to Mound, Louisana bringing 8 oxen to one wagon. The 8 wheel log wagon had wide sheels of 5-6" rims. The back section had double wheels with one following the other. (Tandem effect).

"There was a dummy line that ran into the woods and was used to haul the logs. It had a narrow gauge and reached 4 or 5 miles to the levy. All of the land was in timber. As the timber was cut, the rail road was put in to haul the timber out to the railroad and then carried to the saw mills in Mound.

"Here, they were loaded onto the trains and the cars had short stakes to keep the logs from falling off. The cable that loaded the logs would hook on the car with a hook cable and then slide the load from one to another until the car that had the loader was on was full.

"Sometimes logs were snaked 1/4 mile into the woods and hooked to a mule to be dragged out of the area.

"Before 1917, the sawmill burned and I went to Newalton and worked until the new mill was built. For many years, the Old Negroes would tell how I could "log".

"Papa had 2 teams and was the 'General Boss'. He cut out all the timber and then sold half of his teams and equipment to Mr. Coslow. Before long, Coslow wound up north of Jackson owning everything Papa had. He wanted Papa to let me go over there with him to help him log . Papa may have gone but I know I came back with one team. I was tied up in Vicksburg for 24 hours for inspection.

"Yeager owned the mill and timber at Mound. He gave me money for expenses and Dr. Edwards was to take care of the oxen and mail Yeager the bill. I had put them in a pen and so I released them to cross over the Mississippi River on the ferry boat between 3 or 4 o'clock.

"They were penned on Washington Street and driven down near to the water where the ferry boat was located. The old man was told to allow me to cross with the oxen and for him to send the bill to Mound.

"John was told to phone Yeager and get an OK. John was to go to
the 1st street pass the sea wall if he wanted to call Mound Store
collect.The ferry boat man didn't believe John when he told him
to send Yeager the bill for crossing.

"John didn't know what to do so he talked to the Mound Store
clerk Burley and told him the ferry boat man didn't believe him
and asked him what to do. Burley told John to tell that "bastard"
to come and call himself if he didn't believe John.

"John crossed the team without anymore trouble."

---

continuing Uncle John's narrative....

"The photograph taken in 1914 was printed in the MADISON JOURNAL
in Tallulah,La. The log had 2000 feet in it and Papa had to hook
both teams to the wagon in order to pull it out of the woods.The
leader was a big dark ox named "Kid". His horns were so wide that
he had to turn his head sideways.When a horse and rider met him
they'd better stand still or the ox would rake them."

44-42

State of Mississippi, :
Wilkinson County.   :

For and in consideration of the sum of one dollar ($1.00), receipt of which is hereby acknowledged, I convey and quitclaim unto Walter T. Scott all of my right, title and interest in and to the land in the County of Wilkinson, State of Mississippi, described as follows:

Beginning at a point on the West line of Section 26 Township 4, North, Range 2, West, 18.00 Chains North of the South West Corner thereof; Thence North a long the West line of said Section 36.27 Chains to Pin Oak; Thence East 20.00 Chains; Thence South 18½° W. 7.00 Chains; Thence S. 38½° East, 15.07 Chains; Thence N. 77° E. 11.00 Chains; Thence S. 10½° W. 4.50 Chains to point in Road; Thence Southeasterly with the meanderings of said road to creek; Thence Southerly with said creek to Water Gate; Thence S. 11½° E. 7.50 Chains to a Gate Post on Old Road; Thence S. 84° W. 65.00 Chains to place of beginning, containing 153.73 acres, more or less, and beginning in Section 26, Township 4, North, Range 2, West.

Witness my signature this _30_ day of June, A. D. 1925.

Sam Scott

State of Mississippi, :
County of _Warren_ :

Personally appeared before me, the undersigned authority in and for the said County and State, the within named Sam Scott who acknowledged that he signed and delivered the foregoing instrument on the day and year therein mentioned.

Given under my hand and official seal this _30_ day of June, A. D. 1925.

44-42   _John M. McGiveney_
Justice of the Peace

SAM SCOTT

MITTIE

SAM AND GENE PEEPLES

VIVI DELOACH SCOTT

When Sam Scott moved to Mound, Louisana shortly after 1910, he rented box #16 at the Mound Post Office located in the store by Yeager. He kept this number as long as he lived in Louisana and then his son, John, "inherited" #16.

Today, this store is still in existence, both for the people that live in the area and for the tourist who wish to observe how the people lived in the "old" days.

THE MOUND STORE

44-43

Sam,Gladys and Edward

Herbert,Mittie,John

Gladys and Mittie

Pg. 44-44

CHILD #3:HENRY WILLIAM SCOTT,b.1820 S.C.,d.Mar.10,1888 in
Wilkinson Co., MS.m.Mar.4,1841 (Bk.G.p.86)Elizabeth Jeter,
b.1826,d.ca.1892,dau.of Arglass Jeter and Polly Phipps.
(3 sons)
  1.THOMAS J. SCOTT b.1842,Killed in Va. during Civil War.

  2.ARGLASS WILLIAM SCOTT,b.Apr.15,1852,d.Dec.31,1906,m.
    Sarah(Sallie)Rebecca Holmes,b.Oct.18,1852,d.Feb.3,1941,
    dau.of Phoenix Holmes and Nancy Donnelly.(8 children)
    a)HARRY SCOTT b.1876 d.1897 of spinal meningitis in
      Waco,Texas while visiting his Holmes relatives.

    b) HELEN SCOTT b&d as a infant.

    c) SAM SCOTT b.May 29,1879,d.July 15,1942,m.Vivi
       Ione Deloach b.Dec.18,1882,d.June 15,1945.Sam buried   in
       Tallulah,La.and Vivi buried in Hope Mausoleum,New Orleans
       La.as Vivi Malley. Sam and Vivi m.Wilkinson Co.Ms.
       Feb.27,1902.(Bk. L,p.331) (8 children)

       1.GLADYS SCOTT b.Feb.5,1902,d.May 9,1981,m.Bert Tower
         1917,Bert b.May 3,1886,d.Feb.18,1955.(3 children)

         a) Son,b&d.
         b)CLARA TOWER b.Oct.24,1921,m.May 28,1938 Tallulah,La.
           to Charles Henry (CH)Hodge,b.Jan.24,1917,son of Mittie
           Reynolds and James Madison Hodge from Montgomery,Ala.
           (8 children)
           1.DOROTHY ANN HODGE b.July 12,1939
           2.GLORIA NELL HODGE b.Feb.7,1941 m.Sept.9,1956 to
             Kenneth Laverne Busby b. June 22,1933,son of Fannie
             Muse and Sampson Mcune Busby of Tallulah,La.Both
             born in Vernan Parish,La. (4 children)

             a)DEBORAH DENISE BUSBY b.Nov.8,1957 m.Nov.10,1975
               in Tallulah,to Shelton Ray Bishop,b.Mar.28,1956,
               son of Mary and George Bishop of Pecos,Tx.
               (2 children)
               1.SHELLY DENISE BISHOP b.Nov.10,1978
               2.STACY LARAE BISHOP b.June 17,1980

             b)KENNETH RICHARD(Ricky)BUSBY b.July 6,1959,m.Nov.
               17,1979 to Evelyn Diane Cain Moore,b.Sept.8,1961,
               dau.of Barbara Curtis of Vicksburg,Ms.,and Ralph
               Marcellous Cain of Yazoo City,Ms.(1 child,adopted
               by Ricky)
               1.VENABLE(Trey)CARROLL MOORE BUSBY b. Oct.24,1977

             c)GARY DEWAYNE BUSBY b.June 26,1961 m. June 11,1983
               to Carolyn Coody,dau.of Valie and Buford Coody.
               (1 child)

1.MATTHEW SPENSER BUSBY

3. ELIZABETH JOAN HODGE b.Aug.16,1942,m.Dec.20,1958
   to Thurmon Lejune Busby,(bro.to Kenneth Busby)
   b.Jan.1928   (3 children)
   a)MARGIE LANNELLE BUSBY b.Oct.17,1959,m.Aug.15,
     1981 to James Stewart Morgan b.Apr.14,1952 in
     Panama City,Panama,son of Trobia Moreno Morgan
     and Clifton H.Morgan.(James had two children)
     1.KELLY LYNN MORGAN b. Dec.8,1974
     2.KASEY LEIGH MORGAN b.July 3,1979
     3.LINDSEY ELIZABETH MORGAN b. Jan.20,1987

   b)JAMES GREGORY BUSBY b.Aug.4,1961 m.Sept.19,1987
     Lesley Prince ,dau.of Mr.& Mrs.Linder C.Prince
   c)JOHN PATRICK BUSBY b.Dec.12,1963

4. PATRICIA LOUISE HODGE b.July 12,1944,m.Aug.21,1971
   to Hugh Fairman Acuff,Jr.(2 children)
   a)TONYA LEIGH ACUFF b.Oct.7,1974 Vicksburg,Ms.
   b)HUGH FAIRMAN ACUFF,III(Trey)b.Dec.26,1977,same.

5.JANICE ELAINE HODGE b.Dec.20,1945,m.1st:Sept.23,
   1963 to Alton Earl Ross,son of James D.Ross and
   Fannie Mangum.(1 child,James) Janice m.2nd
   Sept.22,1973 to Ronald Emory Basset b.Jan.1,1949
   son of Bobbie and Clyde Vester Bassett(2children)
   a)JAMES EARL ROSS b. April 7,1965,m.Nov.23,1985
     Linda Sue Lawrence b. Feb.23,1966 m.dau of
     Shirll Massey and Ernest Lawrence.Linda has a
     daughter.(1 child)
     1.KELLY LOUISE LAWRENCE b.June 21,1983
     2.   b.Aug.1987

   b)ANGELIA KAYE BASSETT b.Sept.4,1974
   c)RONALD EMORY BASSETT b.June 27,1977

6.CHARLES HENRY HODGE JR.b.Feb.14,1949 m.1968 to
   Janet Sue Clark b.Mar.3,1950,dau.of Ilene Walker
   and Harlin E.Clark.(2 children) Charles m.2nd to
   Rhonda Mann   (1 child)
   a)CHARLES HENRY HODGE III b. June 6,1972
   b)AMY MICHELLE HODGE b.July 16,1975 Pasadena,Tx.
   c)REGAN MAE HODGE b. Mar.11,1983,Houston,Tx.

7.DONALD ROY HODGE b. Dec.15,1951 m.Oct.4,1976
   Delhi,La. to Pamela Nelson b.Mar.3,1955,dau of
   Fannie Mae Godde and John Nelson of Deliha,La.
   (3 children)
   a)DONNA NICOLE HODGE b.Sept.7,1977
   b)AMANDA DIANNE HODGE b.July 8,1982
   c)JESSICA LYNN b. Oct.9,1986

8.RONALD TROY HODGE b.Dec.15,1951(twin to Donald)m.
July 2,1977 to Jacqueline Eschete b.Dec.25,1957
Natchez,Ms.,dau.of Betty Jo Slampa and James Earl
Eschete.(2 children)
a)JACQUELINE MARIE HODGE b.Oct.28,1978
b)LACEY JO HODGE b. Apr.30,1987

c) ARVEL GRACE TOWER b.Feb.19,1928 m.1st Apr.21,1946
to Joel Glendon(Glen)Barrett of Goodwill,La.b.June
17,1924,son of Virgie and William C.Barrett
(3 children)
1.JOE NELL BARRETT b.April 29,1947 m.Monroe F.Reed
Jr.,son of Monroe F.Reed Sr.of San Antonio,Tx.
(3 children)
a)KHRISTINE DAWN REED b.Dec.17,1971 V'burg
b)KEVIN SHAWN REED b.June 24,1974 V'burg.
c)KELLEY MICHELLE REED b.June 2,1980 Mcghee,Ark.

2.MICHAEL GLEN BARRETT b.Mar.18,1950 V'burg, m.1970
Wanda(Sam)Lee Wahlstrom b.Jan.26,1951 LePanto,Ark.
dau.of Junie Wolfe and Ed Wahlstrom.(3 children)
a)MICHAEL(Mickie)GLEN BARRETT Jr.b.Oct.26,1970
b.JAMES(Jimmy)MICHAEL BARRETT b.Oct.11,1971
c.MYRTTE MICHELE BARRETT b.June 11,1975

3.KENNETH JOEL BARRETT b.July 11,1960 Little Rock,
Ark.
Grace m.2nd.April 10,1977 to Jack Hayne Folk,
b.Oct.5,1924,son of Lucy Sevier and Ben P.Folk of
Tallulah,La.

THE C.H. and CLARA HODGE FAMILY

Dorothy Hodge

C.H. and Clara

2.JOHN SCOTT b.Oct.20,1903 Doloroso,Ms.d.Feb.20,1984
m.Aug.29,1925 to Avis Mae Freeman b. Apr.5,1910,Smith-
dale,Ms.,dau.of Eula Eva Hogan and Ferdanand Columbus
Freeman of Franklin Co.,Ms.(10 children)

a)ALMA MAXINE SCOTT b.Dec.18,1926,m.Oct.22,1944 to
William Elbert Rollins b.June 5,1925,son of Hattie
Dell Rawls and William Elbert Rollins(2 children)
1.JOHN ELBERT ROLLINS b.Mar.26,1946 Winnsboro,La.
m.Wanda Carol Junkin b.Nov.2,1948,dau.of Susie
Lee Long and Willie Wesley Junkin (1 child)

2.DONNA SUE ROLLINS b.Sept.18,1952 Many,La.m.1st,
William Michael Browder,Winnsboro,La.b.Aug.30,
1951,son of Jessie Faye Jennings and James Aubrey
Browder.(1 child).

b)HELEN VIVIAN SCOTT b.Nov.28,1929,m.Dec.7,1945 to
Glen Dewitt Breedlove b. Jan.3,1922,son of Alice
Virginia Moore and Thomas Watkins Breedlove.
(5 children)

1.GLEN DALE BREEDLOVE b. Sept.7,1946 m.Mary Linda
Hines of Bossier City,La.b.Feb.10,1948,dau.of Mary
and William Hines.(3 children)
a)TIMOTHY PAUL BREEDLOVE b.Mar.25,1968
b)TODD LEIGHTON BREEDLOVE b.July 12,1971
c)TYE MICHAEL BREEDLOVE b.July 8,1975

2.RICHARD LAMAR BREEDLOVE b.Jan.26,1948 Lake Providence,La.m.Paula Ann Baker b.Oct.1,19   dau of
Dorothy and Lewis Baker.(2 children)
a)RIVERS LEE BREEDLOVE b. March 28,1971
b)EMILY ANN BREEDLOVE b.Nov.15,1973

3.JUDY ANN BREEDLOVE b&d Sept.7,1950 El Paso,Tx.
4.PATRICIA ELAINE BREEDLOVE b.Jan.8,1951 Tallulah,La.
m.Perry Deacon from New York,son of Millie and
Sanford Deacon.(1 child)
a)DYLAN SCOTT DUNCAN b.July 17,1982

5.DWAYNE SCOTT BREEDLOVE b.Nov.8,1961,Fort Lee,Va.

c)ROSALIE(Rose)SCOTT b.Oct.11,1931,m.Aug.31,1946 to
Dave Moore b. Nov.6,1924,son of Heneretta Thorp
Moore (1 child)
1.RONALD WAYNE MOORE b.July 16,1948 Tallulah,La.m.
Aug.8,1969 Perrilyn Thornton b.   dau.of
Perry Search Thornton and Dorothy Osborn Thornton of
Start,La.(2 children)
a)KENDRDA DEANNE MOORE b.Feb.26,1971,Alsatia,La.

b)ADAM RONALD MOORE b.June 10,1977

d)JOHN HOWARD SCOTT SR.b.Nov.6,1933 m.1st to Mattie
   Ruth Hicks b.Aug.19,1935,dau.of Leon Hicks of
   Madison Parish,La.(2 children)

   1.DEBRA LYNN SCOTT b.Apr.11,1956 Shreveport,La.
     m.1st to Bill Stewart (1 child)
     a)STACEY RENEE STEWART b.Aug.21,1979

     Debra Lynn m.2nd to Richard Styles(1 child)
     b)LINZY NICHOLE STYLES b.May 22,1984

   2.JOHN HOWARD SCOTT JR.b.May 9,1958 Vicksburg,Ms.

   JOHN HOWARD SR.m.2nd to Stella Norcross of
   North Carolina.Stella had three children from a former
   marriage.
   3.AUBREY NORCROSS
   4.CHARLES NORCROSS
   5.PAM NORCROSS m.Steve Eyler (2 children)
     a)MEGAN ROCHELLE EYLER b. 1986
     b)STEPHANY EYLER b.1981

e)MARION BLANCHE SCOTT b.Aug.20,1935 Mound,La.m.Apr.22,
   1955 to William Ary Hillman II,b.July 15,1935,son of
   William Ary(WA)Hillman and Lois Gillman Edwards.
   (2 children)
   1.JACQUELINE NAN HILLMAN b.July 16,1956 Delhi,La.
     m.Oct.19,1979 Robert Jeffery Wright b.July 24, 1956
     Yazoo,City,Ms.(1 child)
     a)WILLIAM BENJAMIN WRIGHT b.Sept.28,1985
   2.WILLIAM ARY (Rusty) HILLMAN III b. Dec.20,1969

f.OPAL PAULINE SCOTT b.May 24,1937 Mound,La.m.Aug.6,
   T.C.(Pete)Self b.Oct.11,1935,son of Bertha Moore and
   J.T.Self.(4 children)
   1.CLYDE ROY SELF b.Sept.11,1956,Stamps,Ark.m.June 18,
     1976 to Cindy Gregory(2 children)
     a)ERICA LYNN SELF b.Nov.7,1979
     b)JARRED MICHAEL SELF b.Oct.29,1981

   2.SHERRY ANN SELF b. Sept.2,1957 Stamps,Ark.m.Feb.10,
     1978 to Buddy Stokes b.May 18,1959,son of Deloras
     Miller and Richard Stokes(2 children)
     a)BRANDI NICOLE STOKES b.Nov.24,1979
     b)MELISSA MICHELLE STOKES b.Mar.26,1986

   3.JOHN TILDEN SELF b.July 24,1958 Bastrop,La.m.
     Elizabeth Rhoden b.Oct.7,1977,dau.of Willie Mae and
     Everette Rhoden.(2 children)
     a)JENNEFER ELIZABERTH SELF b.July 28,1980

    b)JACOB TIMOTHY SELF b.Jan.13,1983

  4.RITA KAY SELF b.Aug.3,1962 Monahans,Tx.m.Mark Young
    Oct.9,1981,son of Evelyn and Mark Young.
g)WILLIAM PAUL SCOTT b.Mar.28,1939 m.Judy Aline Sanford
  Holley b.Dec.27,1943 dau.of Nancy Copeland and Wayne
  Allen Sanford of Rayville,La;.(3 children)
  1.JAMES ALLEN HOLLEY b.Mar.29,1962 d.Oct.9,1983
  2.WILLIAM PAUL SCOTT JR.b.Dec.2,1968
  3.BRIAN SANFORD SCOTT b.Jan.8,1971

h)AMELIA ANN SCOTT b.July 31,1944 m.Dec.8,1962 to
  John Stacy Morgan b.Sept.6,1937,son of Elsie Owens
  and Stacy Morgan of West Carrol Parish,La.(2 children)
  1.STACI LEIGH MORGAN b.Nov.9,1964
  2.KIMBERLY (Kim) MORGAN b.Nov.2,1969

i)MICHAEL WAYNE SCOTT b.June 21,1947,d.Feb.11,1951

j)GEORGE WENDELL SCOTT bdec.21,1950 Tallulah,La.m.Oct.
  4,1975 to Amye Gail Glassl b.Dec.21,1951,dau of
  Ferdinand J.Glassl and Nellie Doris Foster of
  Vicksburg,Ms.(1 child)
  1.ANTHONY JUSTIN (AJ) SCOTT b.Jan.5,1985,Vicksburg,Ms.

John and Avis Freeman Scott's children 1986

Avis with her grandchildren 1986

Avis with more of her family 1986

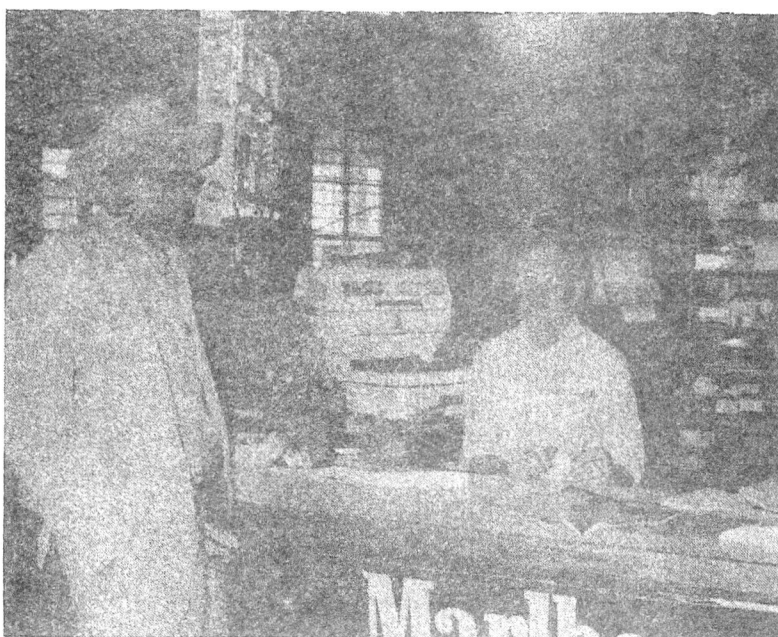

John Scott and Nolan Dickson in the Mound store 1980
Photo by Rick Neuman

Dave,Rose,Brendi,Avis,Opal,Sherry Ann and Michelle 1986

Amye,George,William Avis Rose,Dave,Ann and John

3.HERBERT IVY SCOTT b.Apr.8,1905 Doloroso,Ms.d.May 23,
  1974 Bonita,La.m.Dec.19,1929 to Louine Freeman b.Mar.18,
  1916,d.Aug.12,1982.Both buried in Silver Cross Cemetery,
  Tallulah,La.Louine was sister to Avis,wife of John Scott,
  and dau. of Eula Eva Hogan and Ferdanand C.Freeman.
  (11 children)

  a)EDWARD IVY SCOTT b.Apr.14,1932 Madison Parish,La.m.
    m.1st July 4,1959 Crossett Ark.to Mattie Odell
    Crye,dau.of Rich Turner Crye and Annie Crye.(1 child)

    1.EDWARD TIMOTHY SCOTT b.July 31,1960 New Oarleans,La.
      m.June 25,1983 Shreveport,La.to Gay Gallien,dau.of
      Mr.& Mrs.Joseph A.Gallien of Shreveport

    m.2nd.Estenia Opal Rutledge of Monroe,La.

  b)RAYMOND SCOTT b. Sept.19,1935 Mound,La.m.Sept.21,1953
    to Donna DeVille b. Dec.5,1937,dau.of Bellita S.Smith
    and Claude D.DeVille.Bellita b.Apr.22,1915,Claude
    b.June 10,1903,d.Oct.12,1977.(3 children)

    1.RAYMON DeWAYNE SCOTT b.Nov.21,1954 Bastropo,La.m.
      Sept.24,1976 to Frances Ann Hague b.Feb.26,1954,dau
      of Melvie Sales and Edward Dallas Hague.(2 children)
      a)WENDY ANN SCOTT b.Mar.1,1980 Bastrop,La.
      b)JENNIFER RENEE SCOTT b. Nov.14,1983 Bastrop,La.

    2.RONNIE EDWARD SCOTT b.Dec.2,1955 Bastrop,La.m.June
      5,1976 to Debra Ann Wirt b.June 6,1954 Bainbridge,
      Ma.dau.of Mary Jane Fairfield and Morgan Edwaard Wirt
      of Albany,N.Y.and Atlantic City,N.J.(3 children)
      a)ANNA MICHELLE SCOTT b.Sept.2,1979 Ala.
      b)JO TIFFANY SCOTT b. July 23,1982 Monroe,La.
      c)RONNIE EDWARD,JR.b.June 4,1985 Monroe,La.

    3.MICHAEL RAY SCOTT b.Mar.1,1957 Bastropo,La.m.1st
      Pamela Eileen Parish ,July 3,1976 dau. of Geraldine
      and Fred Parish (2 children)
      a)JESSICA ANN SCOTT b.Oct.12,1978 Emporie,Kansas
      b)RAYMOND MICHAEL SCOTT b.Oct.30,1980 Gulfport,Ms.

      Michael m.2nd to Patsy Jean Cagle b.Jan.31,1944
      Delhi,La.m.Nov.21,1985.dau.of Elby George Cagle of
      Yazoo City,Ms. and Robbie Lee Dixon of Baskin,La,
      Patsy has two children.
      c)DANIEL L.KNOWLES b. Aug.7,1962
      d)KAREN RUTH KNOWLES SAXON b.Aug.1,1965

  c)SARAH ANN SCOTT b.Sept.28,1933,d.Apr.1934

d)BARBARA DELL SCOTT b&d July 17,1937
e)PATRICIA NELL SCOTT b. July 17,1937,twin to Barbara.
  m.Dec.25,1954 Lake Providence,La. to Willie Carl(WC)
  Boswell b. Dec.25,1919 Bartow,Co.Ga.W.C.died suddenly
  in December 14,1987.(3 children)

  1.BOBBY CARL BOSWELL b. Jan.23,1956 Bastrop,La.m.1st
    June 28,1975 Dalton,Ga.to Rose Marie Johnson b.Aug.
    21,1955,dau.of Truman Johnson and Irene Kaugl of
    Tifton,Ga.(1 child)
    a)JOSHUA ADAM BOSWELL b.Feb.25,1977
    Bobby m.2nd Dec.29,1984 to Rebecca (Becky) Lee
    Stambaugh b.Apr.21,1965,dau.of John William and
    Paula Frances Roberts Stambaugh.

  2.HERBERT RANSON (Randy) BOSWELL b.June 2,1958 Dalton,
    Ga.m.Nov.22,1975 Murphy,N.C.to Anita Joyce Rich b.
    Aug.27,1958,dau. of Raymond Laroy Rich and Lela
    Joice Blackwell (2 children)
    a)JEREMY MICHAEL BOSWELL b.Nov.28,1976 Dalton,Ga.
    b)KEITH PATRICK BOSWELL b. Dec.20,1984

  3.KAREN DENISE BOSWELL b. Mar.24,1963 Dalton,Ga.m.1st
    Mar.22,1980 Trenton,Ga.to John Van Jackson Jr.b.
    June 18,1963,son of John Van Jackson Sr.and Janie
    Marie Brooks of Dalton.(1 child)
    a)REBECCA ANN JACKSON b. July 10,1980 Dalton,Ga.

    Karen m.2nd May7,1984 to Rockey Dewayne Harrington
    b.July 10,1962 son of Crystal Vernice Miller and
    Raymond Harrington of Ringgold,Ga.(1 child)

    b)BRANDON DEWAYNE HARRINGTON b. Nov.1,1986 Dalton

f)BLANCHE SCOTT b.July 4,1938.d.1938

g)BILLY RAY SCOTT b.Dec.19,1940 Shreveport,La.m.1st
  Feb.1959 Monroe City,Ind.to Nancy Lou Tomson,dau.of
  Ralph and Nettie Tomson from Washington,Ind.
  (3 children)
  1.MELINDA GAIL SCOTT b.July 9,1960 Washington,Ind.
    m.1st Aug.1978 Vinncenes,Ind.to Robert Earl
    Stevenson b.May 18,1947 Vincennes,Ind.,son of
    Frances Lucy Compling and Donald William Stevenson.
    (1 child)
    a)CHRISTI DAWN STEVENSON b.Nov.4,1978 Vincennes,Ind.

    Melinda m.2nd to Steve Lester Stork b.Aug.2,1955
    Vincennes,Ind.,son of Lester Alexander Stork and
    Claudia Elizabeth Emmons (1 child)

    b)DANIEL RAY STORK b. Jan.18,1986 Vincennes,Ind.

2.LESIA ANNETTE SCOTT b.June 15,1963 Dalton Ga.m.
Jeffery Alan Wade b.Oct.29,1962,son of
Ivan William Wade and Connie Ann Dufon (2 ch)
a)AMBER NICOLE WADE b. Aug.24,1982 Kokimo,Ind.
b)JEFFERY ALAN WADE JR.B.May 4,1984 Kokimo,Ind.
Wade.

3.CATHY RENAE SCOTT b.Dec.2,1964 Dalton,Ga.m.
Robert Warren Emmons b.Feb.5,1960 Vincennes,Ind.
son of Warren Robert Emmons and Glora Neuman.
(1 child)

a)BRITTNEY RENEE EMMONS b.Nov.5,1985 Vincennes,Ind.

Billy Ray m.2nd Dec.2,1966 Eton,Ga.to Brenda Sue
Moore b.Mar.31,1943 Calhoun Ga.dau.of Exie Ylene
Mashburn and Henry Grady Moore of Resaca,Ga.

h)VIRGINIA LOIS SCOTT b.Jan.17,1942 Mound,La.m.Dec.10,
1961 Lake Providence,La.to James Albert Mullins
b.Oct.15,1939 Oscelola,Ark.son of Albert Mullins b.
Sept.28,1912 Hati,Missouri,and Bertha Covine Denton b.
Mar.2,1915 Cardwell,Missouri.(3 children)

1.BERTHA LOUANN MULLIN b. June 12,1965 Heidleburg,
Germany,m.Mack Johnny Harper b.Feb.28,1964 Forest,La.
son of Arnold Joe Harper and Ida Mable Fox .(1 child)

a)JESSICA NICHOLE HARPER b. 1983 Monroe,La.

2.JACKIE LYNN MULLINS b. Sept.20,1968 Lake Providence
La.
3.JIMMY RAY MULLINS b.Jan.12,1971,Monroe,La.

i)SHIRLEY ANN SCOTT b.Jan.15,1943 Mound,La.m.Aug.28,1960
to Edward James Miles b.Mar.30,1939 Tallulah,La. son of
Edward Miles and Lottie Lee Oliveaux of Lake
Providence,La. (4 children)

1.KENNETH EDWARD MILES b.Aug.2,1961 Monroe,La.m.(Lisa)
Melissa Jean Page b. Aug.4,1964 Widner,Ga.dau.of
Billy Gene Page,Sr.and Fannie Lou Martin of
Winder,Ga.(1 child)

a)KENNETH EDWARD MILES ,JR. b.Oct.19,1985
Lawrenceville,Ga.

2.SHELIA ANN MILES b.Oct.29,1962 Monroe,La.m.Robert
Miles Bell b.Sept.17,1956 New Albany,Ms. son of
James Harold Bell and Agnes Ophelia Bell.(2 children)

a)MISTY LYNN BELL b.Apr.22,1979 Monroe,La.
b)STACEY NICHOLE BELL b.April 8,1985 Bastrop,La.

3.JOYCE ANNETTE MILES b.Sept.18,1964 Lake
Providence,La.(1 child)
a)NICKIE MICHELLE MILES b. Sept.2,1985 Vicksburg,Ms.

4.ELIZABETH DENISE MILES b.April 13,1967
Delhi,La.m.Jan.29,1983 Lake Parovidence,La.to Tony
Lee Thornhill b.Jan.28,1964 Ferriday,La.son of Donald
Malvin Thornhill and Sadie Mae Thornton.

j)EDNA EARL SCOTT b.Aug.13,1944 Vicksburg,Ms.m.1st
Lloyd Morris b. Mar.17,1939 Fayette,Ala.son of Garvie
Lloyd Morris and Annie Laboon (2 children)

1.DANNY LOYD MORRIS b.Sept.7,1960 Monroe,La.
(2 children)
a)TIFFANY NICOLE MORRIS b.April 14,1982 Tuscaloosa,
b)SONYA DANIELLE MORRIS b.April 27,1984 Tuscaloosa.

2.SANDY DEWAYNE MORRIS b.Oct.19,1961 Fayette,Ala.
m.Carol Christian b. Sept.20,1962 Cook Co.Ill.dau.of
Ned Eden Christian b.Nov.26,1948 Cook Co.Il,and
Martha Jane Bone b. Sept.28,1948 Cook Co.Il.

Edna m.2nd Barry McMilleon of Bastrop,La.(1 child)

3.BARRY GENE McMILLEON b.Oct.19,1971 Hodge,La.

Edna m.3rd MILTON LEE MUNN JR.b.July 13,1954
Delhi,La.son of Milton Lee Munn,Sr.and Ruth Maxwell of
Oak Grove,La.(no children)
m.4th Jerry Wayne Paul b.May 16,1958 Oak Grove,La.son
of James Kenneth Paul and Mildred Winstead of Oak
Grove.La.

k)BERTHA MAE SCOTT b.Sept.4,1945 m.1st, July 11,1963
Melvin Jordon Herman b. July 13,1944,son of Harry
Herman and Dolly Johnson (5 children)

1.JERREY MELVIN HERMAN b. Dec.5,1963 Lake Providence
La.m.Nov.1,1986 Seoul,Korea to Na Bong Hui b.Sept.
25,1958 Seoul,Korea,dau.of Na Ke Bong and Hong Jong
Won of Seoul,Korea.

2.LISA MICHELLE HERMAN b.Aug.5,1967 Ferriday,La.
m.1st Mar.19,1984 Dalton,Ga.to James Kendall Walling
b.May 22,1963 Dalton,Ga.son of Oliver Walling and
Mabel Walling of Dalton,Ga.(1 child)
a)JAMES BRANDON WALLING b.Oct.20,1985 Dalton,Ga.

Lisa m.2nd June 17,1986 to William Ben Judd b.March 6,1957 of Algood,Tenn.son of Ben Burris Judd and Johnnie Martha Owens of Algood,Tenn.

3.DONNA LOUISE HERMAN b.May 22,1969 Dardanelle,Ark.

4.SHANNA MARIE HERMAN b.June 3,1973 Clarksville,Ark.

5.JONATHAN WADE HERMAN b.Jan.23,1975 Clarksville,Ark.

Lisa married 3rd to Lester Rodgers.

Herbert Scott Family

Louine and Herbert Scott

Neil, Lois with children, Bertha, and Edward

4.MITTIE SCOTT b.Mar.6,1908 Wilkinson Co.Ms.,m.Nov.23,1923
  Summner,Ms.to Roger O'Neal Wilson b.Oct.4,1?0 Kemper Co.
  Ms.,d.Aug.6,1977 Waco,Texas.In 1953,Roger and Mittie moved
  from Drew,Ms.to Waco,Texas where Neil and Ray were living.
  There,years later,Mittie would meet several cousins of the
  Holmes family who had descended from her grandmother,
  Sarah Rebecca's, brothers and sisters.(7 children)

  a)KATHERINE LOUISE WILSON b. Sept.25,1924 Drew,Ms.
    m.1st Mar.25,1939 Drew,Ms. Archie Eugene Peeples
    b.Apr.4,1920,d.Feb.14,1968.Leland,Ms.son of Samuel
    Lee Peeples and Beuna Vista Summers.(3 children)

    Gene m.2nd to Weeze and had one child,
    DONNIE PEEPLES

    Katherine m.2nd Oct.16,1971 Paul Zand Kemp b.Carlsbad,
    N.M. son of Benjamin Willliam Kemp and Mary Jewel
    Johnson
    1.ROBERT EUGENE PEEPLES b. July 22, 1940 Drew,Ms.
      m.May 20,1961 Elizabeth Joan Rubic Kuga ,dau. of
      Frank Munoz Rubic b. Manilla,Phillipines and Emily
      Salcesdo Adenbruck b. Sobu,Phillipines.
      (2 children)Elizabeth had one child from 1st m.to Ken
      Kuga(deceased).

      a)PAULA FAITH KUGA b. Oct.14,1958 m.Dennis Dillard
        son of Eubert Dillard and Lena Mildred Wilburn of
        Tuscaloosa Co.,Ala(1 child)
        1.JUSTIN LEE DILLARD b.Nov.18,1982 West Covina,Ca.

      b)VIRENIA (NIA) GWENDOLYN PEEPLES b.Dec.10,1961
        L.A.Co.Hollywood,Calif.

      c)CYNTHIA DAWN PEEPLES b. Oct.6,1963 L.A.Co

    2.PATRICIA ANN PEEPLES b.Feb.9,1942 Drew,Ms.m.Oct.30,
      1965 Ronald James Lee b.May 30,1938 son of Robert
      Hazeltine and Margeratte Jeanette Bush .Margeratte
      m.2nd to Bryon Lee who adopted Ronald.(2 children)

      a)ERICK JASON LEE b. Oct.5,1970 Ventura Co.Calif.
      b)SEAN MICHAEL LEE b. Aug.16,1973 Waco,Tex.

    3.RICHARD O'NEAL PEEPLES b. Dec.5,1944 Drew,Ms.
      m.Janet McMullen 1964 in Los Angles,Calif.
      (2 children)
      a) TERI LYNN PEEPLES b.June 29,1965 L.A.Co.Ca.
         m.Aug.29,to David Stewlow

      b) KATHERINE TAMMATHA PEEPLES b. June 19,1966
         Clarksdale,Ms.

Richard m.2nd Feb.13,1965 Princeton,La. to Carolyn Ann
Jamar Padgett b.Sept.13,1946.dau.of George Walter
Jamar of Puschopa,Okla and Ida Lou Taylor of Aberdeen,
Caroline has 2 children from her first m.to Lawrence
Joe Padgett.

   c)SHELLI LYNN PADGETT b. May 21,1969 Waco.

   d)CHRISTOPHER BLAKE PADGETT b.DEC.20,1971

b)O'LEVIA NEIL WILSON b.Mar.1,1928,Bared,Mss.m.Feb.22,1944
   Baton Rouge,La.to Ernest Ray Wiese b. Aug.13,1920,
   Moody,Tx.,son of Fredrick Sigmund Wiese b.Nov.15,1892
   Brenham,Tx.,d.May 30,1963 Waco,Tx.,and Lillie Mae
   Edwards of Moody,Tx.b.Dec..31,1896 Moody,d.May 30,1982.
   In 1894,the Edwards moved to Moody from Dalton,Ga.

   1.VIVIAN LOUISE WIESE b. June 6,1946 Waco,Tx.m.Dec.20
      1968 Austin,Tx. to Gary Kim Dodgen b.Sept.4,1946
      Waco,son of William and Ginger Murray Dodgen of Waco.
      (1 child)
      a)TIFFANY ALANA DODGEN b. July 2,1983 Waco,Tx.

   2.SIDNEY RAY WIESE b. Mar.21,1953 Waco,m.July 12,1975
      Dallas,Tx. to Colleen Beth Finklea b.June 22,1954
      Dallas,dau. of Carol Finklea and Helen
      (2 children)
      a)MEGAN NOEL WIESE b.Oct.11,1978
      b)SUMMER KATHLEEN WIESE b.Apr.4,1981

c)VIRGIE LEE WILSON b.Sept.1,1930,d.Sept. 23,1931 of
   diphtheria in Arcola,Ms.

d)ROBERT SAMUEL WILSON b.Apr.12,1932 Vicksburg,Ms.
   m. Oct.2,1957 to Vera Jacquelyn (Jackie) Price,b.June
   9,1936,dau. of Vernon and Beatrice Price of Bertram,Tx.,
   (3 dau.)
   1.AMBER RENEE WILSON b.Sept.5,1958 Austin,Tx.m.May 23,
      23,1980 to Timothy Leigh Taylor of Phoenix,Ariz.
      b.Feb.29,1960.son of Sam and Janie Taylor.(1 child)
      a)RICHARD LEIGH TAYLOR b. Apr.30,1982

      Amber m.2nd Mar.19,1988 Andy Requenez,son of Raul
      and Marianna Requenez of Austin,Tx.

   2.MONICA WILSON b.Oct.2,1959, Austin,Tx. m. Michael
      Maddox b.Feb.1957 (2 children)

   3.Ramona Wilson Copeland b. Apr.5,1962 adopted by
      Jackie's 2nd m.to H.E. Copeland b.Sept.18,1915.

e)ROGER BERNARD WILSON b. Apr.19,1934 Vicksburg,Ms.m.
Oct.2,1954 Killeen,Tx. to Lila (Loe) Nell Dugger
b.Dec.14,1934 dau.of Laura Clara Motl and Benjamin
Franklin Dugger of Killeen,Tx.(2 children)

1.SHERRY THERESA WILSON b. Jan.3,1958.m.April 23,1988
James McLauren Yates Jr.b.July 11,1958,son of James
McLauren Yates Sr.and Alice Walker Yates of Waco.

2.SCOTT ALLEN WILSON b.May 5,1963 m.Dec.14,1984
Bryan,Tx.to Nancy Suzanne Chandler b.Nov.28,1962
dau.of Tom and Willa Dean Chandler of Bryan,Tx.

f)AGNES EFFIE WILSON b.Oct.23,1939 m.July 19,1958 Seymour
Tx.to John Henry Styles b. 1935,son of Lena Mae Brennan
and Samuel Washington Styles of Seymour,Texas.
(4 children)

1.SAMMIE LORIE STYLES (twin) b. Jan.10,1959 Seymour,Tx.
m.Aug.1983,in Houston,Tx.to Ricky Barrett b.Jan.3,
1960,son of Jeneva and Sam Barrett of Houston.
(2 children)
a)JOSHUA RYAN BARRETT b. June 4,1977 adopted by Rick.
b.DANIELLE LAUREN BARRETT b.Apr.28,1985

2.TAMMIE LAURI STYLES (twin)b.Jan.10,1959,d.Jan.11,1959

3.TONI LAURA STYLES b.May 3,1960 Wichita Falls,Tx.
m.Jan.14,1984,Houston,Tx.to Arthur Lopez b.Oct.8,1961
son of Marcus Lopez and Doris Lerma of Houston.
(2 children)
a)ASHLEY LOVE LOPEZ b. Sept.1,1984
b)TAYLOR LEIGH LOPEZ b.Nov. 24,1987

4.JOHN HENRY STYLES JR. b. June 6,1963

John Henry Sr.m.2nd to Laverne McGoo and has an adopted
son Jason Styles b. 1972

Agnes Effie Wilson Styles m.2nd Dec.13,1980 to Harold
Champion Simmons Ph.D. b.Dec.13,1917 Brantford,Ontario,
Canada.Harold was a small child when his father died.He
was reared by his mother,Vra May Simmons and her 2nd
husband,Stanton G. Nichols.

g) EDNA MARIE WILSON b.Feb.11,1942 Vicksburg,Ms.
m.Aug.26,1960 to Jack William Crawford II,b.Oct.31,
1943,son ofJack William Crawford Sr.of Seymour,Tx.
(5 children)
1.CARMEN GAYLE CRAWFORD b.June 1,1961 Wichita Falls,
Tx. m.Dec.25,1984 Delbert Wayne Parker.

2.KIMBERLIE LEA CRAWFORD b.Oct.11,1962 Ft.Worth,Tx.
  m.Dec.8,1979 Chapman Lee Swindell (3 sons)
  a)NICHALOS LEE SWINDELL b.Oct.2,1980 Wichita Falls,
  b)COREY WILLIAM SWINDELL b.Jan.6,1983 Knox City,Tx.
  c)MICHAEL JOE SWINDELL b.Mar.7,1984 Seymour,Tx.

3.JACK WILLIAM (Trey) CRAWFORD III b.Dec.18,1967 Waco.

4.ROGER KELLY CRAWFORD b.July 26,1973 (twin)

5.RUSSELL TRAVIS CRAWFORD b.July 26,1973 (twin)

Ray,Neil,Paul,Katherine,Loe Nell,Roger,Bob,Mittie,Agnes
Thanksgiving 1979 Waco,Texas

Roger and Mittie (Scott) Wilson, 1960

WILSON FAMILY (1950)
Katherine,Bernie,Neil,
Roger,Mittie,Bob
Marie and Agnes

Neil and Katherine
(1930)

Mittie and School friends.Mound,La.(1919)

Marie,Agnes,Neil and Katherine Waco,Tx.

Neil,Marie Bernie,Sam,Agnes,Bob and Greg.
Avis,Mittie,Pearl (1986)

Megan, Summer and Tiffany

Ray and Neil

Christmas 1984. Ray and Neil Wiese's family:
Sid, Colleen, Ray, Tiffany, Vivian, Megan, Gary, Neil and Su

Katherrine and Paul Kemp

Feb.1988.Mittie with Nia,one
of her great,grandaughters.

Ray Wiese,Richard Peeples,and Bob Wilson

5.CARROLL SCOTT b.1910 d.1911 Briars Plantation.

6.SAMUEL PETTIT SCOTT b.Aug.6,1911 Briars Plantation,
near Natchez,Ms.d.Mar.8,1951 Vicksburg,Ms.m.Nov.20,
1935 Port Gibson to Pearl Wright b.Nov.5,1909.d.
1986,dau.of Donnie Eliza Beard and Charlie Buck Wright.
Pearl's son,Bennie was adopted by Sam.(2 children)

   a)BENJAMIN WILLIAM(Bennie)SCOTT b.Sept.29,1927,m.1st.
   Annie May Brown in Jackson,Ms.(1 child)
   1.GWENDLYN IRENE SCOTT m.Richard Parker(2 children)
      a)BRADY PARKER b.Sept.5,1973
      b)BRIAN PARKER b.Jan.6,1971

   Bennie m.2nd Shirley Ann Skaggs from Benton,Ark.
   (3 children)
   2.DEBORAH ANN SCOTT b.Feb.25,1957 m.James Hugley
      (3 children)
      a)BRIDGET MICHELL HUGLEY b.Aug.4,1975
      b)BREA McCALL HUGLEY b.Feb.3,1979
      c)BENJAMIN MATTHEW HUGLEY b.Nov.30,1982

   3.LYDIA MARIE SCOTT b.June 28,1960 m.1st Morris Lee
      German from San Louis,Calif.b.June 6,1959,son of
      Bob and Nancy Marr of Calif.(2 children)
      a)BELINDA KAY GERMAN b.May 26,1977
      b)CHRISTINA MARIE GERMAN b.Mar.12,1979

   4.WILLIAM(Tony)ANTHONY SCOTT b.Sept.19,1961 m.Joyce
      Lynn Slade b. Jan.5,1960,dau. of Sharon D.Coventon
      of West,Tx.(2 children)
      a)TAMEKKA DESHAWN SCOTT b.May 12,1978
      b)CRYSTAL STARR SCOTT b.Jan.13,1980

   b)SAMMIE PETTIT SCOTT JR.b.Sept.22,1936 Vicksburg,Ms.
   m.Dec.29,1956 to Sherry Lynn Jones,b.Dec.26,1936,
   dau.of Glenn Chandler and William Jones(3 children)

   1.GREGORY KEITH SCOTT b.Mar.2,1960 St.Louis,Mo.m.
      Beth Suzanne Hyers b.Aug.22,1963 Bacon Co.Ga.
      dau. of Margaret Peacock b.Pierce Co.Ga.and Chester
      Hyers of Ware Co.,Ga.

   2.KELLY DENISE SCOTT b.July 13,1962 St.Louis,Mo.

   3.DREW ERIC SCOTT b.Oct.19,1967 St.Louis,Mo.

7.EDWARD SCOTT b.1912 d.Jan.9,1918 burned to death while
staying with his grandmother, Lucrecia Jane Deloach,
after his parents seperated.While attempting to save
him,she too, perished.

Sam Scott

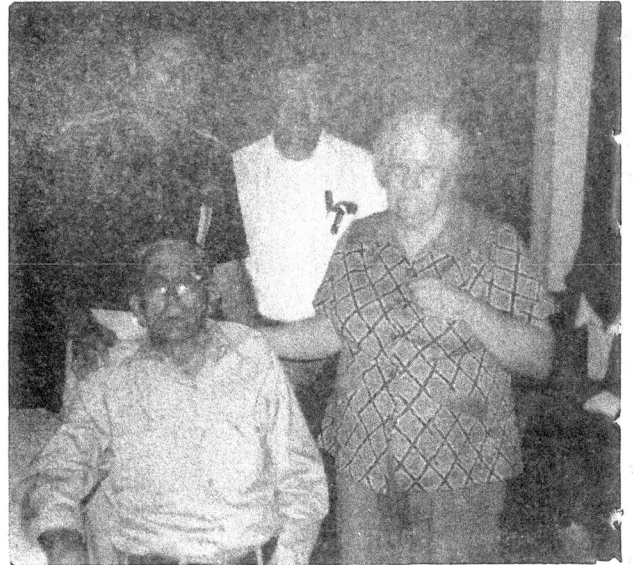

Sam Scott Jr.,Wm.Scott
John Scott and Pearl Scott

Sam Scott Sr.

Sam Scott Jr.and Sherry

8.CLIFFORD EARL SCOTT b.June 5,1914 WWII veteran.
  m.Elizabeth ?   from New Orleans.(2 children)

  a)ELIZABETH SCOTT

  b)Son
  Earl was in the Marines and stationed at Pearl Harbour
  when the Japanese struck during WWII.He was in the middle
  of all the fighting in the islands.The whereabouts of
  Earl is not known to the family,however much effort has
  been made to locate him and his children.

d)DAVIS SCOTT b.Dec.1880 d.   Buried in the Silver Cross
   Cemetery, Tallulah,La.The exact location is not known
   other than it is on the right side of the cemetery as you
   enter and is adjacent to the fence.

   Davis m Apr.20,1904(Bk.N.p.463 Wilkinson,Co.Ms.to
   Hattie Harper Floyd,b.Sept.1875,dau.of W.T.Floyd and Mary
   Ashley.Hattie's 1st m.to W.N.Harper Apr.26,1895(Bk N.p.80)
   produced a son,JAMES b.July 1896 who later died.After
   Harper died,Hattie m.Dave.She died in childbirth while
   living near Waco,Tx.and both she and the baby were buried
   together in a common grave in the old Speigleville
   Cemetery that was later moved to the Chappel Hill
   Cemetery in Waco,when Lake Waco was enlarged.
   (3 children)

   1.DORIS SCOTT b.July 12,1907 m.Sept.5,1925 Wilkinson,Co.
     by Rev.J.C.Lawden,to Harry H.McGraw.b.Dec.21,1903,son of
     William Harry McGraw and Louisa Floyd.m.June 9,1900
     (Bk.N.p.305) (4 children)

     a)HARRY BURNELL McGRAW b.July 20,1926 m.Jan.1,1947 to
       Minnie Louisa(Weeze) Harkey.Weeze m.1st to Vernan
       Middlebrook of Pearl River Co.(1 child)Debra Lee
       b.Aug.16,1945,adopted by Weeze's parents,Margaret
       and Swep Harkey.
       Debra m.Donnie Donald W.King of Pearl River,Ms.They
       have four children.1.Swept,2.Giles,3.David and 4.
       Their home is in Biloxi,Ms.
       Weeze's parents are Margarita May Stout and Swepson
       Fleetwood Harkey.Weeze and Burnell have 3 children.

       1.NANCY LYNN McGRAW b.June 8,1950 m.Dec.9,1969
         to Charles Woodrow Kennedy from Wiggins,Ms.b.Dec
         15,1947,son of Aline and Woodrow Kennedy.
         (2 children)
         a)KAREN LEIGH KENNEDY b.Sept.1,1970 Wiggins,Ms.
         b)KATHRYN LYNN KENNEDY b.Aug.23,1981 Natchez,Ms.

       2.DAVID BURNELL McGRAW MD b.Jan.21,1952 m.Oct.15,1971
         Janet Elizabeth Sorrells b.June 13,1952 ,dau.of
         Robert Sorrells and Betty Higdon of Belzoni,Ms.
         (3 children)
         a)JANET SUZANNE McGRAW b.Sept.1,1974
         b)EMILY SCOTT McGRAW b.June1.1977
         c)MARY MARGARET McGRAW b.Nov.29,1979

       3.LINDA LAVERNE McGRAW b.Oct.20,1955 m.Aug.30,1975 to
         Gerold (Jerry) Howard McDaniels b.Sept.12,1952
         Centreville,Ms.son of Frances Matthews and John
         Deland McDaniels.(2 children)

a)MARY FRANCES McDANIELS b. July 8,1981
b)LAURA HARKEY McDANIELS b. 1984

b)SHIRLEY LA VERNE McGRAW b.July 21,1928 d.Mar.3,1971
m.June 14,1956 to Prentice Hollis Carpenter b.Apr.29,
1929,son of Prentice Carpenter Sr.(3 children)

1.PRENTICE HOLLIS(Bucky)CARPENTER b.June 4,1958
2.HARRY SCOTT CARPENTER b.Oct.9,1961
3.DAVID DALE CARPENTER b.Sept.9,1965

c)THOMAS(Dick)EARL McGRAW b.Mar.16,1930 m.Ethel
Jacquline(Jackie)Sigmon b.Nov.23,1931,dau.of Ethel
and Jacks(BO)Sigmon.(5 children)

1.BEVERLY ANN McGRAW b.Sept.21,1951
2.GINGER LEE Mc.GRAW b.Mar.25,1954
3.THOMAS EARL McGRAW JR.b.Jan.27,1956,d.Nov.1983
4.HARRY McDONALD McGRAW b.Mar.15,1957
5.DORIS MELISSA McGRAW b.Feb.3,1965

2.TOM SCOTT b.Feb.23,1905 d.Oct.11,1971 m.Dec.16,1933 to
Mary Wilna Flowers b.Oct.16,1910 d.Sept.23,1982,dau.of
John Flowers and Vera Leake of Wilkinson Co.Ms.
(3 children)
a)SALLIE VERA SCOTT b.Oct.15,1934 m.Feb.16,1951 to Percy
Edwin Simmons b.Jan.7,1930,son of Clyde F.Simmons and
Golda McGee Hee of Osychia,Ms.(4 children)

1.DEBORAH KATHLEEN SIMMONS b.June 12,1952 m.Mar.12,
1971 James Alford Walker b.Sept.10,1951,son of
Alfred Walker (2 children)
a)LISA MICHAEL WALKER b.May 31,1972
b)BRIDGET LYNETTE WALKER b.Oct.1,1974

2.TERRY LYNN SIMMONS b.Nov.1,1954 m.1st on Mar. 21
1973 Ronald Dowrin Robinson b.Sept.26,1953,son of
Leroy and Niddie Mae Whittley Robinson from
Pinebluff,Ark.(1 child)
a)DEBRA LA SHEY ROBINSON b.Sept.21,1975
Terry Lynn m.2nd.Dec.16,1984 Roy Edward Farmer Sr.
b.Sept.16,1944

3.PERCY RANDALL SIMMONS b.Nov.29,1957 m.July 11,1978
Connie Lynn Johnson b.June 15,1963,dau.of John
Johnson and Loena Ray Johnson from Adam Co.(1 child)
a)CRAIG RANDALL SIMMONS b.Feb.28,1979

4.ELIZABETH ARLEEN SIMMONS b.Feb.23,1960 m.May 6,1977
Carl Eugene Bradshaw b.Dec.10,1953 son of Dorothy
Tracy and James Ray Bradshaw of Adams Co.(1 child)
a)CARL DANIEL BRADSHAW b.Nov.10,1977

b)DAVID EARL SCOTT b.July 27,1936,Bedfort,La.,d.Nov.27
1974,m.Ruth Yvonne Saxton b.April 22,1940,dau.of Elzy
Sylvester and Ruth Charwin Saxton.(3 children)
1.DANNY RUTH SCOTT b.Sept.20,1957 m.Chris Hickman
divorced.(1 child)
a)TIFFANY LEIGH HICKMAN b.April 3,1979

2.THOMAS DeWAYNE SCOTT b.Jan.19,1962

3.WHITNEY DEE SCOTT b.Oct.30,1964 m.Ricky Paul
Davenport Sr.(2 children)
a)AMY RENEE DAVENPORT b.Nov.8,1980
b)RICKY PAUL DAVENPORT JR. b.Aug.31,1982

c)HATTIE EDITH SCOTT b.May 4,1941 Doloroso,Ms.m.Curtis
Savoy Sr.b.May 30,1938 son of Captain Gilbert and
Mammie Savoy.(3 children)

1.SHELIA SAVOY b.Sept.27,1960 m.May 6,1977 Ralph E.
Boyd,son of Ralph E.Boyd Sr.and Janet Boyd.Shelia
divorced (1 child)
a)LISLIE NICOLE BOYD b.Oct.10,1977
2.CURTIS SAVOY JR.b.Aug.28,1961(1 child)by Sandy
Wilson.
a)CHRISTOPHER ALLEN WILSON b.May 3,1982.
3.JOSEPH SCOTT SAVOY b.Nov.21,1962 m.Elizabeth(Becky)
Day.b.May 30,1958 (2 children)
a)THOMAS SPENCER SAVOY b.April 10,1981
4.MARY KATHERINE ELIZABETH SAVOY b.Nov.24,1983

3.INFANT b&d

Weeze,Burnell,Dot McGraw

Dot at school

Harry and Dot McGraw

e)MAJOR JAMES SCOTT b.May 5,1883 d. Jan.2,1941,m.Mar.3,
   1915(Bk.O,p.234 Wilkinson Co.Ms.) in the Buffalo Community
   near Brown's Creek,to Belvia Olevia Johnson b.July 20,
   1891,d.May 14,1985,dau.of Ella Anderson and David Adolphus
   Johnson.Major buried in SCOTT burying ground along with
   his parents,sister Mamie and brother-in-law,Henry Davis.
   Olevia is buried in Woodville. (4 children)

1.GRANTHAM LEONIDAS SCOTT b.Mar.10,1916 Speegleville,Tx.
   d.Oct.8,1986 in Wilkinson Co.Ms. WWII veteran.

2.WILLIE RAY SCOTT b. Nov.2,1917 Woodville Ms.m.Sept.16,
   1937 to Fred Clifton McCarstle b.June 11,1906,Ethel,
   La.,d.Feb.22,1979,son of Eugene Clayton McCarstle
   and Johanna Taylor.Johanna b. Scotland.(2 children)

   a)FRED CLIFTON McCARSTLE JR.b.Aug.10,1939 m.1st Mar.12,
      1963 to Rolilyn Brown McIntoch of Natchez,dau.of Jake
      Walter Brown and Rose Martello of Natchez.Rosilyn had
      a son,Jimmy McIntoch who was adopted by Fred Clifton.
      (3 children)
      1.JIMMY McINTOCH b. Nov.25,1955
      2.FRED CLIFTON McCARSTLE III b.Sept.4,1966
      3.ANNA CATHERINE McCARSTLE b. Jan.20,1969

   Clifton married 2nd Feb.15,1986 to Katie Wise

   b)DONNIS RAE McCARSTLE b. Sept.8,1944,m.June 12,1971 to
      Anthony Lomonaco of New Orleans.They live in Lake
      Charles La.

3.MAJOR LEE SCOTT b.June 7,1923 Doloroso,Ms.m.Apr.9,1950
   in West Virginia to David Speaker. Major Lee d. July 9,
   1983. David d. June 2,1985.David had one son,David
   Speaker Jr.

4.DAVIS ADOLPHUS SCOTT b.Aug.10,1926 Doloroso,Ms.m.July
   5,1947,Woodville,Ms.to Alice Joycelyn White,b.April 5,
   1930 in Centreville,Ms.,dau. of Jones white and Claudia
   Smith. (3 children)

   a)LARRY DAVIS SCOTT b.May 23,1952 m.Dec.12,1971 in
      Pioneer Church on Buffalo,to Carolyn Diane Enis of
      Doloroso.Carolyn b. Aug.14,1952 Centreville,Ms.
      (3 children)

      1.AMY DANILLE SCOTT b. Feb.18,1974 Centreville,Ms.

      2.LORRIE OLIVIA SCOTT b.Mar.12,1977 Centreville,Ms.

      3.VALERIE DIANE SCOTT b. 1980

b)SUSAN LYNNE SCOTT b. Mar.3,1956 Centreville,Ms.m.
April 19,1975 Centreville to John Wayne McDaniel
b.June 8,1955 Centreville.(1 child)

1.LYNDSEY ANNE McDANIEL b. Mar.25,1985

c)WILLIAM KEITH SCOTT b. Aug.20,1960

The State of Mississippi
Wilkinson County

of said County of Wilkinson

Rites of Matrimony between

and Miss. Olevia Johnson Major Scott

Given under my hand this the 3 day of May D 1915

Rev. C. H. Herring
Minister of M. E. Church Southern

MISSISSIPPI'S OLDEST NEWSPAPER - Established 1824

The Woodville Republican.

Publishers - Printers   Woodville, Mississippi 39669   John S. Lewis, Editor

July 8, 1982

Mrs. Ernest R. Wiese
3712 Charlton
Waco, Texas 76711

Dear Mrs. Wiese:

My earliest recollection of Mr. Major Scott dates back to my
very early 'teen age days when I visited his home with my
father, Robert Lewis, who was a dedicated quail hunter. My
father was looking for a bird dog puppy at the time, and had
apparently learned that Mr. Scott had one or more pointer
pups. We picked a liver and white pup from the litter, and
along with Mr. Scott took him across the road to hunt along
a wooded area. After a very short walk the little pup, not
half grown, froze in a beautiful point and I immediately
fell in love with him. As I recall Mr. Scott said that he
did not sell dogs, but he and my father soon struck a barter
bargain, for several boxes of shotgun shells and possibly
a subscription to The Republican.

My father passed away a few years later and I fell heir to
"Ted", as we named the dog. He was far and away the best
bird dog I ever owned and was famed locally for his great
nose and "bottom"(day-long endurance). Ted lived to the
venerable age of 14 years, and his death was a sad day in
the Lewis household. Ever since, when I get together with
other old-time bird hunters to tell tales about our ex-
periences, I always bring up a few stories about "Old Ted's"
exploits. He was truly a magnificent animal.

John S. Lewis
7/8/82
Age 68

66-1

MAJOR JAMES SCOTT

Neil and Aunt Levia

Anthony,Donnis,Anna,Willie Ray,Clifton and Katie

Major and the three
Everette brothers,Tom,Charlie,
and Euall,joined Eugene
Sturgeon to make many hours of
music. These first cousins
shared a love for music that
lasted throuout their lives.
1st row:Charlie,Major,2nd
row,Euall,Tom and Eugene.

Family reunion
1st row: Lonnie Sturgeon,Aunt Bertha,Anne Sturgeon
2nd row: Glen, Harry,Willie Ray and Christine
3rd row: Walter and Leroy

f)HOWARD WILLIAM SCOTT b.Sept.5,1884,d.Dec.7,1955 m.Oct.
17,1906 to Mary Elizabeth Bunch b.Nov.17,1889,d.Jan.29,
1979,dau.of Isaac Bunch and Ella J.McCoy.Both buried in
Woodville,Ms.(7 children)

1.**HARRY LEMEL SCOTT REV.**b.Sept.18,1907,m.Apr.17,1930
to Jewel Edna Duncan b.Aug.19,1911,dau.of Samuel
Rainey Duncan and Nina Mae Wixcon.(3 children)

a)HARRY LEMUEL SCOTT JR.b.Dec.17,1930,d.June 11,1957
Vicksburg,Ms.m.Mary Louise Nosser b.Oct.23,1930,dau.
of John M.Nosser and Effie Mitchell of Vicksburg,Ms.
(1 child)
1.RAINEY NOSSER SCOTT b.Sept.3,1955 m.Nov.13,1977
Denise Brown b.Aug.11,1953 in Attalla,Ala.
Mary Lou m.2nd to Gary Sherman Olin b. July 26,1936,
son of Lawrence and Dorothy Olin.(1 child)
2.JAMES ANDREW OLIN b. Dec.29,1964

b)JOHN LEROY SCOTT b.Oct.19,1938 m.Nov.24,1961 Vicksburg,Ms.to Nora Claire Brooks b.Aug.25,1939,dau.of
Miriam Donald and M.L.Brooks.(2 children)
1)DONALD WAYNE SCOTT b.Aug.9,1964
2)MIRIAM CLAIRE SCOTT b.May 19,1969

c)THURSA MAE SCOTT b.Dec.10,1944 m.Mar.29,1965 Eddie
Dwight Westcott b.Aug.24,1939 in Atlanta,Ga.,son of
John B.Westcott of Phoenix,Ms.and Mildred Jackson of
Atlanta,G.(3 children)
1.MARY BHONNIE WESTCOTT b.Nov.22,1966,d.Dec.26,1966
2.BONNIE MICHELE WESTCOTT b.Apr.14,1968
3.SCOTT DWIGHT WESTCOTT b.Feb.26,1971

2.**NOLAN ARGLASS SCOTT** b.Oct.23,1908 d.Nov.17,1981 m.
Lynsey Lucille Brady b.Nov.29,1908,dau. of Mary Elizabeth
Landcaster,born on the Cherokee Reservation in Anadarka,
Okla., the dau.of Indian Chief, Whitehorse.Lucille's
father was Thomas Carroll Brady of Wichita Falls,Tx.

3.**ROSA LEE SCOTT** b.Dec.3,1910 Speigleville,Tx.

4.**JUANITA (Nita) ELIZABETH SCOTT SCOTT** b.April 29,1916
Doloroso,Ms.m.June 16,1937 Natchez,Ms. to Jewell Leo
Sesser,b.Dec.27,1909 Hot Springs Co.,Ark.,son of Henry
Marten Sesser and Letha Kline of Malvern,Ark.(6 children)

a)JEWELL LEO(J.L.) SESSER b. Sept.28,1939 Doloroso,Ms.
d.May 17,1957 Port Gibson,Ms.

b)HOWARD MARTEN SESSER b.Feb.11,1942 Doloroso,Ms.m.Dec.
24,1964 Mores Island,Calif. to Beryl Malvina Smith

b.Oct.10,1942 Vallejo,Calif.,dau.of Joseph B. Smith
and Malvina Alma Smith of Vallejo,Calif.(1 child)
1.LORI JENNINE SESSER b. Sept.4,1974 Vallejo,Calif.

c)NOLAN TERRY SESSER b.June 4,1944 Maalvern,Ark.m.Dec.24,
1978,Woodville,Ms. to Francis Elizabeth Wilkinson
b.Feb.6,1937 Woodville,Ms.dau.of Jim Wikinson and Oleta
Rodgers Wilkinson of Woodville Ms.(2 children)
1.JIM NOLAN SESSER b.Dec.10,1981,Natchez,Ms.
2.DAVID LEO SESSER b.Dec.5,1983.

d)LARRY DALE SESSER b.June 22,1946 Malvern,Ark.m.Nov.
22,1969 Destrahan,La.to Renee Bergeron b.July 1,1951
dau.of Willard and Madeleine Bergeron.(2 children)
1.MADELEINE NICOLE SESSER b.Dec.16,1977 Destrahan,La.
2.JONATHAN MICHAEL SESSER b.Nov.28,1983 Destrahan,La.

e)ROYCE SCOTT SESSER b.Aug.31,1948 Malvern,Ark.m.Feb.5,
1972 Natchez,Ms.to Marilyn Sue Dossett b.Sept.5,1951
Natchez,dau.of Maudell Barnes and Clarence E. Dossett.
(4 children)
1.RYAN SCOTT SESSER b.Jan.1,1974 Natchez.
2.KATHRYN CLARE(Kacy)SESSER b.July 15,1976 Natchez.
3.ANDREW BRANDON SESSER b.Nov.18,1980 Columbus,Ms.
4.WILLIAM BRENT SESSER b.Jan.18,1983 Columbus,Ms.

f)LETHA ELIZABETH SESSER b.May 7,1951 Malvern,Ark.m.Sept.
27,1975 Natchez,Ms.to Gerry Paul Sumrall b.Oct.27,1954
Natchez,son of Paul L.and Pauline Sumrall.(1 child)
1.MARY ELIZABETH(Mimi) SUMRALL b.June 25,1979 Natchez.

5.AUBREY LEROY SCOTT b.May 3,1914 Speigleville,Tx.m.June
15,1940 to Margaret Christine Beauman b.Aug.17,1921,dau.
of Viola Kethley and Fred Beauman of Warren Co.Ms.
(2 children)
a)PATRICIA JOYCE SCOTT b&d Mar.28,1941.
b)AUBREY LEROY SCOTT JR.MD b.Aug.12,1957 Magnolia,Ms.,
m.Apr.7,1984 Mary Elizabeth Andrews dau.of Jane and
William Hinton Andrews.

6.HOWARD GLENN SCOTT b.Dec.21,1919 Doloroso,Ms.m.Gladys
Merle McCalip b.Jan.4,1921 Monticello,Ms.m.Jan.2,1941
Port Gibson,Ms.,dau. of Fred Willard McCalip and
Rosalie Fortenberry of Columbis,Ms.

7.ELLA MAE SCOTT b.June 2,1926 m.1st Feb.20,1943
Vicksburg,Ms. to J.W.(Jimmy) Jeter b.July 30,1917
Marvel,Ark.son of Edna Frances and Wilman Watt Jeter of
Greenville,Ms.
(2 children)

a)GLENDA KAY JETER b.May 22,1944 Natchez,Ms.m.July 2,

1967 Baton Rouge,La.to William(Bill)Gregory Brundage
b.Oct.18,1934 Monroe,New York,son of Margaret Jane
Newelland Frank Leslie Brundage of Salisbury Mills,New
York.(2 children)

1.LESLIE ELIZABETH BRUNDAGE b.Apr.12,1968 Baton Rouge.
2.WILLIAM GREGORY(Greg)BRUNDAGE b.Nov.8,1974
  Hattisburg,Ms.
b)JAMES POWEL (Bubba)JETER b.Feb.7,1946Natchez,Ms.m.June
  28,1969 Baton Rouge to Louise Conway Oct.25,1947,dau.
  of Robert Conway and Joyce Smith of Mansura,La
  (2 children)
  1.JILL SCOTT JETER b.Sept.29,1972 Baton Rouge,La.
  2.AMY CONWAY JETER b.Oct.28,1975 Layfette,La.

Ella Mae married 2nd on Sept.5,1981 to John Smallbrook
Howkins III,b.Feb.11,1925 of Savannah,Ga.,son of John
Smallbrook Howkins II b.1892 Savannah,Ga.and Alice
Beekman Huger b.Feb.26,1902 Memphis,Tenn.

ELIZABETH BUNCH SCOTT

HOWARD WILLIAM SCOTT

THE STATE OF MISSISSIPPI, } By virtue of a license
Wilkinson County.

From the Clerk of the Circuit Court of said County of Wilkinson I have this day celebrated the Rites of Matrimony between Mr. *Howard Scott* and Miss *Elizabeth Bunch*

Given under my hand this the *17th* day of *October* 190 *6*

J. A. Carter M. B. S Seal.

FOUR GENERATIONS—Four generations of Scotts are gathered in the above picture. They are left to right Howard Scott of Doloroso, Miss.; his son, Harry Scott, Sr., of Vicksburg; Harry Scott, Jr., former resident of Vicksburg attending Mississippi State College and now living in Starksville; and the fourth generation, two-month-old Rainey Nosser Scott.

Howard Scott

Elizabeth and Howard

Nolan, Harry and Nita

Howard, Chester Holmes, and
Charley Everett. (All Holmes
cousins) Waco, Texas.

Nolan, Francis, Nia, Jewel, Leta, Mimi, Jim and David

Harry and Nolan

Jewel and Harry

Reverand Harry Scott

g)MARY (MAMIE) SCOTT b.Jan.20,1886 d.Nov.17,1920,m.Dec.27,
1906(Bk N.pg.583 Wilkinson,Co.Ms.) Henry Davis b.July
26,1876 d.May 6,1944,son of Wm.Henry Davis and Julia
Morris Davis of Wilkinson,Co.Ms. Wm and Julia m.Jan.18
1866,(Bk.K,pg.386) Both buried in Scott burying ground
in Doloroso,Ms.(7 children).

1.LAWRENCE DAVIS b. 1907,d.1951 m.Ruth McKey
   (3 children)
   a)LAWRENCE WILLIAM DAVIS m.barbara Faulkner
     (5 children)
     1.LARRY DAVIS
     2.RICHARD ALLEN DAVIS
     3.BRENDA KAY DAVIS
     4.TIMOTHY DAVIS
     5.PETE DAVIS
   b)MAMIE DAVIS m.John Wright.(3 children)
     1.Cliff Wright
     2.Christina (Tina) Wright
     3.Mark Wright
   c)JANET DAVIS b.1944 m.Kenneth McCaskell(2 children)
     1.JANA McCaskell
     2.ROBERT McCaskell
2.ADDIE DAVIS b.Jan.11,1908 d.Jan.7,1974 m.Clem T.Eidt

3.EDDIE INMAN DAVIS b.Oct.1,1910 d.May 27,1984 m.June
   28.1944,to Mittie Lee Carter b. Nov.17,1917 Ferriday,
   La.dau.Isaac W.Carter b.1875,d.1954 and Mary Amanda
   Carter b. 1879,d.1953 Both parents buried in the
   Pioneer Baptist Cemetery.(2 children)

   a)EDDIE GERALD DAVIS b.Aug.23,1947 m.July 11,1970
     Judy Carter b.Nov.20,1945,dau.of Pauline Living-
     ston and Julius M.Carter of Woodville,Ms. (1 child)
     1.KARA PAULINE DAVIS b.Oct.27,1980

   b)JO ANN DAVIS b. Sept.9,1951 m.June 22,1972 to
     Edward Koch b.Oct.22,1948,son of Ollie Koch and
     Virginia Elizabeth White of Wilkinson,Co.Ms.
     (2 children)
     1.LESLIE HOPE KOCH b.July 2,1976
     2.ELIZABETH LEANN KOCH b. Jan.12,1981

4.BERTICE (Bertie)ELIZABETH DAVIS b.Aug.26,1912 d.Aug.30
   1982 m.Oct.27,1931 to Herbert Nelson Jensen in
   Fayette,Ms. Herbert b.Dec.27,1902 Jefferson Co.Ms.,
   son of Herbert Haynes Jensen and Lelia Ellen Leak of
   Buffalo Community.
   (Lelia's brother Dave Leak,m.Blanche Sturgeon,dau.of
   Elizabeth Holmes Sturgeon,see Holmes reference,.Lelia
   and Dave's parents were Lydia Carter and Fredrick
   Andrea Leak.(1 child)

70

a)HERBERT NELSON JENSEN JR. b. Sept.28,1932 m.Billie
   Hollinsworth b.Jan.17,1956,dau. of Allen A.Hollings-
   worth amd Irma Blakeney (4 children)

   1.ROBERT NELSON JENSEN b.June 21,1957 m.Charlen
      Simmons,dau. of Teresa and Charles Simmons of
      St.Francisville,La.(2 children)
      a)NICOLE TERESA JENSEN b. May 1977
      b)ROBERT BLAKENEY JENSEN b.March 31,1979

   2.JOSEPH ALLEN (Jody)JENSEN b.Dec 1,1958 m.Oct.1980
      Carmine Renee Inman, dau. of Geraldine Cage and
      Brandon Inman. (1 child)
      a)BRANDON GERALD JENSEN b. Jan.13,1984

   3 JANET LYNN JENSEN b. Dec.28,1959

   4.KENNETH BLAKENY JENSEN b. Aug.2,1970

5.WALTER ERNEST DAVIS b.Jan.7,1916 d.Mar.11,1970 m.June
   28,1944 to Tessie McKey b.Feb.25,1926 dau. of Winnie
   Alta Tumey of Liberty Ms. and Troy Lee McKey of
   Centreville,Ms.(3 children)

   a)WALTER ERNEST DAVIS JR.b.Oct.11,1948 m.Apr.15,1976
      Amite Co.Ms.to Ella Rose Smith b.Apr.2,1950,dau
      of Nellie Leona Dykes of Franklin,La.and Albert
      Clarence Smith of Slidell,Ms.(1 child)
      1.KIMBERLY DANIELLE DAVIS b.Nov.5,1977

   b)SUSAN ALYNE DAVIS b.Jan.28,1954 m.Pioneer Baptist
      Church of Doloroso,Ms.to Barry Glenn Williamson,
      b.Aug.17,1954 son of Kathleen Williams and Doyle
      Williamson of Brownwood,Tx.(1 child)
      1.BARRY GLENN WILLIAMSON JR.b Aug.13,1980
   c)WILLIAM HENRY DAVIS b.Sept.5,1964

6.RALPH DAVIS b.July 9,1918 d.Mar.1,1968,m.July 8,1953
   to Mary Holloway b.June 17,1916

7.ARGLASS WILLIAM DAVIS b.June 3,1920,d.Dec.11,1986,
   m.Nov.23,1945 to Marion Klein Hayes of Woodville,Ms.
   dau.of Burgess Rosa Davis and Klein Hayes.

RETIRES FROM SHERIFF'S OFFICE — Arglass Davis, left above, is shown receiving a plaque of appreciation from Wilkinson County Sheriff H. B. McGraw on the occasion of his retirement from the local sheriff's department. Davis was employed with the Wilkinson County Sheriff's Department from August, 1974, and retired effective Monday, July 1. Davis served as the afternoon shift jailer and radio operator at the County Jail and he will be replaced by Anthony David, Jr. The plaque was inscribed: "In appreciation to Arglass William Davis from the Wilkinson County Sheriff's Department for loyal and dedicated service — August 1974 to June 1985."

Eddie and Mittie Davis

Arglass and Burnell

Arglass Davis

DEAN OF STATE SHERIFFS — Wilkinson County Sheriff H. B. McGraw is the oldest sheriff [in years of service but not in age] in the state of Mississippi. On Monday of last week he was sworn in for his seventh term of office, a state record. McGraw served for four years 1960-64 and four more from 1968-72 under the old law which prohibited sheriffs from succeeding themselves. When the legislature implemented the new law making succession legal, effective in 1972, McGraw took office that January and has served continuously since then. He was thus sworn in for his fifth consecutive term last week, bringing to seven the terms of office he has entered. No other Mississippi sheriff can match this length of tenure, state records show.

WOODVILLE REPUBLICIAN Newspaper, January 14,1988
Woodville,Mississippi

Mary (Mamie) Scott Davis

Elizabeth Bunch Scott
and Mary Scott Davis

Tessie, Jo Ann, Elizabeth, Mittie, Leslie, Ruth, and Janet

pg. 71-3

HOMOCHITTO PLANTATION

One of the oldest homes in the northwestern part of Wilkinson County, Mississippi is HOMOCHITTO, located on a plantation of the same name. This home was built during the early 1800's by Hugh Davis. The cottage- type building was constructed from cypress timber cut on the plantation, and hand made bricks were used for foundations and chimneys. Live oaks were planted around the house to form a grove.

It is of historical interest that Jefferson Davis' sister, Lucinda, was married to Hugh Davis and lived at Homochitto as a young bride. Unfortunately, Hugh Davis met an untimely death by drowning in the Homochitto River. It was near the end of her first year of marriage and soon after her husband's death that Lucinda gave birth to a son. Little Hugh spent many of his early days at Rosemont, his grandmother's home. Lucinda Davis remarried to a Mr. Isaac Stamps and Hugh received a good education along with his half brothers and sisters.

Preceeding the War Between the States, the plantation was operated as a self-sufficient unit. Cotton was raised in abundance and ginned at the plantation gin. The cotton and other products were hauled to Natchez or Woodville on wagons. Timber was often floated down the Homochitto River to the Mississippi and on the Plaquemine to New Orleans.

H. Nelsen Jensen, Jr.,

H.Nelsen Jensen Jr.

Bertice Davis Jensen   pg.71-4   Herbert Nelson Jensen Sr

Three heirs of the Davis family were in possession of the plantation in the period following the war. They were Hugh Landon,William James,and Miss Mary Davis. Upon final settlement of the Davis property,Miss Mary Davis,a teacher in New Orleans, became the owner of the Homochitto Plantatioin.

In the 1880's,Miss Davis sold the plantation to Nelson Jensen of Copenhagen,Denmark and members of the Jensen family at this time time occupy the home and operate the cattle and tree farm.

In 1982,Miss Sarah Jensen,sister to Herbert Nelson Jensen, who married Bertice Davis,daughter of Mary (Mamie) Scott,gave me a brief tour of this beautiful home.There are several original pieces of furniture still in the home.When Miss Davis,quite old and living in New Orleans, sold the plantation to Miss Sarah's grandfather,all the furniture that was left in the house came with the purchase.

Seven children were born in the same bedroom where both Sarah and Nelsen's parents (Mr.and Mrs.Herbert Hanes Jensen) died. Afterwards,the children kept the plantation together as all of them love the land and want to keep the home intact.Today,cattle and timber are raised on the 1100 acre plantation.

Nelson (affectionally called "Pappy")Jensen, related a few memories to Joe Johnson and me, about Mr.Eickhoff,the blacksmith whom his grandfather,Nelson Jensen, had hired to work on the plantation.

"He was in Adams County and my grandfather wanted some work done on a wagon. He (Mr.Eickhoff) worked for old man Jim Zeek this side of George Hackett"s up side that hill.My grandfather contacted him and he said 'Yeh,I'll come over there.'And he came over and worked the wagons and done a good job."

"He said, 'If you got a place ,somewhere around here,I'd like to stay.I'd like to stay over here.' My grandfather said ,'I got a house over there...' Joe, (Joe Johnson) where you shot that deer that time,right over there in that corner...what we called old wheat house...,and he done a little work on the chimney and he stayed there and then later,he built his own house."

"You know,Joe,on the bridle hill leading off to the swamp and below those old slave quarters. That's were the old man died.

"I carried him to Natchez and told them to take care of him and whatever charges had to be,I'd take care of them.

"I remember having a row with this old fellow--his sons are real prominent up there now--he wanted to buy some kind of special robe for this old fellow and I said,naw,naw,I talked to this old man (Mr.Eickhoff)and he told me,'Don't you go to no trouble...not a DIME for expense.Just take a sack or something and take me up on that Indian mound and drop me in there and shove some dirt on top of me.'

"And that was his bird...he wasn't particular about any of it. 'But don't go to any expense.' That was the German,you know. Beat anything you ever heard of.

"He wouldn't throw away anything.He'd take the tinfoil out of Old George Washington Smoking tobacco and roll it up about the size of a gallon bucket and tie a string or something around it and lay it over there.

"He'd take any can and take it to his anvil and flatten it as pretty as you please.Then he'd punch a hole in it and he had a wire with a little washer on it. When he got the wire full,he'd bend the wire over.

"And he'd say,'The first time you go to town I got some junk'. He'd throw all that stuff in there and I'd make the man give me a ticket of what it was and how much he paid for it.

"That was the way they were taught.He told me that he was taught his trade in a school in Germany. When he got through,his last examination was to go into sort of lobby and he was given a set of tools.

"But,they'd let you look at them and then take the chisel,a draw knife,your hatchet or any other instrument with an edge on it and beat it across the anvil and just ruin it and give it back to you.

"Then,when you pass and come out the other door over younder,the other fellow there inspected your tools and they'd better be fixed and he'd give you a ticket or a diploma.

"My grandfather said that over in Denmark,you had a little reference book,pocket book of some kind, and you'd give it to the fellow when you caught up with what you're doing. He'd write down what labor you did. He said he'd worked a many a day for 10 cents per day.

"It took him six weeks to come from Denmark on a cattle boat.Now, you can eat your breakfast here and dinner in London.Mr.Eickhoff had G.A.E. on all his tools.Gustavious Aldophus Eickhoff...he always wanted to carry his own weight.

"He was way up in age when he died. He was crippled and I hauled his wood for him. He had some kind of infection from his knees to his ankle and stayed very sore. He use to go down to the river

...there's a big ole spring there and he'd carried a a half barrel to put his legs in it. He claimed the minerals helped him. He thought we hung the moon.

"He could take a plow share that the point was gone,put a new point on it and temper it.They talk about the Englishman but no body can temper like the Germans. "

"When Mr.Eickhoff died,my little ole boy and I went to the hospital in Natchez and got him.We wrapped him in a blanket, placed his body in my vehicle and brought him back to the plantation.We buried him according to his request. There was no body else except my Mother ,sister and a couple more. We buried him and I said a little prayer over him."

h)WALTER THOMPSON SCOTT SR. b. July 29,1891 d.Nov.17,1959
   m.Dec.31,1926 Wilkinson Co.Ms. to Mary Jane Dawson
   b.Apr.26,1904 d. Apr.26,1965,dau.of Mary Jane Wilkinson
   and Lewis William Dawson of Wilkinson Co.Ms.(2 children)

1.WALTER THOMPSON SCOTT JR.b.Oct.26,1928 m.Mar.5,1950
   Marie Louise Frank b. Nov.6,1928 dau. of Lawrence
   James Frank and Delchesia Louisa Vincinelli (5 children)
   a)KAREN YVONNE SCOTT b. May 31,1952 Fort Smith,Ark.
      m.Aug.10,1974 Natchez,Ms.to Ronald Glen Mayers
      b.Feb.1,1952 (1 child)
      1.ANN MARIE MAYERS b. Sept.8,1981 Cleveland,Ms.

   b)LINDA ANN SCOTT b.June 10,1954 m.1st Ronald Sanders
      son of Pat and J.Y.Sanders of Vidalia,La.(1 child)
      1.TAYNA ELIZABETH SANDERS b. Dec.9,1972

      Linda m.2nd to Alex Pearson Oct.13,1973 b.Aug.24,
      1950 Morresville,Ind.,son of Alex Vincent Pearson
      and Estelle Frye. (2 children)

      2.WALTER VINCENT PEARSON b. May 5,1977 Natchez,Ms.
      3.JESSICA LYNN PEARSON b. Sept.7,1978 Natchez,Ms.

      Linda m.3rd.to Lonnie Eugene Lipe b. Jan.14,1944,son
      of Claude Eugene Lipe and Virginia (Virgie) Lipe.
      (1 child)
      4.SARAH LEANNA LIPE b. Jan.23,1983 Natchez,Ms.

   c)LAWRENCE (Larry) WALTER SCOTT b. Feb.14,1956 Natchez,
      m.Aug.5,1978 to Angela Sue Braley b. Aug.1,1950 in
      Springhill,La.dau.of John R.Braley and Nellie Ruth
      Dean. John's father was Jessie F.Braley b.1890,d.1966

      (Name changed in 1800 as the German spelling was
      Brachley). John's mother was Gladys D.Duncan b.1888
      d.1978. Nellie's father was Darious A.Dean b. 1891,d.195
      and her mother was Lilliam M. McKeithen b. 1890,d. 1983.

   d)MARILYN SUE SCOTT b. Oct.11,1957 m.Feb.14,1976 Natchez,
      Ms.to Hale Edward Roberts Jr.b.Nov.29,1952,son of Marjori
      Eloise Halstead from Boston,Mass,and Hale E.Roberts Sr.
      from Jackson,Ms. (2 children)

      1.GEOFFREY HAYDEN ROBERTS b. Sept.6,1976 Staten Island,NY
      2.HAMILTON "SCOTT"ROBERTS b. May 5,1981 Jackson,Ms.

   e)PATRICIA GAIL SCOTT b.Apr.16,1960 m.Raymond Gousett

      1.CHRISTOPHER SCOTT b. Nov.12,1980 Natchez,Ms.

2.SHERRY MAE SCOTT b.Feb.15,1936 m.Sept.10,1955 Woodville
  Methodist Church to Joseph Densel Johnson b.Jan.14,1930
  from Simpson,La.son of Elizabeth Martin and Joseph
  Fountain Johnson of Simpson.(2 children)

  a)JENNINE DENISE JOHNSON b. June 5,1962 Natchez,Ms.
    m.May 28,1983 to Luther Rudolph Wilson b.July 20,1960
    Natchez,son of Marguerite Whitlington and Ernest
    Rudolph Wilson.(1 child)

    1.JOSEPH RUDOLPH WILSON b. Oct.29,1986

  b)JOSEPH DENSEL JOHNSON JR. (Joe D.) b.Apr.20,1966
    Natchez.,d.Mar.4,1983.

Bernie and Sherry

Neil and Olevia

Mary, Walter and Mittie

Roger and Walter

1950 Visit to Doloroso, Ms.
Walter and Mary Scott's home

Ray, Walter, Roger,
Bernie and Mary

WALTER AND MARY SCOTT'S HOME

Walter and Mary

...MARRIAGE LICENSE:...

The State of Mississippi, Wilkinson County.

To any Judge, Minister, Justice or any other Person Lawfully Authorized to Celebrate
The RITES OF MATRIMONY:

YOU ARE HEREBY LICENSED TO CELEBRATE THE

:RITES OF MATRIMONY:

BETWEEN

Mr. *Walter Scott*

AND

Miss Mary Dawson

and for so doing this shall be your warrant.

Given under my hand, and official seal this 31st day of December
in the year of our Lord One Thousand Nine Hundred and Twenty-Six

W. J. Stewart Clerk.

By _____ D. C.

TI STATE OF MISSISSIPPI, }
   Wilkinson County.   } BY VIRTUE OF A LICENSE.

From the Clerk of the Circuit Court of said County of Wilkinson I have is day
celebrated the Rites of Matrimony between Mr. *Walter* *ti*
and Miss *Mary Dawson*
Given under my hand, this the 31st day of December A. D., 1926.

Rev. G. P. McKeown [Seal]
Minister M. E. Church, Gloster

1918 Walter on left with
WWI friends

Ray,Sherry,Walter

Marie and Walter

CHRISTMAS 1980 Doloroso,Ms

Sue and Larry

Ronald and Karen

...This log barn was built of peeled pine logs. Even the rafters were of peeled pine logs and all the roof was split boards. All of thse boards were hand wrought as well as the crib and the boards sealed up the inside. The only bought material were the nails.

All the neighbors pitched in. Mr.McCarstle, Uncle Major, Uncle Howard, Tom, Eddie and all the Davis boys halped. Nobody had money to buy bought materials. In fact, that same year,Daddy los quite a few of his cattle because he couldn't buy any feed to feed them. I suspect he lost fifty head of cattle that year. the just starved to death.

Moss is good feed for cattle. Timber wasn't worth anything then,so cutting a tree didn't mean a thing then. You cut a tree down now,you've cut down a good bit of money....

WALTER THOMAS SCOTT JR.

Joe D. Johnson

Joseph Rudolph Wilson

Joe, Sherry, Jeanne and Rudy

73-5

3. **MAJOR E.SCOTT** b.1863 d. 1882-82 m.Ida Bryan Nov.10,1881
Wilkinson Co.Ms.(Bk L,pg.507).Major died shortly after his
marriage to Ida.He is buried in the Scott burying ground
next to his father,~~Argless~~ *Henry* .

Ida Bryan Scott later m.Nov.15,1894 to J.S.Cobb.(Bk N,pg.51
Wilkinson Co.Ms.) Ida was the grandaughter of Caleb Swayze
(Will June 1883,pg.20-23) On Mar.17,1883,Argless Scott
borrowed $110.00 from Ida to make a crop.The debt was
cancelled Jan.24,1894.

C.A. Cobb, Chancery Clerk:—

Please mark satisfied
and cancelled the trust deed to Ida Scott
from J.T. Sturgeon, recorded in Book JJ. p. 488.
the same having been paid.

J.S. Cobb

WILLIAM AND LAVINIA SCOTT
Child #4:SAMUEL B. SCOTT b.1824 Fairfield County,South Carolina,
d.Feb..1868 Catahoula Parish,La.m.Apr.19,1851 Concordia Parish,
La. Susannah Turner Bruce.Susannah was the widow of John N.Bruce
(m.Wilkinson Co.Ms Dec.10,1835).

Susannah and John N.Bruce had two children,Robert J.W.Bruce and
Mary Ann Bruce.Samuel and Susannah had one child,Daniel,who lived
only a few days after Susannah died on May 11,1852.

John N.Bruce was the brother of William G.Bruce who had married
Samuel's sister,Ann Scott on Nov.2,1850,Concordia Parish,La.

These events set the stage for a legal battle between William
G.Bruce and Samuel B.Scott which lasted nearly twenty years.

When Samuel married Susannah,she had inherited from her husband
John, one half of a tract of land that John and William had
bought jointly in Franklin Parish.Besides land in Concordia
Parish,Susannah also had heired land from her own family
(Elizabaeth Turner ,wife of Benedict Dukes,in Baton Rouge).Bruce
believed that this land and property rightly should go to the two
children of Susannah and John.

In June,1852,Samuel asked to be appointed tutor of Susannah's
children and claimed a portion of Susannah's estate through their
child Daniel,that had not survived.

Susannah's two brothers,James Madison Turner and Henry Clinton
Turner of Union Parish objected to the tutorship of both Samuel
and Bruce. Tutorship was given to H.G.Turner.

In 1853,Bruce was appointed tutor.Samuel asked the District Court
of Louisana for permission to sell a portion of the land in order
to clear debts to Mary Ann (Bruce) Gibson,wife of Rendon M.
Gibson.She and her husband had brought judgement against Samuel
and Wm.G.Bruce for $1,400.00 plus interest.In 1854,Samuel settled
Mary Ann Gibson's interest in the estates for $772.50.

The land in Corcordia Paish was advertised at a sheriff's sale
and Samuel was the highest bidder.He bought 399 acres for
$300.00.

In June 1853,William G.Bruce was named tutor.In 1854 he ordered
Samuel to file a report on the estate.In 1857,he charged that
Samuel had begun overseeing Susannah's place in June ,1851 and
that Samuel owned nothing but his horse when he married
Susannah.He also claimed that since Susannah's death,Samuel was
not taking proper care of the plantation and slaves.
(A guardian was then known as a "tutor")

Samuel B. Scott

Samuel explained that 1853-54 were depression years and he was forced to hire out the Negroes.Meanwhile,through the remaining years,the tutorship moved back and forth between the Bruce family and the Turner family.In 1856,there was an opposition of heirs filed in Catahoula.B.& E.Duke paid money that was due Susannah in 1852 and W.W.Bruce was appointed tutor to Robert D.Bruce and John Calper and his wife,**MARY ANN CALPER.** Evidently,Mary Ann had remarried.Samuel also received $230.00 of this money as his share of Susannah's estate.

This infighting ended by 1859. All the property was ordered to be sold and divided except those tracts in Franklin and Concordia Parishes.Eventually,the sheriff seized Samuel's land and personal property for judgement amounting to $459.

All of the animosity or ill-will faded over the years as both Samuel and William B. were still "family". In the diary of Aeolian,she frequently mentions " Uncle Sam"and" Uncle Ben" visiting.

In the Catahoula Parish Courthouse in Harrisonburg,I found 74 seperate documents as well as numerous receipts which covers these years.It was not until July 11,1859 that a final settlement was made.Nevertheless,problems still arose until Samuel died.

At Samuel's death in 1868,William G.Bruce asked to be the admininistator of the estate but Benjamin,the brother of Samuel opposed.Benjamin was named administrator but he too,died before it was completed.Therefore,William G.Bruce became administrator of both Samuel and Benjamin's estate.

STATE OF LOUISIANA, PARISH OF CATAHOULA,
Eleventh District Court--Clerk's Office.

I *W. W. Bruce* do solemnly swear that I will faithfully discharge the trust reposed in me by my appointment as *Tutor* to *Robert*

J. W. Bruce

minor heirs of *J. N. & Susanah Bruce*, deceased, to the best of my knowledge and understanding, agreeable to law, so help me God.

Sworn and subscribed to, this 28 day of

April A. D. 1856 before me,

C. E. Duke Clk

W. W. Bruce

STATE OF LOUISIANA, PARISH OF CATAHOULA,
Eleventh District Court--Clerk's Office.

I *W. G. Bruce* do solemnly swear that I will faithfully discharge the trust reposed in me by my appointment as *under Tutor* to

Robt J. W. Bruce

minor heirs of *J. N. & Susanah Bruce*, deceased, to the best of my knowledge and understanding, agreeable to law, so help me God.

Sworn and subscribed to, this 28th day of

April A. D. 1856 before me,

C. E. Duke Clk

W. G. Bruce

76-1

Ann Scott Bruce

Saml B Scott

1852		To G B May Dr	$	C
April 7		Balance on last years acct	44	25
April 29	"	visit Wife pres & med	4	00
30	"	visit " pres & med	4	00
May 2	"	visit " pres & med	4	00
4	"	visit " pres & meds	3	00
7	"	visit " pres & med	3	00
8	"	visit " pres & med	3	00
"	"	Call (evening) 6 hours attent.	6	00
10	"	visit pres & med	3	00
"	"	Call evening attent. all night		00
11	"	visit Wife pres & med	3	00
"	"	visit " evening attent. all night		00
18	"	visit Child pres & med	2	00
23	"	visit " (H. Lake) pres & med	6	00
24	"	visit " " " "	6	00
26	"	med & pres Babe	2	00
			$ 85	25
			73	00
			14	00
			$59	90

Recd payment   G.D May

100
73
27~

59. 00
34 25
93 25

Sam¹. B. Scott Esq &c

New Orleans Octob. 23. 1852

To Oakey & Hawkins Dr

S. B. Scott	2 Pieces Ky Linsey 44½ Yards	35¢	15.58
Black River	1 Barrel Flour		4.25
	1 Barrel Mess Pork		17.00
	8 Pairs Russett Brogans		8.00
	3 Pairs Mud Boots	$2¼	6.75
	Drayage to Lelia		.50
			52.08
	Commission on purchase a 2½ do		1.30
			53.38

Received, Trinity, La, March 24th, 1853
from Sam¹ B. Scott, two dollars, in full
for publishing notice of application for administration on estate of Susanna Scott, dec'd
T. W. Graves
Ed & Prop'r
Sm. Advocate

$200

76–3

WILLIAM AND LAVINIA SCOTT
Child #5:ANN SCOTT b.June 6,1826 Fairfield Co.SC. d.Catahoula
Parish Aug.12,1864 m.Nov.5,1850 to Willliam G.Bruce b.Jan.1,1823
Wilkinson Co.Ms.d.Mar.8,1891 Catahoula Parish.La.

According to their daughter Aeolian's (Olie)diary that Dr.Jon
Campbell of Natchez so graciously allowed me to copy,Ann and Wm.
had children that are not listed in the BRUCE Bible.The few pages
of the diary that still exists, mentioned "Oscar" dieing and also
"two little sweet babies".

In the 1860 census record of Catahoula Parish,pg.22,#206-226,9th
Ward,Trinity,La.records:
```
     Bruce,W.G.      36   b.Ms   farmer    $17,200    $500
          ,Ann.      33   b.SC
          ,N.C.       9   b.La (Charles N.)
          ,A.E.       7   b.La (Aeolian E.)
          ,W.J.       3   b.La (Walter J.)
          ,W.J.    7/I2   b.La. male
```
This last child is not listed in the Bible.

Aeolian was 13 years old when she wrote the pages that are still
in existence.It is a compilation of boats that traveled up and
down the Black River each day and the visitors, both relatives
and strangers that touched her life.These pages describe the
fever from which they all suffered,the deaths,the school days,as
well as the affection that she held for her brothers,father and
someone she called "sister".

Her "Uncle Ben"(Benjamin C.Scott) may have been injured in the
Civil War as Olie mentioned him using a cane and then later in
the year,Uncle Ben moved down to live with "Uncle Sam".(Samuel
B.Scott)

On Wednesday,Aug.23,1865,she wrote,"About eleven (11:00)Oscar
took the fever.He is so sick.We had Dr.May with him.Pa was up
with him all night."

On Thursday,Aug.24,She continued,"Sweet Oscar is very low.Not
expected to live. OH MY GOD ! Poor Sweet Oscar died this evening
at sundown.Oh,it is hard to part with him."

On Friday,Aug.25,"Little Oscar was buried today at five(5:00) in
the rain. The Work of GOD be Done."

Another poignant entry was on Saturday,November 11,1865.She wrote
"Pa,Buddy,Walty and I went over to our old place and took the two
little sweet children up and brought them over here and buried
them by Ma and Oscar."

William G.Bruce and Anne Scott's first born was Charles Ney
Bruce.
    a)CHARLES NEY BRUCE .b.Sept.23,1851 d.May 10,1908 m.Dec.2,
    1891 Annie Rourke Campbell b.June 8,1902 d. Oct.1904
    (1 child)
        1.OLIE MAY BRUCE b. 1903 m. Hayden Ellis.Olie May's
          parents died when she was a small child and on
          Sept.30,1925,she petitioned the court at Catahoula
          for the land that she had inherited from her
          father,C.N., to be given to her.The court agreed
          and she received the middle portion (113 acres)
          acres)of the original William Scott land which
          consisted of 333 acres.(Conveyance Record Bk,6,
          p.495)
    b) AEOLIAN "Olie " BRUCE b.Dec.12,1854 d.Oct.4,1875 m.Sept
    21,1869 to Major Seab Washington Campbell b.1838 d.July
    31,1889.(2 children)
        1.ANNIE "Olie"CAMPBELL b.Feb.26,1873 m.Charlie N.Beard.
          Dec.29,1891 (Vol II,p.3,CATAHOULA PARISH MARRIAGES,
          by Haley)

        2.HOWARD PRESTON CAMPBELL b. Dec.25,1874 d.June 10,1955
          m.Feb.6,1901 Hattie Olie Cross b.June 5,1881
          d,Nov.25,1874.dau of Jonathan Simms Cross(10th
          child of John Presberry Cross and Phoebe Steele),
          and Addie Lanehart.Both buried in Fort Hill Cemetery,
          Harrisonburg,La.(4 childrn)
            a)SEAB W.CAMPBELL b.Lismore,La 1902
              d.Ferriday,1936 m.Nov.9,1929 to Ambolean Prince.

            b)ADDIE BRUCE CAMPBELL b.Lismore,1904
              d.Natchez,1968 m.Nov.19,1932 Jesse Stallings
              Burris

            c)JONATHAN CROSS CAMPBELL SR. b.July 10,1906 d.
              Natchez,1966 m.Oct.16,1931 Edna Woods b.Sept.15,
              1912 Woodville,Ms.(1 child)
                1.JONATHAN CROSS CAMPBELL JR.MD b Jan.4,1939
                  m.Aug.19,1960 Natchez,Ms.Nan Yvonne Nevels
                  dau of Katie Beatrice Jones and James Julio
                  Nevels of Vicksburg,Ms.(5 children)
                    a)PATRICK HOWARD CAMPBELL b. Oct.12,1961
                    b)JONATHON CROSS CAMPBELL III
                      b.Mar.2,1964
                    c)EMILY VIRGINIA CAMPBELL b.Jan.12,1970
                    d)SEABORN WOODS CAMPBELL b.Jan.12,1977
                    e)KATHLEEN EDNA CAMPBELL b.May 7,1978

    4.ANNIE CAMPBELL b.Sept.7,1909 Parham,La.d.1909

The sale of the SCOTT land by Dr.Jon Cross Campbell a few years
ago,marked the end to a SCOTT descendent owning this land.

Dr. Jon Campbell with
grandparents instruments

Yvonne and Jon

Jonathan Cross Campbell Jr. family, 1979
Jonathon, Patrick, Yvonne, Kathleen, Seaborn, Jon, and Emily

MAJ. SEBORN CAMPBELL

AEOLIAN BRUCE CAMPBELL

EDWARD PRESTON CAMPBELL AND HATTIE OLIE CROSS

Benjamin Scott

WILLIAM AND LAVINIA SCOTT
Child #6: BENJAMIN C.SCOTT b.June 6,1826 Fairfield County,SC,
d.Oct. 1866 Catahoula Parish,La.(Twin to Ann.)

Benjamin C.Scott was a veteran of the Civil War.He served with
the Co.A.,17th La.Inf..and he enlisted at Camp Moore,La..He was
captured at Vicksburg,Ms.July 4,1863 and paroled June 6,1865.

Ben never married and at various times,lived with his brothers.
In 1865 he was using a cane which indicates that he had been
wounded in the war

When Samuel B.Scott,his brother died,Ben was named as the
administrator over the wishes of his brother-in-law Wm.G.Bruce.
However,before the estate could be settled,Ben also died and then
Wm G.Bruce was named adminstrator.

By 1865,Wm.G.Bruce had acquired the 1/7th portion of two of Ann's
brothers,Major A.,and Henry William.This ,along with his wife's
1/7, gave him 3/7 portion of the 333 acres.As administrator of
both Samuel B.and Benjamin C.,he was able to gain another 2/7
ownership by Dec.1.1877.(Bk P, p.527 Catahoula Parish,La.)

Not until after the death in 1868 of John W.Scott ,was Wm.G.Bruce
able to gain John's 1/7 interest.Also,in 1879-80,Walton J.Bruce
(Wm.G's son) bought another 1/7 interest for $200.00 from the
heirs of Thomas Francis Scott who lived in Texas.Davis Winfield
of Limestone Co.Tx.,Sally A.Callicoatte of Camp Co.Tx.,Frances
Marion Scott Sr. of Coryell Co.,and Lavinea Scott Poer of Hill
Co.Tx.(Conveyance Bk I,p.80-81,1879-80 Catahoula Parish,La.)

On Dec.3,1890,(Deed Bk CB,5,p.228,Catahoula Parish) the Tensas
Basin Levee Board District conveyed to Wm.G.Bruce all right,title
and interest to this section of land of 333 acres.As a result of
this document,he was able to obtain a clear title to the land.

WILLIAM AND LAVINIA SCOTT
Child # 7: JOHN W.SCOTT b.Oct.14,1834,Ms. d.Jan.20,1868 Concordia
Parish,La.buried in the SCOTT CEMETERY.m.Jan.15,1859 to Sarah B.
Magoun b.1838 Ms.,dau.of Dr.C.S.Magoun (MD)of Concordia Parish.

In the 1860 census pg.795 lists both John and Dr.Magoun families
```
#2   Magoun,C.S. 45 physician & farmer  $50,000    $5,000 b.NH
           ,C.A. 46                                        b.Ms
           ,S.P. 18   cadet
           ,O.E. 15
           ,M.M.13              all children b.Ms.
#3 Scott   ,J.W. 25  farmer                                b.Ms.
           ,S.B. 21                                        b.Ms.
           ,H.A. 6/12                                      b.La.
```

John was a veteran of the Civil War and probably was another ill
or maimed individual who did not return home in good health.He
did not live but a short while after returning home,as he died
in January before the youngest child,Nellie was born in May.
John's tombstone is one of the oldest stones still standing in
the SCOTT CEMETERY.

In 1864,dated "Flourry Mound",John's brother-in-law,Wm.B.Bruce
applied in John's behalf,to the government for "help to clothe
families since the fall of Vicksburg".A law had been passed for
this situation and there were many wives and children in
Catahoula and Concordia that were in desperate need.Among the
long list,were Sarah and her children,Hellen,4 and Cyrus,2.
WmG.Bruce served as a Notary Public in Concordia Parish,La.

John and Sarah had 3 children.In the appraisment of his estate on
July 14,1870,there were 3 milk cows and calves at $90.00,2 yoke
of oxen at $120.00,5 dry cattle at $50.00,and 60 head of hogs at
$5.00 each.Total of the estate was $560.00.Witness:B.C.Scott
(Benjamin C.Scott was his brother)

> a)HELEN ANN SCOTT b. Nov.4,1859 d. May 12,1923 m.1st,July
> 22,1875 to Henry H.Foreman.
>
> m.2nd to Charlie Burley   (8 children)
>
>> 1.RENA TAYLOR
>> 2.LOIS CAMPBELL
>> 3.RUTH SHANE
>> 4.MARION BURLEY
>> 5.OVID BURLEY
>> 6.WILLIE BURLEY
>> 7.WALTER BURLEY
>> 8.CYRUS BURLEY
>
> b)CYRUS SCOTT b. 1861

John W. Scott

c)NELLIE MAGOUN SCOTT b.May 21,1868,d.Mar.15,1953 m.1st Joel
B.Burley Aug.3,1885,(2 children)

    1.CALVIN SCOTT BURLEY b.1890 d. 1972
    2.ETTA OLIVIA BURLEY b.Aug..8, 1892 m.John Gelston
    b.Dec.29,1887 of Columbia,SC.(2 children)
        a)NELLIE ELIZABETH GELSTON b.Feb.23,1918,m.May 5,
        1951 to Mr.HARPER
        m. R.H. BLAKENEY

        b.DOROTHY GELSTON
    Etta lives with Dorothy in Columbia,S.C.

Nellie m.2nd Cyrus B.Burley Jr.Nov.7,1895
b.Nov.10,1869,d.Apr.8,1963

NO. 197   License
John W. Scott   &   Sarah B. Magougn
1859

STATE OF LOUISIANA,
Parish of Concordia.
NINTH DISTRICT COURT.

To any Justice of the Peace or Minister of the Gospel, duly authorised to celebrate Marriages within this Parish—GREETING:

YOU are hereby specially authorised, and empowered to unite in the Holy Bonds of Matrimony Mr. *John W Scott* a resident of *Concordia* and *Miss Sarah B Magoun* a resident of *Concordia* and the same being done you will make a formal act of your proceeding in the presence of three or more witnesses as the Law directs, which you will return, together with this License, with all convenient speed.

Given under my official signature and the impress of the Seal of my Office, at Vidalia, on this *Fifteenth* day of *January* A. D. Eighteen hundred and *fifty nine*

[signature]

STATE OF LOUISIANA,
Parish of Concordia, } ss.

BE IT REMEMBERED, That on this *20th* day of *January* Anno Domini, Eighteen hundred and *fifty nine* by virtue of the above License, I, *J A Routon* a Minister of the Gospel proceeded to Celebrate the Rights of matrimony at the Residence of Dr Magoun in said Parish, and joined together in the Holy Bonds of Matrimony Mr. *John W Scott* Parish of *Concordia* and *Miss Sarah B Magoun* of *Concordia*

The same being done in the presence of *Wm G Bruce, Major &* *Scott and J C Godwin* competent witnesses, who have signed this certificate with the said parties, and me, the said *minister*

Witnesses
M A Scott
W G ——

John W Scott
Sarah B Magoun
J A Routon

JOHN W. SCOTT

MAJOR SCOTT
CEMETERY

80-3

Daniel Jackson Scott

WILLIAM AND ANN SCOTT
#7 child:DANIEL JACKSON SCOTT
DANIEL JACKSON SCOTT b.1800 Fairfield Co.S.C.,d.June 23,1878
Fairfield Co.S.C.

Throughout the years that Daniel J.Scott lived,he was the
mainstay of the family.He served as administrator of his mother's
estate,Major's estate,and James's estate.As mentioned before,
Daniel traveled extensively from South Carolina to Mississippi
and Louisana keeping in touch with all members of the family.In
addition,he bought and sold land and slaves in all of these three
states.The legal documents of these transactions give credence
that Daniel was blessed with common sense and had acquired a vast
knowledge of legal transactions.

At his death in 1878 at the age of 78,he was living close or with
his sister Sarah Carmen.To all appearances he had no wife nor
children although in the 1820 census,line #158 lists Daniel
between 16 and 26.(We know he was 20) and a female between 16 and
26-assumedly a wife.His mother Ann was #157 as well as his
brother William Scott.

By the time of the 1830 census,William,Henry and John W.Scott
were already in Wilkinson County,Mississippi.In Fairfield County,
there was a Daniel Scott listed on p.390,line 9,with only 1 male
between 10 & 15,1 male between 20 & 30,and 1 male between 40 & 50
living in the household.But,in any event,no proof can be derived
that this was OUR Daniel.

Nevertheless,in the 1840 census,p.169,line 21-25,Daniel Scott was
listed with a female between 40 & 50 and a male between 20 &
30.Daniel was at that time,40 years old and living next to his
brother George.There is a possibility that his wife was named
Martha Ann (Bill #1852 #30) Joint answer of Nanthaniel B.Holly &
Chas.A.Holly to cross bill of Daniel and Martha Ann Scott.

It is also clear that in the 1850 census,Daniel was living alone.
p.223,line #347 lists Daniel as being 50 years of age,born 1800
and a " Rancher",rather than a" Planter".Personal wealth was
$3,500.00. Then too, Daniel was a neighbor of his brother George.

After Daniel's mother,Ann,died,the "Homeplace of 100 -115acres
had been acquired by his sister,Sarah Carmon".(Bk SS p.289,1850
on Scotts Branch)Two years later in 1852,(Bk TT,p.299)Daniel
bought the William Scott homeplace from Sarah and John Carmon.

The land seemed to fluctuate between 100 and 115 acres throughout
the years.After Daniel died in 1878,Thomas Scruggs made the
statement on July 8,1878 that he had been asked by several heirs-
in-law to be made administrator. He stated that Daniel's property
value did not exceed $1,200.00.Sarah objected, as she was the
nearest surviving kin and thus,was named adminstratrix.

However,she also declared that she and a nephew, John Cross and two neices,Nancy Haigood and Eliza Parnell were the only next of kin of Daniel.This,of course,was not true as there were others, besides John P.Cross, in Louisana and Mississippi.

On Sept.12,1879,Henry William Scott of Wilkinson County,Ms. and John P.Cross of Concordia Parish,La. issued a complaint against Sarah Carman. It mentioned the amount of $735.00 in regards to Daniel's estate.(Bk AF p.532 and Bk AF p.476).

On July 26,1878,Thomas Anderson,Samuel L. Crawford and Nathan Roberts were named as appraisers.It was declared that Daniel's personal property consisted of $1,250.00 and the land was distributed as follows:

100 Acres Adj Owens & Scruggs to Sarah's son,Samuel C.Carman (Homeplace)   (Bk AF p.532 1879)

350 Acres Mill Tract to Andrew Y.Milling (Bk AF p.492 1879)

120 Acres to William A. Clark Adj Boyd & Scott (Bk AF p.476 1879)

40 Acres to C.E.Leitner Claxton River Place (Bk AF p.471 1879)

80 Acres to C.E. Leitner Claxton Home Place (Bk AF p.470 1879)

In 1887,Sarah's son Samuel C.Carman sold the 100 A "Home Tract" to his sister,Martha A.Carman (Bk AL p.288 1887)It was only four years later that Samuel bought it back.(Bk AO p.497 1892)

State of South Carolina }
County of Fairfield }

We the undersigned appraisers appointed by the Judge of Probate for Fairfield County having first taken and subscribed the oath prescribed by law, do certify that we have estimated and appraised the property set forth in the following inventory and that it contains a true and perfect inventory of all and singular the goods, chattels and credits of Daniel Scott deceased made by and shown to us by Sarah Cannon Administratrix of the said deceased, and by us viewed and appraised.

2 Chairs 25 Cupboard 1 25 Book Case 30	
2 Quilts 2 feather Beds	10 —
Lot Old Iron	1.50
Balances	1 50
Lot tools	3 00
14 00 lbs lint cotton More or less in 3 Bales @ 9c	126 00
Sorrel Horse (Butler)	10 —
75 Bus Cotton seed, 8c	6 00

Brot over

Set plow gear	.15
2 old Wheels & Spade	1.00
1 Large pot 1 oven	1.50
Ceder press	1.50

Cattle

Black Bull	8.00
Spotted	10.00
Red heifer	5.00
Brindle	8.00
Cream	10.00
Cow & Calf (Rose)	10.00
heifer	7.00
Cow & Calf (Brandy)	12.00
Cow & Calf (Pink)	10.00
Ox (Bill)	10.00
10 head Hogs	20.00
Broad Ax Spirit level & Mill saw	3.50
Well chain	.25
Gold Coine	40.40
Silver coine	6.25

Notes & Mortages

Geo Scott	
Goodwin Steel	129.68
James B Gibson	30.00
Wesly Watt & J H WilRose	15.00
James H Steel Doubtfull	70.00
John Copland	700.00
E A Gibson	25.00
C H Scruggs Doubtfull	23.??

Sarah Scott Carmon

WILLIAM AND ANN SCOTT
8 child: SARAH SCOTT b.1801 Fairfield Co.S.C. d.after 1879 as
she was the administratorix of her brother,Daniel's estate.
m.John Carmon.
The 1850 census states:p.285,line 277-78
    Carman,John   48 Shoemaker b. Burlingauche $3500.
      ,Sarah   49   Fairfield
      ,Wm.   26
      ,Martha 22
      ,Sarah   19
      ,Susannah 12
      ,Jane   10
      ,Samuel 8
      ,Jesse   4
      ,William 3
The 1870 census states: p.10,line 81
    Carmon,John   65   Farmer   b.SC $155.00
      ,Sarah   69   b.SC
  Scott ,Susannah 4   b.SC
  Carmon,John   3   b.SC

    p.24,line 189,list two sons of Sarah and John:
    Carmon,Samuel 27   Farm laborer
      ,Jesse   23   Farm laborer

As mentioned before,Sarah was the adminstratrix of her brother
Daniel's estate in 1878.No other information is known of her
personally.Refer to Daniel Jackson Scott for further information
concerning the SCOTT HOMEPLACE.

When Sarah's son Samuel C.(b.1843)died, his will was probated
Feb.24,1904.(DB 74 p 47)Also,(FF Co.Deeds AL/288 and AO/497 names
Martha A.Carmon as wife of Samuel C.Carmon.) Frank Jernigan
shared the contents with me:
1.His son E.G.CARMON would have 2 mules,1 bull headed heifer and
   35 acres with my dwelling house bounded by N.D.Roberts,E.by
   A.S.Scruggs,S.by Wm Boyd,W.and remainder of 100 A.
2.Son J.W.CARMON 40 A.in N.part of this my home place bounded by
   35 A.willed to E.G.,Robertrs,Lyles and Scruggs.
3.Grandson SAMUEL J.(S,I)CARMON remainder of home tract,33
A.bounded by Roberts and land willed to E.G.and J.W.
4.Grand daughter RUTH A.CARMON Brown Cow and sewing machine.
5.Daughter ANNIE MAT HARRRISON (wife of Augustus Harrison)her
   mother's bed and bedding.
   Daughter 40 A.on S.side of Matthews Place bounded by J.A.Hagood
   Jane Moore,and J.W.Boyd to remainder of the Matthews Tract.
6.Son E.G.CARMON remaining 20 A.of Matthews Tract.If he should
   die without heir,property goes to Samuel J(I,S).
7.Son JOHN A.C.CARMON $80.00.
No mortgages may be given on this property and the children can
only sell to each other but to no others.
Sons J.W.and E.G.CARMON Exec.

In this will of Samuel C.Carmon, the daughter listed as Annie Harrison ,was the wife of Augustus W.Harrison.One of their daughters was GUSSIE LEE HARRISON. Frank wrote,on Nov.2,1986,that he had visited with Miss Gussie Lee and she told him that the A.W. Harrison "Home Place" was the WILLIAM SCOTT land.

She remembered that when she and her sisters were small children their father took them to the old Scott house to see a buzzard nest there.It was an old log house and the roof had fallen in.

Miss Gussie Lee died on Oct.3,1985 at the age of 80.Frank had intended to return for another visit but" time takes it's toll". Her obituary read as follows:"She was born in Fairfield County and was a daughter of the late Auguster W.and Annie Carman Harrison.She was a member of Union Memorial Presbyterian Church and a retired employee of Southern Maid Garment Co.

Surviving are nieces,Mrs.Naomi Miller of Winnsboro and Mrs. Minnie Carman of Columbia; and nephews,Creighton Robertson of Winnsboro and Leroy and Edward Robertson of Columbia."

Today,the land is owned by a timber company.

James Scott

=WILLIAM AND ANN SCOTT
#9 child:JAMES SCOTT b.pre 1805 d.July 2,1844 Fairfield Co.S.C.
It is suggested that James was the youngest of the family as
Sarah was born ln 1801 and William did not die until 1805.Also,
whenever there would be a list of the heirs,James was always
last. Since he was an unmarried adult at the time of his death in
1844,it is possible that he was in frail health.

It was evident that James had been ill for several months, as
John Cross had cared for him during his illness.On January
25,1845,he presented a bill for "Board and Attention during
Sickness from 8th of March to 2nd day of July $50.00".He also
stated that as of February 10,1845,he had not been paid.
(FF Estates,Box.81,pkg.164,2,6,15,7,&9)

The final return was made on January,1848. The eight heirs John
Scott, Elizabeth Cross,George Scott,Henry Scott,William
Scott,Sarah Carman,Ann Scott and Daniel Scott received $18.75
each. Elizabeth Cross had died leaving two children,John P.Cross
and Susannah Stanton who each received half of her share.

James died July 2,1844.It stated that he was unmarried and had no
children.Also, his brother Major was already dead as well as his
sister, Elizabeth who had married Samuel Cross.His brother,Daniel
Scott was appointed administrator.

State of South Carolina,
Fairfield District } In the court of ordinary

To John R. Buchanan Esquire ordinary in &
for the District of Fairfield in the State
aforesaid.

The Petition of Daniel Scott of the
District and State aforesaid. respectfully
Sheweth. That James Scott late of the District
and State aforesaid, departed this life on the
second day of July A.D. 1844, intestate, being
possessed of some small personal property.
That said intestate left neither wife nor
child; but left a mother, and brothers &
one Sister, & the children of a deceased sister,
his heirs at law.

Your petitioner, a brother of said
intestate, prays that administration upon
the Estate of said deceased may be granted
to him.

And your petitioner will ever pray.

Sept. 2d 1844 —

Daniel Scott

Related Families

Geter / Jeter

WILLIAM JETER'S WILL
March 1797

Last will and Testament was proven in Open Court by the Oath of Edmund Holleman and ordered to be Recorded March Term 1797

In the name of God Amen.The twenty fifth day of November in the year of our Lord one thousand seven hundred and nineth three. I WILLIAM JETER of Edgefield County and Ninety Six District in the State of South Carolina and being aged and feeble of body but of perfect mind and memory thanks be to God for the Same and therefore calling the Mortality of my body and knowing that it is appointed for all men once to die do make and ordained this my last Will and Testament that is to Say Principally and Just of all I Recommend my Soul into the hands of Almightly God who gave it and my body I recommend to the Earth to be given a Decent like Christian Burial at the discretion of my Executors of Nothing Doubting but at the General Resurection I Shall Receive the Same again by the mighty power of Almighty God and receive the Same Salvation through the ?   ots of our Blessed Lord and Savior Jesus Christ and as ? ing Such worldly Estate wherewith it hath Pleased God to bless me in this life I give demise and dispose of the same.In the following manner and form.

Imprimis Item:I lend my beloved wife MARGARET JETER all my whole and state both real and personal that I am now possessed with her lifetime or widow hood.

Item: I give and bequeth unto MARGARET my dearly beloved with one Feather bed and Furniture being the bed we now usually ly upon(or in)one Dark bay mare known by the Name of Fancy,one cow and Calf and three Heads of Sheep.

Item: I give and bequeath unto my well beloved JOHN WILLIAM JETER four hundred acres of Land,one Negro man named Ned,one feather bed and furniture all which being put onto his possession with other household Furniture as likewise to him and his heirs forever.

Item:I give unto my Daughter PARTHENY VAUGHN one hundred acres of Land, one feather bed and furniture, one mare,saddle and bridle, with all and which I had formerly had given her and put into her possession unto her and her heirs forever.

Item:I Give and bequeath unto my Daughter ANCRIDGE HOWLET the Goods and Chattles that I formerly lent her and also a Debt of twenty one pounds two Shillings and Eight pence half penny Virginia Currency now due to me by Cradock Vaughn unto her heirs forever and also one hundred acres of Land which I give unto my Grandson Seth Howlet lying between the Mire branch and the red Lik branch.

Item:I give and bequeath unto my Daughter CALPHARNA BAKER one tract of Sixty acres of Land,two mares,a saddle and Bridle,and other household Furniture which I had formerly given and put into her possession to her and her heirs forever.

Item: I give and bequeath unto my Son HAL JETER a Wagon and horse which I now have lent him.All my land my Son Hal Jeter lying from the back line to the old road formerly runing by Samuel Mills on both Sides Gunnells Creek,to him and his heirs forever.

Item:I give and bequeath unto my son JOSEPH JETER one Negro Girl Called Edy to his and his heirs forever.

Item:I give and Bequeath unto my Son CORNELIUS JETER one Mullato boy Called Baron and one cow and calf which he now has in his possession to his and his heirs forever.

Item: I give and bequeath unto my Son JOSEPH JETER two Negroes known by the Name of Jack and Hannah,one hundred acres of Land and Plantation where on he now lives together with a Negro boy known by the Name of Phill which Land and boy he now has in possession,to him and his heirs forever.

Item: I give and bequeath unto my Son ARGULUSS JETER one Negro boy known by the Name of Isaac,one Sorrel Stallion Called Speddill which he hath now in his possession,to him and his heirs forever.

Item:I give and bequeath to my Son ELIAZER JETER the Plantation and Land whereon I now live up Gunnels Creek to the road Dividing Between Hal Jeter that has been heretofore mentioned,one Negro boy Names Sam,one Cow and Calf,one black Stallion Colt,three head of Sheep and one Feather bed and furniture to him and his heirs forever.

Item: I give and bequeath to my Daughter ELIZABETH CRUZE one Negro girl called Jude,one Negro boy I give to my Grandson WILLIAM CRUZE named Boy,to them and their heirs forever.

Item: I give and bequeath unto my Daughter SARAH CROSSBY one Negro girl called Edy which she now has in possession,to her and her heirs forever.

Item: I lend unto my Daughter NANCY MOSELY during her life one hundred acres of Land adjoining Jn'Kilcrease and Henry Key Surveyed for me and granted to me by the Honble.At her death,I give unto my grandson GEORGE MOSELY,son of Nancy Mosely,all the aforesaid land of one Hundred acres and fifteen Pounds Sterling after the Death of my wife which I Desire may be put to Lawful Interest til his arrival to twenty one years of age.
Item:I give unto my Daughter DELILAH GARRET,one feather bed which she has received to her and her heirs forever.

87

Item: I give and bequeath unto my Daughter PRISCILLA MOSELY one cow and calf,to my grandaughter SALLEY MOSELY,Daughter of Priscilla Mosely,one hundred and twenty acres of land lying on the upper Side of the Red Lik branch waters of Gunnals Creek.

Item: I lend unto my Daughter PEGGY KILCREASE one Negro Girl called Tamer and one feather bed which she now has in possession and one Bay Stallion Colt known by the name of Jubiter and if She dies without leaving (an heir?) I pray to be divided as is hereafter mentioned and I give unto my grandaughter PEGGY KILCREASE one Hundred and fifty acres of Land whereon she now lives provided that there Should not be a charge made of a Certain Sorrel Horse by Minor Kilcrease,husband of my Daughter Peggy against my estate.

Item: I leave all my Estate that has not ben heretofore mentioned to be divided in the following manner(viz)
---one sixth part to HAL JETER
---one sixth part to CORNELIUS JETER
---one sixth part to ELIAZER JETER
---one Sixth part to GEO MOSELY,son of my daughter Nancy Mosely
---one sixth part to SALLY MOSELY,daughter of my Daughter Pricilla Mosely
---one sixth part to my Daughter PEGGY KILCREASE

Item: I do constitute and ordain MARGARET JETER,my beloved Wife,my friends JOHN MARTIN and my son HAL JETER,my Sole Executors of this my last will and Testament and I do utterly disallow and revoke,disannul all and every other former Testaments,Legacies bequeaths and Excutors by me in any wise before named Wills and bequeathed and confirming this and no other to be my last will and testament.

In witness whereunto I have set my hand and seal this Day and year first within written.Signed,Sealed,and adknowledged.

In presence of
EDMUND HOLLEMAN
MERRYMAN COOK
ELEANOR COOK

Interlined before assigned the words,and if she dies without
?   I prae to divided as is hereafter mentioned of a certain Sorrel Horse.

Between the years of 1790 and 1810, Americans had settled in the western part of the original 13 Colonies and along the banks of rivers west of the Appalachian Mountains. As the colonies became more crowded,the westword movement increased during the years preceding the war of 1812.

The settlement of William Jeter's will could have been the beginning of Argulass's movement which eventually ended in Wilkinson County,Mississippi.The census record of 1790 (the first United States census) shows that the members of his family were the only JETERS in the state of South Carolina at this time. However,in 1813,Argulass married Polly(Mary) Phipps of Wilkinson Co.,the daughter of Henry Phipps.

The spelling of the JETER/GETER name would virtually become a seesaw. Until the years around 1860,both spellings were sometimes used in both the marriage bond and the marriage ceremony.But today, the spelling'GETER' is the dominant spelling used by the descendents still living in Wilkinson Co.

In his will of 1840,Arguless identified several of his children: STERLING,JUNE,NANCY,JANE,ELIZABTH,LUCINDA,ARGLESS,AND DAVIS (BK M.pg.150,Wilkinson County,Mississippi)

ARGLES JEETER'S WILL
Will 1840

Know all men by these present that I Argles Jeeter of the county and state aforesaid for and in consideration of the natural love and affection which I have for my wife MARY JEETER and my children STERLING JEETER,JUNE AND NANCY JETTER,JANE JEETER,ELIZ-ABETH JEETER,LUCINDA JEETER,ARGLES JEETER AND DAVIS JEETER, and for and in consideration of the sum of ten thousand dollars to me in hand paid by them have given,granted ,bargained,sold,conveyed and confirmed and delivered and by these presents do give,grant,-bargain,sell,convey,confirm and deliver unto the said MARY JEETER for and during the term of her natural life,and after her death to my children above named their heirs and assigns forever reserving to myself out of the same a suficient yearly support during my life all the following described property to wit:

One tract or parcel of land lying and being in the said state and county conveyed by HENRY PHIPPS to said JEETER by deed bearing date the second day of April A.D.1840.,and being on Pineywood Creek,a branch of the Buffaloo Creek,and bounded as follows:

Begining at a gum tree on said Phipps Easterly line runing thence North 14@,W.120 perches to a Magnolia,thence South 32@ E, 130 perches to a small Magnolia,thence North 84@ E, 110 perches to the begining as described in said deed.Containing one hundred acres more or less,also the following dscribed land lying in said County containing sixty acres more or less and bounded as follows to wit: On the south by public lands,and East of said lands of said JEETER and the heirs of JAMES PHIPPS,being the same conveyed by THOMAS ELLIS and wife to said JEETER by deed bearing date 12 th day of February AD 1835. Also the following tract of land.:

Lying in said county containing forty seven acres and forty three hundredths of an acre more or less and known as fractional section No.27 Township No.4 Range,No.2 West and being lot No.2 of said section,and being the same conveyed by JOHN STROTHER and wife to said ARGLAS JEETER by deed bearing date the 16th day of January AD 1837.

Also the following described tract of land lying in said county containing twelve acres more or less begining at an Iron Wood at the South West Corner of MR.WHITES line and runing thence North 84@ East,twelve and one half chains to a white Oak,thence extending South Eastword so far as to include twelve acres of land as described in a deed from HENRY PHIPPS and wife to said JEETER,bearing date the 2nd day of October AD 1819.

The forgoing tracts of land constituting the tract of land on which said ARGLES JEETER resides.

Also the following negro slaves to wit:BEN,JIM,DICK,CHARLES,TOM, LEE,SAM,HENRY,MARY,RACHEL,HARRIET,and LUCY.Also all the Horses, Mules,Wagons,Carts,Hogs,Sheep,Oxen. Cattle and farming utensils of every name and description on said land or belonging to said ARGLES JEETER. Also all the household and kitchen furniture belonging to said ARGLES JEETER, Also all the crops of cotton, Corn,or other things raised on said land in the present year 1840.

Together with all the here ditamends,priviliges and advantages belonging or in anywise appertaining unto the above described premises,To have and to hold the above granted,bargained,and described premises with the appurtenances unto the said MARY JEETER during the term of her natural life and at her death unto the said STERLING JEETER,JUNE and NANCY JEETER,JANE JEETER,ELIZA-BETH JEETER,LUCINDA JEETER,ARGLES JEETER and DAVIS JEETER,their heirs and assigns forever,reserving always as aforesaid out of said property a sufficient yearly support to the said ARGLES JEETER during the term of his natural life.

In witness whereof the said ARGLES JEETER hath hereunto set his hand and seal this twenty first day of September in the year of our Lord one thousand and eight hundred and forty.

Signed,sealed and delivered in the presence
of Y.Davidson
State of Mississippi   his
Wilkinson,County,   ARGLES X JEETER
                                                    mark
Personally appeared before me a Justice of the peace in and for said county,ARGLES JEETER who acknowledged that he signed,sealed

and delivered the foregoing deed and instrument in writing as his act and deed on the day and year therein written.
Given under my hand and seal this 21st day of September AD
TRUMAN POWELL
Justice of the Peace

As mentioned before,Argulas's marriage to Polly Phipps in 1813 was the first indication that he was in the state of Mississippi.In fact,their marriage was the second Jeter marriage recorded in the Wilkinson County marriage book;the first was of a William Jeter to Elizabeth Morgan in 1808.

When listing in chronological order the marriages of the Jeter/Geter family ,one point emerges. The John W.Jeter who married Charlotte Lambert in 1820 in Feliciana Parish, Louisiana(now East Feliciana),probably was a brother to Argless. In William Jeter's will,he mentiones a son, John William Jeter as his oldest son. John W.Jeter and wife Charlotte of Feliciana Parish,later moved to Wilkinson County and lived in the vicinity of Arglus and Polly.The name of STERLING was used in both families for their respective sons. Therefore, hopeful that some of the descendents of John and Charlotte will someday uncover proof or disproof of this assumption,information on both John and Argulas are included.

ARGULUS JETER b.1770 South Carolina.,m.Polly (Mary) Phipps on April 22,1813 in Wilkinson County,Ms. (MB A,pg.259)Polly was the daughter of Henry Phipps,and also the sister of Phebe Phipps who married a Sterling Jeter in 1817.
Argulus and Polly had 10 known children:Sterling,June,Nancy,Jane, Elizabeth,Lucinda,Martha,Argles,Eugenia(Ugenia)and Davis.

CHILD #1.STERLING JETER b.1815,m.Nov.8,1838(MB F.pg.260 Wilkinson Co.Ms.)to Narcissa Swayze b. 1815.Narcissa probably related to Caleb Swayze b. 1820 who m.Sterling's sister Nancy Jeter in 1839.Sterling and Narcissa had two children.
    a.WILLIAM JETER b. 1844
    b. DAVIS JETER b. 1849

CHILD #2.JUNE JETER (possibly a twin to Nancy.)
CHILD #3.NANCY JETER.b.1820 m.May 2,1839 (MB F,pg.280 Wilkinson Co.Ms.)to Caleb C.Swayze b. 1820.In 1850,Nancy and Caleb had one child listed in the census.
    a.MARY JANE SWAYZE b.1841 (later to marry Lewis H.Bryant on Jan.14,1858)
In Caleb C.Swayze's will dated June 22, 1883,several grandchildren are listed as recipients of his estate.Nancy is not mentioned.He gave his land known as the James Swayze place situated near the Homochitto River consisting of 120 acres, to his grandaughter IDA ISABEL SCOTT (who had married Major E.Scott

on Nov.10,1881.Major was the son of Henry Scott and Elizabeth
Jeter).Ida was the daughter of Lewis H.Bryant and Mary Jane
Swayze.After the death of Major,she married J.S.Cobb.

To his grandchildren Mary Ann McNeely and Caleb Swayze
McNeely,he gave his homeplace situated on Buffalo Creek which
consisted of 336 acres.To his grandson John Ford McNeely he gave
247.32 acres.All were children of Murdock D.McNeely.He added the
provision that if any should die without heirs,the estate should
be redivided among the living heirs. Nancy Downs was to have the
80 acres that he had set aside for her natural life and in
closing,he named his cousin James P.McNeely as his "sole
executor" of his last will.Witness were A.W.Lanehart,J.K.
Sessions,and Jas.M.Sessions.

CHILD # 4: JANE JETER b.1822,m.Feb.8,1844(BK G,pg.266)
1st to Ferdinand C.Ford.Divorced.Two children.
    a.Oliver Ford b. 1845
    b.Eugene Ford b.1847
    Married 2nd Jan.11,1852(MB I,pg.133)to Thomas Brannon b..SC,
1795,d.Sept.3,1864.Thomas's first wife was Patsy White who died
in 1849.Those interested in Thomas's 1st marriage lineage should
contact Mrs.BC Walker,PO Box 179,Roxie,Ms.39661.

In the 1850 census,Argulus Jeter was 70 years old and a
widower.He was listed as living with Thomas Brannon along with
both families.In the slave schedule of 1850,both men had several
slaves and many acres of land. Evidently,they were farming
together as a unit.

1850 CENSUS:
    BRANNAN,THOMAS.b.1795 55 male,planter,#3,300 b. SC
    NEWMAN,Nancy, b.1838(dau.)m.Jan.5,1847 (MB H.pg.136)
            ,ALEXANDER b. 1822
            ,Martha b. 1848
    Brannon,Thos.b. 1830   20
            ,W.W. b. 1832   18
            ,A.(G or J.)b. 1838   12
            ,Harriet C. b. 1840 10
            ,John A. b. 1842   8
            ,Doug. C. b. 1844   6
    JETER,ARGLESS 70,b. 1779 planter $960 b. SC
            ,Mary   40 b. 1810
            ,Argless W. b. 1830   20
            ,Jane b. 1822 28
    Ford ,Oliver b. 1845 5
            ,Eugene b. 1847 3
By 1860 Jane and Thomas had 5 children of their own.Davis,Mary
Lucenda,C.A. Virginia E. and Violet.

1860 CENSUS:
    BRANNON,THOS 66
            ,Jane 38

```
                   ,A.J. 23
                   ,Ford 20
                   ,Douglas 19
        Ford       ,O.T. 16 (Oliver T.)
                   ,Eugene 12
        Brannon Davis A. 8
                   ,Mary Lucenda 7
                   ,C.A. 5
                   ,Virginia E.  3
                   ,Violet 1
```
By 1870,Thomas had died leaving Jane a widow of 48.The 3 youngest children listed in 1860 did not appear.The only child younger than Mary Lucenda was Benjamin,age 9.

1870 CENSUS:
```
        BRANNAN ,JANE 48
                   ,Davis  18
                   ,Lucenda 17 (She would later marry Wm.A.K. Cooper
                           Dec.16,1874)
        JETER   ,Rufus S. 20.(This is the Sterling Rufus Jeter who
                   married Laura M. Cage in 1872.(MB L.pg.219)The
                   family relationship is presently unknown.
                   Nevertheless,Rufus,as he was known,was very close to
                   the Jeters and the Scotts and was called"cousin".
                   In the 1900 census, Rufus and Laura had eight
                   children.(Notice the changed spelling to Geter)
                   1.Elen L. Geter   b.1874
                   2.Duncan C. Geter b.1876
                   3.Virginia(Jenny)E.Geter b. 1880 (m.G.A. Rawarth on
                      June 14,1905(BK N.pg.505)They were married by the
                      Rev.Brown,son of the minister who m.Rufus and
                      Laura.  G.A.and Jenny had 3 children and made
                      their home on the "Old Cage Place".
                      a)Laura Raworth m.T.W. Walsh .Lives in Baton
                         Rouge,La.
                      b)Helen Rawarth m.Stewart B. Curry .Lives in
                         Woodville,Ms. Has Rufus Jeter/Geter Bible.
                      c)George Raworth
                   4.Mary S. Geter b. 1883
                   5.Nellie Geter m. Alec K.Farrar 1907
                   6.William Geter b. 1887
                   7.Rufus Geter b. 1888
                   8.Frances Geter b. 1990

        BRANNON ,BENJAMIN W.b.May 1862,m.Oct.6,1886 to Lydia
                   Netterville b. Sept.1863.(5 children in 1900
                   census)
                   1.Benjamin J. Brannon b. July 1889
                   2.Anthony Brannon b. June 1891
                   3.Edna E.Brannon b. Oct.1893 m.Oct.26,1915 to
                   J.A. Massey.
```

Harry Scott indicating where the original Thomas Brannon home was once located. Land now owned by Joe and Sherry.

HARRY SCOTT AT FORMER LOCATION OF BRANNON HOME

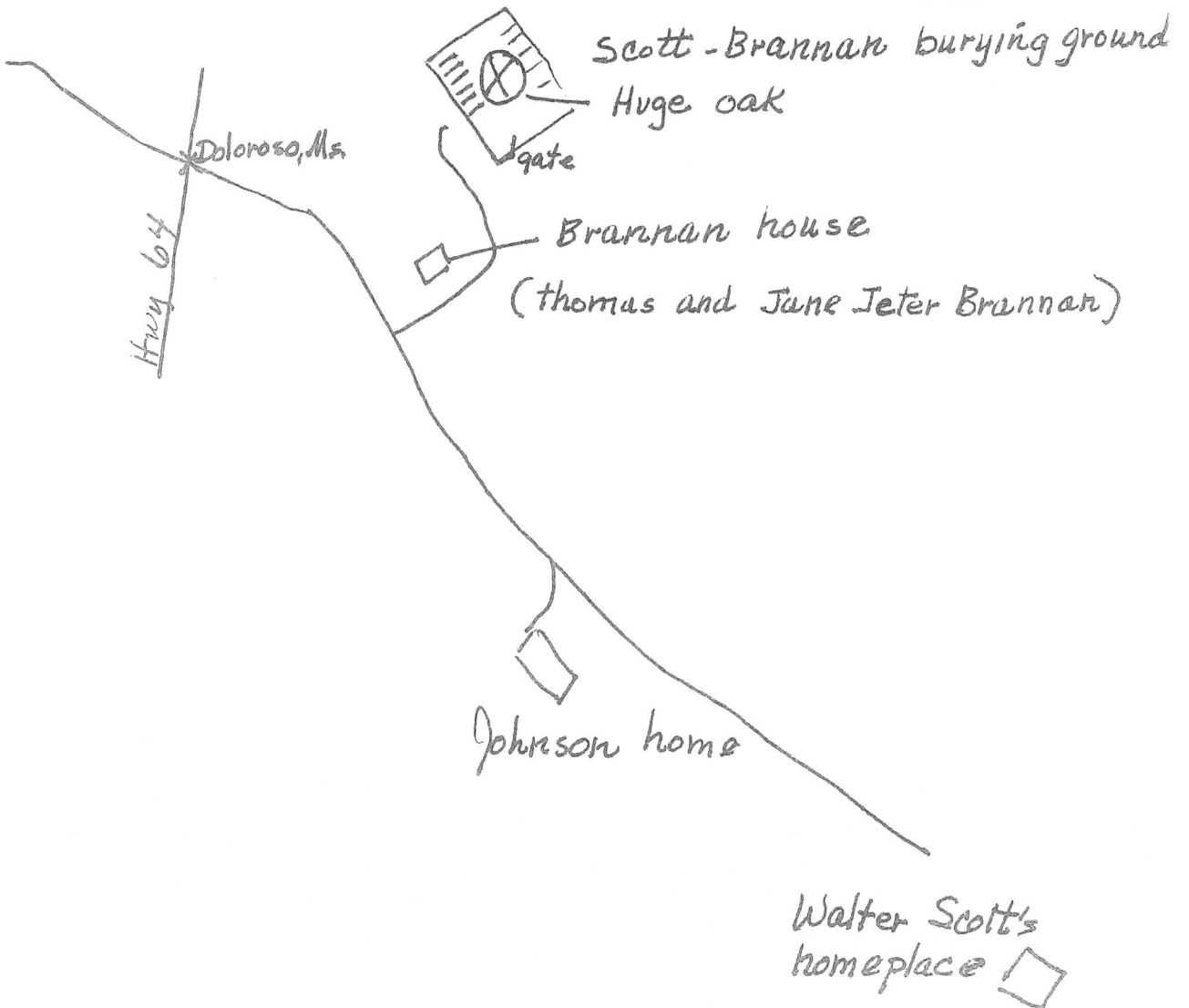

Scott - Brannan burying ground

Huge oak

Doloroso, Ms.

Hwy 64

gate

Brannan house

(thomas and Jane Jeter Brannan)

Johnson home

Walter Scott's homeplace

    4.Lucinda Brannon b. Aug.1896
    5.Anita Brannon b. Oct.1898 m.Aug.22,1923 to Edward
      Carey Corley.

(Davis A. Brannon,Jane and Thomas's oldest son,died before 1900
but was married on Apr.11, 1878 to Mary E.Netterville b.
1854,dau.of R.E.Netterville.In 1900 census,Davis and Mary had two
children.
        1.Viola E.Brannon b.June 1879
        2.David Brannon b.Mar.1881 m.Sept.8,1912 Sallye
          Petty.Mrs.Sallye Brannon was for many years the
          county clerk of Wilkinson County,Ms. In 1979,Mrs.
          Brannon wrote me"...I'm going to photostat copies
          for my husband's cousins that are living,as well as
          the "Ben Brannan" who married a sister to my
          Mother-in-law who was the wife of Davis A.Brannon
          who according to your data was 8 yrs of age in
          1860.They had a daughter who was 13 months old when
          her Father died and she was pregnant with the baby
          that I married.He was named for the Father,David
          Arglass Brannan who has been dead twenty four
          years....I'll be 88 in Nov.and am living alone in
          my home...."

On Aug.16,1878,Jane partitioned the government on behalf of her
husband,Thomas Brannon,Private in the company commanded by
Captain Engles in the War of 1812. His physical description was
as follows: 17 years of age,born in S.C.,a farmer,height 5 feet
and 10 inches ,dark brown hair and grey eyes.She stated that she
was married May 1,1851 by H.R. Davis JP.Also,since Thomas had
died near Cold Springs on Sept.3,1864 ,she desired a widow's
pension.

CHILD #5: LUCINDA JETER b.1823 m. ? Womack (BK G.pg.11)
CHILD #6: ELIZABETH JETER b.L825 m.Mar.4,1841(BK G,pg.86) to
Henry William Scott b. 1820 Fairfield Co.S.C.Henry's father,
William Scott was neighbor to the Parhams in Catahoula
Parish,La.The area is still known as the "Parhams
Community"Elizabeth and Henry had 3 children.
    a)THOMAS J.SCOTT b.1841,d.in Civil War.
    b.ARGLASS WILLIAM SCOTT b.April 15,1852 d.Dec.31,1941
      m.Sarah Rebecca Holmes,b.Oct.18,1852 d.Feb.3,1941.Sarah
      was the daughter of Phoeix Holmes and Nancy Donnelly.
      (8 children)
      1.Girl stillborn
      2.Harry Scott (Henry) b. 1876 d.1895 Waco,Tx.while
        visiting Holmes relatives.
      3.SAMUEL SCOTT b.May 1879 d.July 15,1942 m.Vivian Ione
        DeLoach .
      4.DAVIS SCOTT b.Dec.1880 m.Hattie E.Harper Floyd.Both
        Hattie and her stillborn baby are buried in Waco,Tx.

94

5. MAJOR JAMES SCOTT b.Apr.5,1883 d.Jan.2,1941 m.Belvia
   Olevia Johnson.
6. HOWARD WILLIAM SCOTT b.Sept.5,1884 d. Dec.7,1955 m.
   Elizabeth Bunch.
7. MARY (Mamie) SCOTT b.Jan.20,1886,d.Nov.17,1920 m.Henry
   Davis.
8. WALTER T.SCOTT b.July 29,1891 d. Oct.18,1959 m.Mary
   Jane Dawson.
   c) MAJOR E.SCOTT b. 1862 d. 1882-83.m.Ida Isabell Bryant
   (grandaughter of Caleb C.Swayze) Ida m.2nd Nov.15,1894
   to J.S.Cobb.

CHILD #7:MARTHA MATILDA JETER b.ca 1823 Land record(BK G,p.734)

CHILD #8 ARGLESS WILLIAM JETER/GETER b.1830 SC,d.May 25,1892
Wilkinson Co.Ms.m Feb.27,1856 to Catherine Audrey Parham b.1840
Parham Community,Catahoula Parish,La. and d.1820 in Wilkinson
Co.Ms..They were married by Rev.T.A.Routon,Minister(Witnesses:
F.Ruth,John W.Scott and S.L. Land.Catherine's father,Peterson
G.Parham was b. in Va. and her mother,Sarah A. Kilsey was b. in
Ga. Peterson and Sarah m.Dec.26,1828 Wilkinson Co.Ms.(BK E,pg.74)
The 1900 census states that Argless and Catherine had 10
children.(William Herman,Arglass P.,Elizabeth,Fredrick Hayes,
Henry Pickney,Dulcie R.,Sarah,Mary Ellen, and twins,Luther and
Bobbie).However, by 1900,only 4 were living.Henry Pickney,and two
grandchildren,Leona B.Curtin and Grover C. Curtin were members of
the household #42.These children were Doris Carter's half brother
and sister.
   a) WILLIAM HERMAN GETER b.1863,d.July 1896 of pneumonia.
      m.Nov.25,1886 to Hattie J. Curtin.(4 children)
         1. ALMA GETER.m.Eddie Davis
         2. VIRGINIA GETER
         3. HERMAN GETER
         4. WHITNEY GETER m.   Flavia (2 children)
            a) Whitney GeterJr.
            b) Marion Geter

   b) ARGLASS P.GETER b.1869 d.before 1900.m.Ella Archie May
      23,1889 (BK M.pg.222)(2 children)
         1. EDNA MAE GETER b.1889 m.Charlie Haag. Dec.30,1912
            (BK.O,pg.230.)
         2. LEO ARGLASS GETER b.1891 m.Emilie Leake June 11,1916

            a) LEO ARGLASS GETER JR.b.Apr.19,1917,d.Dec.30,1980 m.
            Jan.9,1947 Ardis Carter.
               1. Ann Marie Geter m. Mr.Rosso
               2. Jerry Leo Geter m.Joette Denise Gonsoulin July
                  19,1980,dau. of Mr.& Mrs.Joseph Charles
                  Gonsoulin.
            Leo died and Ardis m.Cliff Cobb

b)HENRY LEE GETER

c)MARY ELLA GETER m.1st Calvin Berry
   (2 children)
   Mary m.2nd Dorsey Trevillion
d)KATHERINE GETER m.1st Jimmy Rodgers
   (1 child)
   Katherine m.2nd.   Story
e)ALEC BOYD GETER m.Bernice Carter
   1.Alec Boyd Geter Jr.
   2.Robert Geter
e)WILLIAM BOYD d.young

c)ELIZABETH JANE (Bessie)GETER b. 1873 m.1st Oct.7,1890
  (BK pg.159)to J.W.Curtin.
   1.Leona Curtin b. April 1892
   2.Grover C.Curtin b.April 1893
   In 1900,both children were living with grandparents.
   Elizabeth m.2nd Oct.6,1890 (BK N.pg.236) to William James
   (Will) Carter,brother to Lewis Carter who married Mary
   Holmes.Jim and Lewis's father was John Carter.
   3.JUDSON CARTER died at 3 months.
   4.LEE CARTER died at 4 years.

   5.MONA DORIS CARTER b.Mar.11,1911 m.W.Vernan Carter
     b.Sept.16,1903 d.Mar.22,1978.W.Vernam was the son of
     Isaac Carter and Mary Carter and grandson of Isaac
     Abraham Carter and Martha Jane Netterville.Isaac A.
     and Martha J. were married May 6,1878(BL.pg.408).
     Isaac and Mary are listed as Family #285 in the 1900
     census,and were newlyweds.

     a)WILLIAM VERNAN CARTER JR.b.Dec.23,1927 m.Edith
       Reece b. Dec.22,1928.
        1.Dorothy Loraine Carter b. June 29,1949
          m.Roger Craine b.
           a)Dorothy Laverne Craine b.
           Dorothy,Roger and 15 months old Dorothy
           Laverne were killed in an automobile
           accident on Mar.22, 1978.
        2.Mona Laverne Carter b. Mar.31,1953 m.Warren
          Wood Whitaker b. Oct.31,
           a)Mona Lynn Whitaker b. Oct.20,1970
           b)Lacy Ann Whitaker b. July 23,1980
           c)Warren Wood Whitaker Jr. b. June 29,1981

     b)MARY ELIZABETH CARTER b.Sept.7,1929 m.Henry
       Parham Geter b. Mar.24,1924,d.1949 in an
       accident.Henry P.was the son of Henry Parham
       Geter Sr.and Eunice McGraw.
        1.William Parham Geter b.Feb.5,1949
        2.Henry Parham Geter III b. Feb.9,1950

96

In July ,1982,while visiting Doris, I was told a sweet and gentle story that her mother had told her.
"Mother and Mr.Jim Curtin lived in the old Curtin home.When her mother,Elizabeth Jane Gerter,was married to her first husband,Jim Curtain,Doris's mother was called "Bessie".

Her Grandma Curtain,(Bessie's mother-in-law)would say,"Bessie,now don't get scared now,but you're going to see Old John Curtain come out yonder and hang his clothes on that fence".
Her mother said they'd be sitting out on the porch and Grandma Curtain would say,"Yes,he'll be here in a few minutes...(this would be her husband)to hang his clothes out."Doris's mother said she never did see him but Grandma Curtain always did.She always wondered if the poor old soul imagined that she saw him or if she really DID see him.

Bessie never did say anything to hurt her feelings but Grandma would say"Just watch Bessie,John has a WHOLE TUB of clothes to hang out".

Doris's parents met at a dance at Grandpa Geter's house. Bessie had married a Curtain and Jim had married a Rabb.Jim's wife,Elizabeth E.Rabb had died in childbirth leaving him with three children who were raised by Grandma Rabb.Jim told Doris that Bessie was his "first" love.They had met and married each other after both spouses had gone.

    d) FREDRICK HAYES GETER b.Apr.1875 m.Nov.3,1898 to
       Amanda Rabb b. Feb,1882.(BK L.pg.408)
        1.HENRY PICKNEY GETER m.Littie Ogden July 29,1919
         (BK.O,pg.364)
           a)HENRY PICKNEY GETER JR. m.Eula Sanders
             1.Mary Geter
             2.Dolly Geter
             3.Hazel Geter
             4.Jane Geter
             5.Leroy Geter
           b)MABEL GETER m. 1st Leonard Nettles
             1.BETTY JEAN NETTLES m. Lawrence Kyser
               (2 children)
             2.EVA MAE NETTLES
               (2 children)
             3.J.B.NETTLES m.Mildred Rodgers
               a)Rodgers Nettles
               b)Charles Nettles
               c)Frances Nettles
               d)Bonnie Nettles
               e)Jennings Nettles
               f)Brenda Nettles
               g)Linda Nettles

4.GLEN BOYCE "SONNY" NETTLES b.1940 d.May 4,
   1983 m.Virginia Carver.
     a)Robbin G.Nettles
     b)Keith Nettles
     c)Redina Nettles Graham
     d)Michelle Denise Nettles
   Mabel m.2nd.to William Versie Thompson

c)CLIFFORD AUBREY GETER b.Feb.22,1912, d.Apr.26,
   1983.m.Etta Sanders,dau.of Malva Nettles and
   Dennis Sanders.
     1.Dennis Aubrey Geter d.Aug.14,1967 m.Geraldine
       Netterville.
       (2 children)
     2.William Lee Geter m.Ernestine Westberry
       (4 children)
     3.Freddie Geter m.Erline Roberts
     4.Cecil Geter m.   Walker
     5.Louise Geter m.Alvester McKlemurry
     6.Mary Katherine Geter Moak
     7.Margaret Ann Geter Murray

d)CLINTON GETER m.Mildred Vines .Clinton and
   Mildred had three sets of twins.
     1.Shirley Geter m.Thomas Velter
     2.Barbara Geter m. Sonny Brown
     3&4 died
     5.Donald Geter
     6.Ronald Geter
e)EDNA GETER m.Jim Nettles

f)DULCIE GETER m.1st Herman Temple
   (2 children)
   Dulcie m.2nd Delcy Ray Merritt
   (5 children)
   Dulcie was reared by Bessie Geter Carter

e)HENRY PARHAM GETER b.July 21,1879,d. Sept.11,1946 m.1st to
   Kate A.Carter on June 30,1905 (BK N,pg.508).
     1.LEV MAGRUDER GETER b.June 20,1906 d.Feb.28,1960
       m.Bernice Leake
         a)LYDIA ANN GETER m.July 1980 Jack Hude III,son of
           Jack Hude Jr.and Mrs. Wm.Barton Swinny.

Henry m.2nd Feb.11,1915 (BK O,pg.230) to Eunice McGraw
b.July 4,1892,d.Feb.11,1968.
     2.ARGLASS WILLIAM (DOC) GETER b.Apr.16,1916 m.Jewel
       Alma Roudolph.
         a)ROUDOLPH (RUDY) WAYNE GETER b.1941-42 m.Rosie

```
        b)RODNEY GETER (MD) m.Caroline Doll
            1.John Geter
            2.Curtis Geter
            3.Kay Geter
        c)JUDITH LYNN GETER b.Sept.3,1948 d.Nov.17,1983 m.
          Tom Lavin MD.
        d)KERRY ANN GETER m Henry Mertz
            1.Tracy Mertz
            2.Mellisa Mertz
            3.Henry Mertz Jr.
        e)CARYE GETER  m.Shawn

3.JIMMY V. (Sook) GETER b.Jan.10,1918 m.Theodore Leake

4.ADRIAN GETER b.Feb.14,1919

5.KATHERINE (TOOTSIE) GETER b.Apr.24,1921 m.G.J.Mahaney
        a)MARTHA MAHANEY  m.Ray Gardill
        b)MICHAEL GETER MAHANEY  m.Carrie
            1.Rachel Mahaney
6.GORDON (BUD)GETER b. 1923 d.Mar.26,1982 m.May 26,1946
  Phyllis Vasquez.
        a)KATHLEEN GETER m.1st Ron Hensarling
            1.John David Hensarling
            2.Robin Hensarling
            3.Brian Hensarling
        Kathaleen m.2nd to Dan Daley

        b)ELLA SUSAN GETER b. Aug.3,1948 m.R.E.Roddy
          Simmons b.June 1968
            1.Jennifer Ann Simmons
            2.R.E.Simmons III
            3.Jonathan Gordon Simmons

        c)GORDON LOUIS (BUBBA)GETER b.Aug.21,1957
          m.Aug.17,1979 Evelyn Robertson.
            1.Gordon Joseph Geter b. Mar.23,1981
            2.David Brandon Geter b. Nov.30,1985

        d)PHYLLIS LEISA (SISSIE) GETER b.Aug.21,1957
          twin to Gordon Louis,m.1st Mike Ingram.
            1.Benjamin Drew Ingram b.Jan.5,1982
          Phyllis m.2nd Paul Boteler
            2.Christopher Kyle Boteler b. Dec.2,1984

7.HENRY PARHAM GETER b. Mar.21,1925 m.Mary Carter,
  b.Sept.7,1929.dau.of Mona Doris Carter and William
  Vernan Carter.Henry Parham died 1949 in an
  accident.
        a)WILLIAM PARHAM GETER b. Feb.5,1949
        b)HENRY PARHAM GETER III b.Feb.9,1950
```

f)DULCIE R. GETER m.William L. Hayes Jan.28,1875 (BK L,pg. 330)
William was Chancery Clerk of Wilkinson Co. for many years.
  1.BELL HAYES m.Tom Wood
      a)TOM WOOD JR.
      b)CLYDE WOOD m.Dottie Steele
          1.Dorothy Gayle Wood m.W.R. Spell Jr.
            a)Brian Spell
            b)Melissa Spell
  2.KATE HAYES m.Josh Billings
      a)RUTH BILLINGS m.John Cortelyou
  3.LILLIAN HAYES m.L.T. Ventress
      a)JAMES ALEXANDER VENTRESS m.Ann Catchings
  4.JOHN T. HAYES
  5.ANNIE IRION HAYES
  6.
  7.
g)SARAH GETER

h)MARY ELLEN GETER

i)BOBBY GETER

j)LUTHER GETER (twin to Bobby)

CHILD #9: EUGENIA (UGENIA) JETER :No information available other than her father's will.

CHILD #10: DAVIS JETER :No information available other than his father's will.

PHOENIX (PHINEAS)G.HOLMES b.1819 Ms.d.after 1880 m.Nov.23,1849
    Nancy Donnelly b. 1830,d.after 1880.(MB 1,pg.34,Wilkinson
    Co.Ms)dau of Nancy Atisberry and William Donnelly.

    Phoenix's father was born in Tenn.,and absolute proof of
    his name is unknown at the present time.Rebecca,the mother,
    was b.1790 Ms.m 2nd Feb.19,1829 to Williamn Haslip(Hazlip)
    in Adams Co.Ms..Rebecca and Wm.combined two families in
    this marriage and also produced a son,Samuel W.Hazlip in
    1832.

    According to William's will that was filed Mar.11,1845,he
    named his Wife Rebecca and released to her all the property
    she owned at the time of their marriage and also gave her
    the sum of $500.00.

    To John Hazlip,$50,to Nancy Wood,Charlotte Galtry,Mary Rabb
    and Eveline Haslip,$100.00 each. All other possessions were
    to go to his youngest son,SAMUEL W.HAZLIP.

    William also mentioned that "The negro boy,Jack,is the
    property of the heirs of Thomas Holmes,dec'd,as he was
    bought with their money".He named Wiley Wood and John Hazlip
    as guardians of Samuel.

    In the census of 1850,Wilkinson Co.Ms.,Rebecca Haslip was
    listed as the head of the family.Phoenix and Nancy H.were
    newly married and living with Rebecca along with Minerva,28,
    who later m.Joseph Byes,Sametrus(Samuel)18,and Theadore,5.

    In Rebecca's will of 1852,she gave her negro man Squire to
    her grandson,Theadore.To her daughter,Minerva Bias,her
    cherry bedstead and side saddle.Her other household items,
    stock of cattle,hogs and horses were to be sold and the
    proceeds were to be equally divided between daughters Eliz-
    beth Ford,Sarah Chandler,Emmeline Holmes,and Minerva Bias.

    She gave her son,Phoenix G.Holmes $5.00 and to her grandson
    Thomas W.Holmes(son of Phoenix)$100.00.To her grandchildren
    Eugenia J.and Sardinia S.Holmes,children of her son R.S.C.
    Holmes dec'd,$2.00 each.To her grandson William H.Campbell,
    she gave $4.00.She also left her clock to her son Samuel

    Last,her "esteemed friend",John J.Chandler was named as her
    executor.

101

Holmes

Family #321:Chandler,John J.Chandler   56
                    ,Virginia R.   11
              Bias,Minerva   44
            Holmes,Theodore   13
                   ,Eudoria   6
                   ,Menia   1
(John was the husband of Phoenix's sister,Sarah Chandler)

    #322:   Wood,Wiley M.   83   b.Tenn.
                 ,William N.   57
                 ,David H.   21   b.Ms.
                 ,Douglas   19   b.Ms.
           Gibson,James   28   b.Tenn
                 ,Mary   23   b.Ms.
          Hazelip,M.(Miss)   48   b.Ms.
             Ford,Robert   12   b.Ms

    #323:   Scott,H.W.   40   b.S.C.
                  ,Eliz.   34   b.Ms.
                  ,Thomas J. 19   b.Ms.

    #330: Hazlip,Sarah W.   28   b.Ms.
                ,Martha   23   b.Ms.
                ,Mary   3   b.Ms.
                ,Lilla   2   b.Ms.
                ,Wm.F.   1   b.Ms.
*****   SCOTT,A.W.   8   b.Ms.
    (Arglass William Scott was to marry Sarah Holmes
    in 1876.He was the son of H.W.Scott,#323)

          HOLMES,P.G.   40   b.Ms.
        Donnelly,Sarah   57   b.Ms.
          Holmes,Nancy   30   b.Ms.
                ,Thos.W.   9   b.Ms.
*****   ,SARAH   7   b.Ms.
                ,Amanda   6   b.Ms.
                ,Wm.F.   4   b.Ms.
    (Sarah Donnelly was the mother of Nancy)
        Hornsby,Wm.(F,T?)   4   b.Ms.

    #334: Hazlip,Samuel   28   b.Ms..
                ,Martha   23   b.Ms.
                ,Mary   3   b.Ms.
                ,Lilla   2   b.Ms.
                ,Wm.J.   1   b.Ms.
    (Phoenix's half brother)

                        102

```
#337:  Holmes,Wm.A.            47      b.Ms.
        ,Emeline               48      b.Ms.
        ,Wm.H.                 20      b.Ms.
        ,Maria                 18      b.Ms.
        ,Elizabeth             16      b.Ms.
        ,Rufus                 14      b.Ms.
        ,Alice                  7      b.Ms.
    (Emeline was Phoenix's sister mentioned in the mother's
    will)


Wilkinson Co.Ms. COLD SPRINGS District Beat 4 1870 Census

Family #241    Haslip,S.W.(Samuel) 38    b.Ms.
                ,Mary L.           32    b.Ms.
                ,Mattie             7    b.Ms.
                ,Samuel             4    b.Ms.
                ,John N(or W)       3    b.Ms.
                ,Babe            1/12    b.Ms.
                ,Martha            32    b.Ms.
    (Last record found of Samuel's family in Wilkinson,Co.)



            Haslip,Eveline        58    b.Ms.
                (With Douglas Wood family)

# 242    Holmes, Emeline         58    b.Ms.
          ,Maria L.              28    b.Ms.
          ,Rufus                 24    b.Ms.
          ,Alice                 17    b.Ms.
          ,Theodore              23    b.Ms.
    (Emeline,widow of Wm.A.and also sister to Phoenix)


Wilkinson Co.Ms.COLD SPRINGS District Beat 4 1880 Census

Family #25    Felter,Elison A.    63
               ,Benjamin A.       29
               ,Susan             17
               ,June S.           15
               ,W.A.              11
               ,Alice              9
               ,Nancy              8
               ,Rosa E.            6
               ,Elison          2/12
    (Ellison A.Felter m.Mary Ann Roddy Oct.1,1849.It
    appears that she had died since the baby was born.
    History would repeat itself with the death of her
    daughter,Prudy on Oct.11, 1899 after giving birth
    to her baby,David).
```

```
Family #26        HOLMES,WM.F.        23        b.Ms.
                  ,Prudy             22        b.Ms.

   #31            Holmes,P.G.        63        b.Ms.   Tenn.  Ms.
                  ,Nancy             50        b.Mo.   Mo.    Ms.
                  ,Amanda            26        b.Ms.
                  ,Mary M.           18        b.Ms.
                  ,Elizabeth         12        b.Ms.
                  ,Francis (Frank)  9        b.Ms.

    #73           SCOTT,ARGLUS W.    28        b.Ms.   Ms.    Ms.
                  ,Sallie            28        b.Ms.   Ms.    Ms.
                  ,Henry(Harry)       4        b.Ms.   Ms.    Ms.
                  ,Samuel(Sam)        1        b.Ms.   Ms.    Ms.


    #77           SCOTT,HENRY H.     60        b.SC    SC     SC
                  ,Elizabeth         55        b.Ms.   SC     Ms.
                  ,M.E.(Major)       17        b.Ms.   SC     Ms.

    #81           EVERETT,W.T.       22        b.Ms.   Ms.    Ms.
(William T.Everett  m.Amanda Holmes in 1886 and moved to
McLennan .Co.Tex..His father, Dr.T.J.Everett,had left Amite
Co.Ms.after the Civil War and practiced in McLennan Co.
until his death in 1892)


Wilkinson Co.Ms.COLD SPRINGS District Beat 4 1900 Census

Family #3         Farrar,T.H.        56        b.Ms.
                  ,Ella C.           45        b.Ms.
                  ,Alex K.           20        b.Ms.
                  ,Mary H.           19        b.Ms.
                  ,Thornton H.       15        b.Ms.
                  ,Ann W.            12        b.Ms.
                  ,BENJ.F.           10        b.Ms.
                  ,Henry E.           8        b.Ms.
(Benj.F.Farrar m.Amanda Carter,the dau.of Mary M.Holmes
  and Lewis Christopher Carter.Descendents in Waco,Tex.)


   #15            STURGEON,JOHN      42        b.Ms.
                  ,ELIZABETH         31        b.Ms.
                  ,Blanche           10        b.Ms.
                  ,Eugene             8        b.ms.
                  ,Hartsel            4        b.Ms.
                  ,Horace             1        b.Ms.

         (John m.Elizabeth Holmes in 1883)
```

```
#187        SCOTT,ARGLESS W.    47      b.Ms.
            ,Sarah R.           47      b.Ms.
            ,Samuel(Sam)        21      b.Ms.
            ,David(Dave)        19      b.Ms.
            ,Major              17      b.Ms.
            ,Howard             15      b.Ms.
            ,Mary(Mamie)        13      b.Ms.
            ,Walter              8      b.Ms.

#207        HOLMES,FRANK J.     29      b.Ms.
            ,Lula E.            26      b.Ms.
            ,David               4      b.Ms..
            ,Leon                2      b.Ms.

#208        HOLMES,WILLIAM      45      b.Ms.
            ,Chester            15      b.Ms.
            ,Nannie             13      b.Ms.
            ,Karie              11      b.Ms.
            ,Everette            9      b.Ms.
            ,Hellin              5      b.Ms.
            ,Davis            8/12      b.Ms
        (Many descendents of William F.Holmes are living
        around the community of Crawford,Tex.,about 30 miles
        west of Waco.)
```

McLennan Co.Texas 1900 Census Sup.Dist.#9 Speegleville Village

```
Family #189   EVERETT,WILLIAM   42      b.Ms.
              ,Amanda           39      b.Ms.
              ,Thomas           13      b.Ms.
              ,Charlie          11      b.Ms.
              ,Euell             2      b.Ms.
```

Wilkinson Co.Ms.1910 Census Beat 4 ,Apr.16,Friendship Road

```
.Family #4            STURGEON,JOHN (S.) 52 m.26 yrs.
                      ,Lizzie       41 12 ch. 8 liv.
                      ,Blanche      20
                      ,Eugene       18
                      ,Hartsell     13
                      ,Horace       11
                      ,Kate          9
                      ,Alonzo        7
                      ,Mary          5
                      ,Elmo        1yr.6mo.
        (John and Lizzie lived all their lives in the same
        home.The "Old Sturgeon Home" is still owned by
        their descendents. They are buried in the HOLMES
        burying ground on Hwy 65 east of Hwy 61 south.)
```

```
#15        CARTER,LOUIS      42   m.19 yrs.
                ,Mary       47   3 ch. 2 liv.
                ,Manda      16
                ,Casey       4
           HOLMES,LULA       35 sis.-in-law wd.5 ch.3 liv.
                ,Dave       14
                ,Lizzie      6
                ,Mary        3
```
(Lula would later move to Waco,Texas along with
Louis and Mary and would remarry.Their descendents
are still in Texas)

```
#94        SCOTT,SAM         30 m.8 yr.
                ,Viva       26 5 ch.5 liv.
                ,Gladys      7
                ,John        5
                ,Hubert E.   4
                ,MITTIE      2
                ,Carroll    4/12
```
(Sam and Vivi moved to Mound,La.where he was a
logger.Three more children were born and then
they seperated.Vivi went to New Orleans and Sam
stayed in Mound.Mittie boarded with families in
order to stay in school.

```
#100       SCOTT,HOWARD      25 m.3 yrs. 2 ch.
                ,Lizzie     19
                ,Harry       2
                ,Nolan      1yr.8 mo.

#101       SCOTT,SALLIE      54 wd. 7 ch. 6 liv.
                ,Dave       28 wd. (3 ch. 2 liv.)
                ,Walter     17
                ,Tom         5 (grandson)
                ,Dorris      3 (grandaughter)
```
(Sallie and Argulass's oldest son Henry(Harry) had
died in 1897 in Waco,Texas of spinal meningitis
while visiting his Aunt Amanda and Uncle William
Everett. Dave's wife ,Hattie Harper Floyd,had died
in childbirth while they,too,were living in Texas.
Both Hattie and baby were buried together .)

```
#102       DAVIS,WILLIAM H.  33  m.4 yrs. 2 ch.
                ,MAMIE (MARY) 21
                ,Lawrence    2
                ,Addie       1 yr. 3 mo.
```

PHOENIX (Phineas)G.HOLMES b 1819 Ms. d.after 1880.m.Nov.23,
    1849,to Nancy Donnelly b.1830,d.after 1880.(MB 1,pg.34,
    Wilkinson Co.Ms.) dau.of Nancy Ellsberry and William
    Donnelly.(7 children)
1.THOMAS W.HOLMES b.1851 d.before 1870

2.SARAH REBECCA HOLMES b. Oct.18,1852,d.Feb.3,1941,m.
    Feb.8,1876(MB L,p.331 Wilkinson Co.Ms.)to Argulass
    Scott b. Apr.15,1852,d.Dec.31,1906,son of Henry W.
    Scott and Elizabeth Jeter.(8 children)See SCOTT
    information,child #3)

3.AMANDA ELIZABETH HOLMES b.Aug.1855 d.1928,m.April 4,1886
    Wilkinson Co.(MB M,pg.98)Wm.T.Everett,b.Aug.1857
    son of Dr.T.J.Everett .(see 1880 Census #81)(3 sons)
    Amanda and Wm.buried in Chapel Hill Cemetery,Waco.Tx.

    a)TOM JEFFERSON EVERETT b. Jan.3,1887 d.June 29,1958.
      m.Gertie Carter b.Nov.27,1884,d.Dec.28,1951,both
      buried in the Pioneer Baptist Church Cemetery at
      Doloroso,Ms.

    b)CHARLIE EVERETT b.Dec.29,1888 d.Aug.2,1976 m.Dora
      McClelland in McLennan County.Dora b.May 12,1895,d.July
      26,1975.Both buried in Waco Memorial Cemetery.

    c)EUALL EVERETT b.Dec.5,1897 d. Sept.4,1976,m.1919 to
      Mettie McClelland. Mettie b.June 20,1898 and is a sister
      to Dora. Both were dau.of Otis Ocar McClelland and
      Rachel Tazewell who came from Illinois and settled in
      the Crawford community.Euall buried in the Waco Memorial
      Cemetery.The McClellands in Crawford Cemetery.

The Everett men and several of their cousins were
accomplished musicians. For many years,the music of their
guitars,violins,and mandolins floated out through the
airwaves around the Waco area.

Their string band was known as the TOM CATS and played
regularly on radio station W A C O twice a week,on
Wednesday and Saturday.

At one time,the radio station held a contest to see how
far the air waves carried their music.The winner lived in
east Texas,close to the state of Louisana.

"Cousins": Charlie,Major
Scott,Euall,Tom and Eugene
Sturgeon. Waco,Texas

Mettie McClelland Everett

Charlie,Dora,Euell,Mettie,Tom and Gertie.Photo made
at Alonzo (Lonnie) Sturgeon's home,Doloroso,Ms.

pg. 107-1

4.WILLIAM F. HOLMES b.Jan.1855,d.Aug.6,1928 m.Jan.20,1880
    W.A. Felter 's home in Doloroso,Ms.to Prudy Felter,b.1856
    d. Oct.11,1899,Wilkinson,Co.Ms.dau. of Elison A.Felter and
    Mary Ann Roddy who were m.Oct.1,1849(see census #25,1880)
    (8 children)
  a) FANNIE HOLMES b.& d.Aug.1882
  b) CHESTER HOLMES b.Mar.1885 d. Paris Tex. 1953-54.
    m.1st to Lenner Hogan (1 child)
    1.LONNIE HOLMES b.   d. 1980
      (Adopted by Will George of McGregor,Tx.)
    m.2nd to Lula McDonald Dec.1,1925 who d.1934
      (Twin boys)
    2.DAROLD SUFORD(Pete) HOLMES b. June 21,1928 m.1950 to
      Sadie Irene Moore b.Jan.3,1930 of Powderly,Tx.dau.
      of Dyer Moore and Ellen Morris.(1 child)
      a)NANCY GAIL HOLMES b. Aug.14,1956 m.Brandt Dickey
        b.Feb..21,1954,son of Dorothy and Charles Dickey.
        (2 children)
        1.LAURA ELLEN DICKEY b.May 19,1981
        2.LYDIA CAROL DICKEY b. Sept.4,1984

    3.HAROLD BUFORD(Jack) HOLMES b. June 21, 1928 m.Helen
    Newman dau. of Griffin and Cleo Newman of Minter,Tx
      (1 child)
      a)DONNA KAY HOLMES b. 1955 m. Randy Meeks
        (3 children)
        1.JENNIFER PAIGE MEEKS
        2.JUSTIN MEEKS
        3.SARAH MEEKS

  c)NANNIE M. HOLMES b. Aug.31,1886 d.Feb.4,1972,m. June
    23,1912 to Neal Shillings b Sept.10,1891,d.Mar.29,
    1975 (2 children)
    1.baby
    2.BONNIE SHILLINGS b.Nov.16,1915 m.July 14,1936 to
      Hershal Ray Gassaway b.Sept.6,1913,d.Aug.6,1984,
      son of O.L.Gassaway and Cora Lee Bankhead of Bolling
      Green,Ky.(1 child)
      a)CLYDE RAY GASSAWAY b.Sept.21,1938 m.Apr.21,1968
        to Patsy Louise Jones ,b.July 2,1939,dau.of Thurman
        Jones and Lillie Mae McCarver .(2 children)
        1.MICHAEL (Mike) TIMOTHY GASSAWAY b.July 2,1958
          m.Feb.12,1984 to Karen Ashley b.Mar.1984,dau of
          Mr.& Mrs.Jim Ashley.
        b)CHRISTOPHER CHAD GASSAWAY b.June 13,1969

  d) KEARIE HOLMES b.Aug.1889 d.May 9,1909 (measles)

  e)EVERETT L.HOLMES b. Jan.15,1893 d.Mar.12,1947
    m.Dec.27,1914 to Alma Bost ,b.Aug.27,1895,d.Nov.1977
    dau. of Robert Bost and Margaret Adella Graves.
    (11 children)

1.ROBERT WILLIAM HOLMES b. Apr.21,1916 d.Feb.25,1978
  m.Nov.12,1938 to Annie Lee Alexander at Patton,Tx.
  in the home of Carl and L.Z.Jaynes home.(2 children)
  Annie is the dau.of Lottie Maddox.
  a)LYNDA JEAN HOLMES b.Mar.14,1946,m.Jan.30,1965 to
    Stan Mitchael.(2 children)
    1.GAYLE LYNN MITCHAEL b. Oct.10,1966
    2.CHRISTIE LEA MITCHAEL b.Dec.28,1972
  b)TONY LAY HOLMES b. Aug.12,1958

2.HAZEL MARY HOLMES b. Sept.9,1918 McLennan Co.Tx.
  m.Jan.7,1938 McGregor,Tx.to Claude Brown Hawkins
  b.Oct.26,1909,d.Apr.1987,son of John Hawkins of
  China Springs,Tx.and Annie Brown of Crawford.
  (2 children)
  a)MARY LaJUANA HAWKINS b. Aug.7,1940 Waco,Tx.m.
    June 27,1958 to Billie Carl Westerfield b.Aug.14,
    1939,son of Carl and Rosemary Pollard Westerfield
    of Oglesby,Tx.(2 children)

    1.GINGER KAY WESTERFIELD b. Feb.2,1960 Clifton,Tx.
      m.Jerrell Martin,son of William Harold Martin
      and Peggy Miles Martin.(2 children)
      a)SHANDA NICOLE MARTIN b.Feb.1,1980
      b)BETHANI JO MARTIN b.July 23,1982
    2.LANE WESTERFIELD b. July 16, 1968

  b)ARLEEN GAIL HAWKINS b.Sept.8,1951 m.Dec.8,1973 in
    Crawford,Tx.to William Bays Atkins III b.Dec.8,
    1951,son of William Bays Atkins Jr.and Lanell Dale
    Turner of Fort Worth,Tx.(2 children)
    1.BRADY GARRETT ATKINS b.Dec.7,1978
    2.ASHLEY KATHERINE ATKINS b.Oct.14,1981

3.WAYNE(Red)STERLING HOLMES b. Oct.25,1920 m.Sept.22,
  1945 Toledo,Ohio to Mary E.O'Connor b.Oct.7,1919
  Toledo,dau.of Michael J.O'Connor and Laura Bior.
  (5 children)
  a)KATHLEEN ANN HOLMES b.June 24,1946 m.Nov.7,1968 to
    Arthur Lee Gibbs.b.Sept.10,1947,son of James
    R.Gibbs and Mary Thomas (2 children)
    1.MARK R.GIBBS b.May 21,1970
    2.CHRISTOPHER GIBBS b.Nov.28,1972

  b)CAROLYN MARIE HOLMES b.Dec.12,1949 m.Nov.15,1969
    David M.Lehsten b.Sept.16,1948,son ofJohn Lehsten
    and Margaret McCarthy.
    1.DAVID M.LEHSTEN b.May 12,1969
    2.MATHEW WAYNE LEHSTEN b.Apr.19,1973
    3.LISA M.LEHSTEN b.Apr.6,1970
    4.KATHERINE LYNN LEHSTEN b.July 19,1983

c)MARILYN JEAN HOLMES b.Apr.12,1958 m.Mar.18,1978
Morewci,Mich.to Robert Sloan b.Aug.23,1954,son of
Ray Sloan and Lois Burrow(2 children)
1.DOUGLAS J.SLOAN b.Aug.19,1979
2.DANIEL R.SLOAN b.Dec.19,1984

d)TIMOTHY MICHAEL HOLMES b.Oct.1,1955 m.Aug.1978
Toledo,Ohio to Gail Glenn b Dec 27 ,dau.of Thomas
and Eileen Glenn.
e)GERALD WAYNE HOLMES b.Sept.24,1951 m.Oct.2,1971
Toledo,Ohio to Rebecca J.Thomas b.June 28,1950.
dau. of Albert Thomas and Virginia Wilhelm (1 son)
1.GERALD W.HOLMES b.June 17,1976

4.EARL EVERETTE HOLMES b.Sept.26,1922 m.Aug.11,1945
Waco,Tx.to Dollie Pearl Williams b.April 18,1919 dau.
of Frank Fuller Williams and Corrine Davis.(1 child)
a)Walter S.(Bud)Terry b.Sept.9,1960.Caldwell,Tex.
Foster son.

5.MEARL ALMA HOLMES b.Sept.26,1922 m.May 1945 Crawford
Tex.to Buster Morgan b. April 25,1918 Winters,Tx.
son of Reuben Morgan and Lulu Morgan.Ruben from North
Carolina and Lulu from Indian Gap,Tx.(3 children)

a)DEANNA COONER (2 CHILDREN)
1.AMY ELIZABETH HARRIS b. Oct.16,1979
2.JONATHON BOYD HARRIS b.Aug.18,1972
b)RICKY MORGAN b. Jan.9,1954
c)RANDY MORGAN b. Jan.9,1954(twins)m.Renise Blair
b.Dec.4,1952

6.RAYBORN(Ray)JAMES HOLMES b. May 6,1925 d.Feb.15,1987
m.1st: Thelma Callie Mae Jones . (3 children)

a)PAMELA JANE HOLMES b. Nov.27,1950 Clifton,m.May 16,
1970 Waco,to Donnie Ray Clapp b.   d.Apr.4,
1986,son of Tillman Clapp and Marie Parson from
Potosi,Mo.(2 children)
1.DONNIE RAY CLAPP JR. b. Oct.4,1971
2.CHRISTINIA RENEE CLAPP b.June 11, 1978

b)JAMES RODNEY HOLMES b.Feb.23,1955 m.Oct.23,1978 to
Audrey Denise Carlile b.Aug.24,1957,dau.of Maybelle
Melton and Jim C.Carlile .Maybelle from Bertram and
Jim from Oak Allen Tex.(1 child)
1.VALERIE DENISE HOLMES b. Feb.21,1980

c)PHILLIP ULAS HOLMES b. Jan.12,1963 m.Jan.5,1985 to
Denise Moore b. 1962.

7.EDWIN (Ed)LEE HOLMES b.June 15,1928 m.May 22,1948
  Valley Mills Tex.to Margaret Annell Walker b. Dec.31,
  1928,dau. of Floyd Bruce Walker and Artie Lee
  Honeycutt (1 child)
  a)DON ALLEN HOLMES b.Jan.3,1949 m.June 5,1970 Golinda
    Baptist Church to Debbie Grusendorf b. Aug.3,1951
    dau of JoAnn Hurst & Earl Grusendorf (2 children)
    1.JIMMY DON HOLMES b. May 22, 1971
    2.HOLLY AMANDA HOLMES b.Mar.15,1975

8.BOBBY EUGENE HOLMES b.June 4,1930 m.Dec.9,1949
  Pasadena Tex. to Margaret Ruth Boggs
  b.Jan.4,1930,dau of Rossie LaFaye Boggs and Alice
  Catherine Saunders.(6 children)
  a)MICHAEL WALLACE HOLMES b. Aug.11, 1950 Pasadena
    m.Barbara Mae Thomas (1 child)
    1.MICHAEL LEE HOLMES b. Feb.26,1981
  b)GARY EUGENE HOLMES,b.Oct.23,1952 m.to Lisa Sheppard
    (2 children)
    1.ALLYSON DENISE HOLMES b. Aug.26,1978
    2.CHRISTOPHER NEAL HOLMES b.Mar.26,1982
  c)JOEL DAVID HOLMES b. Feb.14,1956 m.to Maggie
    Gonzales (1 son)
    1.MARCUS GONZALES HOLMES b.Aug.18,1980
  d)ROBERT KEITH HOLMES b.Oct.2,1957 m.Dec.20,1986.to
    Glenda Walker (1 child)
    1.Sarah Walker
  e)JEFFREY SPENCER HOLMES b.May 26,1965 Beaumont
  f)JAMES ANDREW HOLMES b.Oct.10,1966 Beaumont
    (Both Jeffery and James engaged at this moment.)

9.WILLIAM CHARLES HOLMES b. Sept.23,1932 m.Crawford
  Joyce Allyne Pieper b. July 7,1936 dau. of Elsie
  Sandhoff and Edmond Pieper .(2 children)

  a)DAVE KENT HOLMES b. June 8,1956 m.Nov.19,1977 to
    Marla Kay Symank b. July 6,1958 dau of Ervin E.
    Symank and Dorothy L. Schmalriede of McGregor,Tx.
    (2 children)
    1.JILL ELAINE HOLMES b. Nov.24,1983
    2.AMY MICHELE HOLMES b. June 25,1985
  b)SHARON RAE HOLMES b.June 11, 1958 m.Clifton,Tx. to
    Terry Westerfeld b. Nov.18,1958,son of Helene
    Schulte and Ray Westerfeld (1 child)
    1.STACIE RENEE WESTERFELD

10.JOE ALLEN HOLMES b. Aug.1,1934 m.Waco to Louise
   Halford b.Sept.6,1940 dau. of Joe T. Halford and
   Lottie Eliot. (4 children)
   a)DUB ALLEN HOLMES b. July 28,1960 Clifton,Tx.

        b)KIMBERLY KAY HOLMES b. July 4,1962 m.Sept.6,1980
          Crawford,Tx.to Ronnie Buice,son of Barbara Stewart
          and Lawrence Buice.(1 child)
          1.LINDA KAY BUICE b. June 17,1983
        c)GREGORY LOUIS HOLMES b. Sept.8,1968 Clifton,Tx.
        d)SANDY JO HOLMES b. July 11, 1971 Clifton,Tx.

     11.JIMMY WELDON HOLMES b. July 5,1939 m.May 19,1957 to
        Zo Nelda Bond.b.Dec.19,1938 dau. of Ida Bernice
        Morgan and Walter Arlis Bond.(2 children)
        a)DARRELL GLEN HOLMES b. Sept.22, 1959 m.Sept.10,
          1983 to Teddie Lou Belknap b. Oct.11,1961,dau.of
          Gwindle Williams and Wray Belknap.(1 child)
          1.ASHLEY MICHELLE HOLMES b. Feb.21,1986

        b)DANIEL KYLE HOLMES b. June 22, 1962 m.Aug.10,1985
          to Kimberly Wagenschein b. Aug.21,1965,dau. of Paul
          Wagenschein and Mary Alice Parsons.(1 child)
          1.BRITTANY DANIELLE HOLMES b. July 28,1986

  f)HELLEN LOU HOLMES b & d.Jan.15,1893,(twin to Everett L.)

  g)HELLEN LOU HOLMES b.Aug.25,1895 d.July 13,1964 m.Feb.11,
    1912 to Otis Alfred Bost b.Jan.30,1891 d.Oct.22,1970,son
    of Robert Bost and Adella Graves of San Marcos,Tx.
    (7 children)
    1.ADELENE BOST b.Jan.12,1913 d.aug.16,1943 m.Jan.1932
    to Wm Bryan Mosley b. 1907 d.Dec.1958.(1 child)
    a)WM.BRYAN MOSLEY b.Mar.16,1934,d.Aug.13,1980

    2.CLIFTON OTIS BOST b. Apr.28,1915 m.1942 to Doris
      Lovelace b. Mar.15,1923 Axtell,Tx.,dau of "Hosie
      Lovelace.(1 child)
      a)GWENDOLYN BOST b. Jan.20,1943 Waco,m.1st to John Boyd
      (1 child)
      1.JOHN DAVID BOYD b. Sept.13,1963 Dallas
      Gwendolyn m.2nd to Troy Suggs (1 child)
      2.MIRIAM ELIZABETH SUGGS b.Sept.14,1970 Dallas

  3.DELLA BOST b. July 30,1917 m.June 13,1945 to Oather(OL)
    Lee Copeland b.Feb.24,1916,son of Wm.Edward Copeland
    b.1884 in Ala.and Pocahontas Bryant.b.1888 in La.Wm.
    and Pocahontas lived in Peoria,Tx.Wm.m.1st Janie Gillis
    cousin of Pocahontas and had 11 children in all.
    1.Myrtle,2.James Westly,3.Ruby,4.Willie.Janie died and
    William and Pocahontas had :5.Herbert,6.OATHER,7.Sybil,
    8.James,9.Berlie, 10.Helen,and 11.Ola Mae.

    Della has been my most valuable assistant in gathering
    this information on the WILLIAM F.HOLMES descendents.She

HELEN AND OTIS BOST

Clifton and Adelene Bost

David Holmes, Bill Holmes
and Chester Holmes

and Oather have "hung" in there with me from the very
night that I met them. She has been my "co-pilot" and
friend and I appreciate her interest and attitude.This
compilation could not have been as complete without her
assistance.

4.CARLENE BOST b.Nov.23,1921 m.Oct.16,1944 to Levi(LD)
  Davis Alexander b. Feb.25,1920 son of Dora and Summers
  Alexander .(1 child)
  a)PHYLLIS ALEXANDER b. Feb.16,1949 m.June 1969 to
    Ronnie Turner b. Feb.16,1948,son of Juanita and Boyd
    Turner. (3 children)
    1.AMY TURNER b.June 6,1973
    2.RHONDA TURNER b. Jan.8,1975
    3.AMANDA TURNER b.Dec.15,1981

5.RICHARD BOST b.July 1,1925 d.Mar.1979 m.Dorothy Best
  from Portland,Oregon.(5 children)Richard and Dorothy
  divorced.Dorothy remarried and had another child.
  All children took her 2nd husband's name which is
  unknown.
  a)LINDA BOST
  b)RICKY BOST
  c)TERESA BOST
  d)SHELIA BOST
  e)BECKY BOST

6.O.A. BOST b.June 3,1930 m.Sept.4,1948 to Mildred
  (Milly)Lorine Snider b.Mar.16,1932,dau.of Robert
  Samuel Snider and Florence Dormae Warren of McGregor
  Tx.(1 child)
  a)RANDY LEE BOST b.Jan.16,1966 m.July 19,1886 Jamie
    R.Weiss of McGregor,b.Mar.27,1965 dau. of Billy Gene
    Weiss and Marsha Ann Novacic .Marsha b.Akron,Ohio.
    1.SHAD ANDREW BOST b.Feb.11,1987

7.DONALD LEE BOST b. Sept.4,1934 m.Aug.1,1969 to Nancy
  Dobbins b.Oct.20,1939 dau.of Sidney Byrom Dobbins and
  Nancy Collette Biggs .(3 children)
  a)1.KATHLEEN BOST b.June 12,1959
  b)JOHN DAVID BOST b.July 24,1961 m.Oct.1,1982 to Donna
    Lynn Burnett b.Oct.15,1962.
  c)SHELLY COLLETTE BOST b. Jan.8,1983

h) DAVIS R. HOLMES b. Sept.1899 d. 1903. Davis's mother died
   a few days after his birth.He was never a strong child.He
   was cared for by his sister,Nannie,until the family
   decided to make their move to Texas. William's sister,
   Elizabeth Sturgeon convinced him to leave the child with
   her family.William later returned to Doloroso on a visit,
   and took his son to join his family in Texas.

5.MARY M.HOLMES b.Nov.1862 d.1923 m.Mar.23.1891 Lewis
  Christopher Carter b.Mar.1868 d.Nov.1955.(MB M,pg.270
  Wilkinson Co.Ms.)Lewis was from the Buffalo Community
  between Doloroso and Woodville Ms. Mary and Lewis moved
  to the Speegleville Community near Waco,Tx.where they
  farmed.Both are buried in the Chapel Hill Cemetery
  located in the "Old Speegleville" cemetery that was moved
  to Chapel Hill when Lake Waco was enlarged.(4 children)

  a)SARAH AMANDA CARTER b.Sept.15,1893 d.Jan.14,1977 m.1919
    to Benjamin Franklin Farrar Sr.b.July 12,1889,d.Aug.25,
    1973,son of Ella C.Ford and Thornton H.Farrar (MB L,pg.
    434,Wilkinson Co.Ms.)Thornton's grandparents were Alex
    K.Farrar who m.Ann Mary Dougherly Apr.29,1836(MB A.pg.
    28 East Feliciana Parish La.)Sisters and brothers :Alex
    (A.K.)b.Nov.1879 m.Nellie Geter June 3,1907(MB N.pg.593
    Wilkinson Co.Ms.);Mary H.b.1881 m.Wm.F.Best Oct.2,1902
    (MB N.pg.395 Wilkinson Co.Ms.);Thornton H.b.Jan.1885
    Ann M.b.May 1887 m.Sidney B.McCaleb Sept.10,1914(MB O
    pg.212 Wilkinson Co.Ms.)and Henry E.b.1891.

    Amanda and Ben are buried in the Speegleville Cemetery
    along with her parents.(4 children)
    1.MARY ELLA FARRAR b.Mar.8,1921 m.Aug.27,1942 to Brady
      Odell Everett b.Jan.4,1920,son of Ruth Madison Bell
      of Waco and Levi Bart Everett of Coryell Co.Tx.
      (2 children)

      a)BRADY LYNN EVERETT b.Feb.14,1947 m.Aug.31,1967 to
        Linda Lou Bush b.Sept.12,1946 dau.of Delia Mae Nix
        and Joseph Larkin Bush of McLennan Co.Tx.
        (3 children)
        1.DAVID LYNN EVERETT b.Dec.19,1968
        2.SCOTT BRADY EVERETT b.June 22,1976
        3.CHRISTI LEIGH EVERETT b.Dec.27,1978

      b)STEPHEN LEE EVERETT b.March 21,1951 m.June 5,1970
        to Cindy Lee West b.Feb.23,1953 dau.of Beryl Keith
        West and Mildred Arlene Bagley of Adamsville,Tx.
        (2 children)
        1.STEPHEN KYLE EVERETT b.Aug.26,1974
        2.KACIE LEE EVERETT b.Apr.14,1977

    2.BEN (Speedy) F.FARRAR JR. b.Feb.18,1927 m.July 8,
      1950 to Helen Christine Smith b.Sept.26,1931 dau.
      of John L.Smith b.May 15,1905 and Fannie Lee Chandler
      b.Jan 21,1909 from Mt.Calm,Tx.(2 children)
        a)SUSAN DIANE FARRAR b. Oct.7,1950
        b)DAVID LEE FARRAR b. Jan.21,1969

3.PARNELL FARRAR b.July 1,1923 m.Sept.23,1961 to Mary
  Larlene Cochrum b.Dec.11,1920 dau.of J.T.Cochrum and
  Martha Jane Brunson of Limestone Co.Tx.Larlene has
  two children by 1st marriage.

  a)SANDRA ANN THETFORD b. Sept.8,1942 m.J.D.Willingham
    b.Nov.6,1940,son of Alvin and Kathleen Willingham
    of McClennan Co.Tx. (3 children)
     1.JEFFREY WILLINGHAM b.Feb.24,1969
     2.ANN LARLENE WILLINGHAM b. June 21,1971
     3.ALISA KATHLEEN WILLINGHAM b.June 21,1971(twins)

  b)FELIX NELSON THETFORD b. June 10,1945 m.Laura Gayle
    Herron b. Nov.12,1945 dau.of Alvin and Lucy Herron
    of Brownville,Tx.(1 child)
     1.ROBERT NELSON THETFORD b.Jan.19,1983

4.CORDELL FARRAR b.July 1, 1923 m.Mar.6,1943 to Mary
  Lois Ramsey b Jan.26,1925 dau.of Raymond Ramsey
  b.Mar.8,1902,and Oma Gunn from West,Tx.(2 children)

  a)CORDELL WAYNE FARRAR b.July 15,1944 m.May 11,1963
    to Sylvia Annet Stephen b.Aug.11,1946 dau. of
    Dorothy and Maravyn Stephens of McLennan Co.Tx.
     1.RANDALL WAYNE FARRAR b. Feb.18,1964
     2.SHELIA ANNET FARRAR b. July 15,1967
     3.KEVIN SCOTT FARRAR b. June 4,1970

  b)DERRELL GENE FARRAR b. Apr.23,1949 m.1st Paula
    Kay Plymell June 1,1968,dau. of Mr.& Mrs.Beth
    Plymell of Fort Worth.(1 child)
     1.DERRELL GENE FARRAR JR. b.Dec.15,1968
    Derrell m.2nd to Donna Avent Childress b.Dec.23,
    1950 .Donna has a daughter.
     2.AMY DAWN CHILDRESS b. Sept.9,1973

b.CASEY CHRISWELL CARTER b.Sept.1895 d. Sept.20,1924
   m.Jessie Richards. (1 child)
  1.VERNAN CARTER married and had two children.His wife
   remarried .Information on his family is unknown.

c.ESTELLA CARTER b Apr. 1900 died 1906,buried in Ms.

These two Holmes sisters
married and settled in
McLennan Co.Tx.

Mary Holmes Carter

Amanda Holmes Everett

6.ELIZABETH HOLMES b. July 7,1868 buried in Holmes Cemetery
on "Old Hwy 65",west of Hwy 61 south.d.July 12,1950
m.Dec.19,1883 (MB M pg.16,Wilkinson Co.Ms.,) to John T.
(Johnny) Sturgeon b.Dec.1857 d.Nov.17,1941 son of Hiram
Sturgeon and Clarinda Cole (MB I pg.311,July 22,1855)in
Wilkinson Co.Ms.,(11 children.)By 1900 there were eight
born,but only four living.

a)BESS STURGEON b. and d.as an infant.

b)BLANCHE ESTELLE STURGEON b. Dec.23,1889,d.Mar.28,1980
m.Aug. 25,1920 David Frederick Leak b.May 14,1890
d.Apr.1,1959(2 children)

1.FREDERICK ANDREW LEAK b.July 13,1921 m.Jan.13,1947
to Doris Birdwell b.Dec.5,1924,dau.of Archie David
Birdwell and Velma Smith Crouch of San Augustine
Tx.(1 child)
a)JANET LYNN LEAK b.Oct.10,1948 m.Aug.23,1969 to
Dalton Craig Jaynes b. Mar.5,1949,son of Dalton
Henry Jaynes and Jo Beth Campbell.

2.MARY RUTH LEAK b. Jan.9,1925 m.Dec.19,1952 Raymond J.
Parkins b.Dec.6,1926,son of Eva Maude and John Henry
Parkins Sr.(2 children)
a)JOHN DAVID PARKINS b. Oct.8,1953
b)RAYMOND DANIEL PARKINS b.Dec.24,1955

c)EUGENE THOMAS STURGEON b.Dec.13,1891 d. May 13,1987
m.Ola Olevia Broussard Sept.19,1914 (MB O.pg.216
Wilkinson Co.Ms.)Eugene buried in the Scott Cemetery,
Concordia Parish,Louisana.
Ola b.Feb.3,1897 dau.of Louis Frank Broussard and Olevia
Crane of Monterey,La.,Concordia Parish.(1 child)

1.JOHN MILLARD STURGEON b.Aug.16,1915 Speegleville,Tx.
d.Nov.18,1981 m.Feb.14,1937 Margie Calhoun b.Sept.14,
1919 dau.of Jessie Calhoun and Ellie Nora Wilson
(2 children)
a)LINDA JUNE STURGEON b.Feb.24,1945 m.Dec.22,1963
William (Billy Green,b.Nov.1,1945,son of Bruce Green
and Jeanne Mae Ford .(3 children)
1.SHANNAN LYNN GREEN b.July 14,1967
2.JUSTIN TERRELL GREEN b.Sept.12,1969
3.RICHARD KYLE GREEN b.Nov.27,1972

b)JOHN MILLARD STURGEON b. Jan.27,1942 m.June 14,1963
Johnnie Ruth Bryan b.Aug.28,1946 dau.of Johnny
Bryan and Mabel Jones Bryan(2 children)
1.JOHN MILLARD STURGEON III b.Oct.15,1970
2.JAMES IRA STURGEON b.Dec.6,1972

d)DEDDIE HOLMES STURGEON died young

e)HARTSELL LAURA STURGEON b.Apr.19,1896 d.Sept.24,1974
  m.Louis Victor Broussard(bro.to Ola Broussard Sturgeon)
  b.Dec.21,1892 d.May 20,1939.M.Aug.10,1918.Both buried
  Rice Cemetery,Monterey,La.Hwy 129.(1 child)

    1.CORNELIA ADELLE BROUSSARD b.May 26,1919 Monterey,La.
      m.Feb.24,1943 Natchez,Ms.to Virgil Golson Wright
      b.Apr.11, 1918 Gilead,La.

f)HORACE B. STURGEON b. Aug.5,1898 m.Mar.11,1924 (BK O,pg.
  542 to Addie Stewart.(2 children)

    1.FRANK STEWART STURGEON b.Dec.22,1931 d.July 2,1983
      m.Jan.15,1950 to Louise Penuel Stueg.b.Nov.13,1926
      d.Nov.9,1975.(2 children)
      a)FRANK STEWART STURGEON JR. b. Jan.2,1951
      b)JOHN ALVY STURGEON b. Feb.21,1952

    2.GRACE STURGEON b. July 31,1934 m.Truit Perryman.
      Horace m.2nd to Cleo Crunp b.Apr.15,1900
      d.Aug.15,1960 (1 child)

      a)INDIA ANNE STURGEON b. Sept.27,1942 m.Ronnie David
        Veralin (2 children)
        1.ANGIE VERALIN b. Jan.3,1964
        2.RONNIE VERALIN b. Oct.1,1964
      Horace m.3rd.Jan.22,1963 to Ella Swindle

g)KATE STURGEON b.Jan.20,1901 m.June 5,1922 to Howard
  Wright b.Sept.9,1883 ,d.Aug.4,1961 Evergreen Cemetery
  (1 child)
    1.EVAN MILLER WRIGHT b.Mar.6,1926 m.1950 Kathryn
      McCurley.

h)ALONZO HACKETT STURGEON b. Feb.25,1903 m.Aug.12,1927 to
  Mamie Susan Ellis b.June 9,1907 dau.of Henry David Ellis
  and Martha Susan Partridge of Norwood,La.(5 children)

  a)JOHN HENRY STURGEON b. Dec.3,1928 m.Nellie Crapp.
    (2 children)
    1.MARY NELL STURGEON b. Nov.5,1951 m.1st Feb.20,1971
      William Frank Maxie b. Oct.12,1950 son of Wm.Warren
      Maxie Jr.and Dorothy Nell White.Grandson of
      Wm.Warren Maxie Sr.and Florence Mae Hutton.
      William and Mary divorced Apr.23,1981.(2 children)
      a)MELISSA JANE MAXIE b. Sept.1,1971
      b)REBECCA LYN MAXIE b. Dec.11,1976

2.VALENCIA LYNN STURGEON b.June 27,1955 m.1st to
  Martin B. Halloran Jr. (1 child)
  a)SARAH JOHNELLE HALLORAN b.Nov.1,1981 d.Nov.2,1981
  Valencia m.2nd to Tommy McLeod. (1 child)
  b)Daughter born 1986

b)ALONZO HOLMES STURGEON b.Dec.13,1931 m.Dec.4,1953 to
  Betty Jane Moore b. Sug.26,1932 dau. of Tobie Delton
  (T.D.)Moore and Nellie Morris.Nellie, dau.of Chalmers
  Morris. (1 child)
  1.ALONZO HOLMES STURGEON JR. Aug.28,1965

c)MAXIE EUGENE STURGEON b.Mar.31,1934 d.Sept.7,1985, m.
  Mar.9,1957 Gloria Clarke b.Sept.27,1940 dau.of Claude
  Clarke and Doris Wheeler   (3 children)

  1.SUSAN ELISE STURGEON b Feb.4,1963 m.Steve Calvin
    Idom b. Sept.30,1959,son of Calvin and Ida Idom
    (1 child due in Oct.1987)
  2.HIRAM EVANS STURGEON b.Oct.5,1964 m.May 21,1987 to
    Carolyn Christine Byrd b.Oct.21,1965,dau.of Judy
    Byington Byrd McGrew and James Byrd.
  3.STARLA ELIZABETH STURGEON b.July 30,1968

d)LTC CHARLES ELLIS STURGEON b.Feb.2,1937 m.Oct.22,1960
  to Mamie Inez Green b.June 1,1939 dau. of General Gile
  Green and Sarah Barbara Rice of Monterey,La.
  (4 children)
  1.CHARLES ELLIS STURGEON JR.b.Oct.10,1961
  2.JOHN ROBERT STURGEON b. Jan.10,1963
  3.JAMES ANTHONY STURGEON b. May 22,1964
  4.PATRICK SCOTT STURGEON b. May 20,1967

e)LOUIS VIRGIL STURGEON b.Jan.15,1942 m.Oct.29,1961 in
  Hattisburg,Ms. to Catherine Irene Reed.b.Mar.7,1942
  Dallas,Tx.,dau.of Alvin Cecil Reed and Irene Leake of
  Crosby,Ms. (3 children)
  1.LOUIS VIRGEL STURGEON JR.b.May 2,1962
  2.CATHERINE YVETTE STURGEON b. June 17,1963
  3.CECIL REED STURGEON b.Nov.19,1964

Elizabeth Holmes and Johnnie Sturgeon   1938

Blanche

Lonnie and Mamie

LONNIE AND MAMIE

HOLMES BURING GROUND
NEIL AND HERBERT JENSON

STURGEON HOME--ELGIN

118-2

MAJOR AND THE THREE EVERETTE
BROTHERS, TOM, CHARLIE,
EUALL, AND EUGENE STURGEON

EUGENE AND OLA STURGEON

118-3

Mr. and Mrs. Eugene Sturgeon

HIGH WATERS were many during the early days on Black River. The old Sturgeon home went through many of them, as evidenced by the above picture.

OLD HOME BEHIND THE NEW HOME

7.FRANCIS (FRANK) HOLMES b. Apr.1871 d.June 28,1908
  Wilkinson Co.Ms.m.Dec.27,1894 (MB N.pg.55) Lula Belle
  Smith b.Dec.1874,Wilkinson co.Ms.d.May 24,1961,buried in
  Rosemound Cemetery in Waco.Tx.as Lula Sterling.After
  Frank died,Lula moved to Waco along with her children
  to live close to Frank's sister,Mary Carter. Lula re-
  married 2nd to Clyde Cleary(no children) and 3rd to a
  Sterling.(no children)(4 children with Frank)

  In the June 30,1983 issue of THE WOODVILLE REPUBLICAN
  Vol.159,Woodville,Mississippi,in the "Backward,turn
  backward,Oh Time,in thy flight...." column of 75 years
  ago in 1908,states the following:"Mr.Frank Holmes died at
  his home in this town on Tuesday morning and his remains
  were taken to Cold Springs on Wednesday morning and
  interred in the family grounds..."
  This referred to the HOLMES CEMETERY on "Old Hwy 65",
  west of Hwy 61 south.

  a)DAVID EUGENE HOLMES b. Jan. 1896 d.June 11,1950.m.
    Ruby Brown of Crawford,b.Sept.6,1899,dau. of Theodore
    Brown and Eva Farmer of Crawford(2 children)

    1.MOSELLE HOLMES b.June 12,1919 m.Nov.16,1940 to Harley
      Vivian Johnson b.Nov.1,1918 son of Theo Burrel Johnson
      and Willie Bell Bird of Coryell,Co.Tx .(2 children)

      a)VIVIAN ANNE JOHNSON b.Apr.8,1946 m.May 18,1968 to
        John Everette F.Skinner III b.Aug.5,1945,son of E.S.
        Skinner Jr.and Ethel Irby.

      b)DAVID BRYAN JOHNSON b.Aug.28,1953 m.Mar.15,1974 to
        Brenda Kay Riley Sept.15,1956 dau. of Johnny J.Riley
        and Ann Matthew.(2 children)
        1.DAVID BRYAN (Scooter)JOHNSON JR. b. Nov.28,1976
        2.JUSTIN SCOTT JOHNSON b. Jan.14,1981

    2.WILLIAM ROBERT(Billy Bob,also Bill) HOLMES b. July 3,
      1924 Crawford.d.July 26,1982 Temple,Tx.m.June 22,1949
      to Martha Jeanette Guerin b.Nov.21,1928,dau.of Henry
      Howard and Lillian Ellen Guerin (3 children)

      a)DEBORAH JEAN HOLMES b.March 26,1951 Waco,Tx.m.May
        13,1972 to Michael Van Donnelly b.May 22,1942.
        (2 children)
        1.LARRY WILLIAM(Billy)DONNELLY b.Feb.23,1973 Temple.
        2.AMANDA BETH DONNELLY b. May 14,1976 Temple,Tx.

      b)PATRICIA DIANE HOLMES b.Nov.23,1953 Waco,m.Sept.16,
        1972 to John Elliot Turnbull b.Apr.17,1951
        (2 children)

1.TIMOTHY LAND TURNBULL b. Dec.18,1973 Temple,Tx.

2.JENNIFER HOPE TURNBULL b.Feb.10,1976 Waco.Tx.

c)DAVID EUGENE HOLMES b.Aug.19,1955 Waco,Tx.m.Aug.1,
1974 to Brenda Kay Hutka b.Oct.22,1955 Temple,Tx.
dau.of Johnnie Edward and Bernice Agnes Hutka.
(2 children)
1.ANGELA DAWN HOLMES Aug.8,1980 Temple,Tx.
2.JOSHUA EDWARD HOLMES b.June 8,1983 Temple,Tx.

b)LEON HOLMES b. Mar.1898

c)ELIZABETH HOLMES b.Jan.8,1903 d.Jan.31,1987 m.Taylor.

d)MARY HOLMES b.Jan.,24,1907d.May 5,1971 m.to Lenard Q.
Sloan b.Dec.28,1902,d.Sept.10,1941(1 child)

1.THOMAS ROY SLOAN b.Mar.25,1928 d.Oct.8,1950
Mary m.2nd to Mr. O'Dell .Buried in the Rosemound
Cemetery,Waco.

WILKINSON COUNTY MARRIAGE BOOKS 1805-1899
SCOTT

ARGLASS SCOTT to Sarah Holmes Feb.8,1876 BK L,p.331
DAVE SCOTT to Hattie Harper Apr.20,1904 BK N,p.462
HENRY SCOTT to Sarah Henninton Jan.12,1822 BK D,p.181
HENRY W. SCOTT to Elizabeth Geter Mar.4,1841 BK G,p.86
HOWARD SCOTT to Elizabeth Bunch Oct.17,1906 BK N,p.570
MAJOR A. SCOTT to Celia Ann Sapp Dec.6,1840 BK G.p.66
MAJOR A.SCOTT to Nancy A.Comer Dec.24,1843 BK G,p.252
MAJOR E. SCOTT to Ida Bryan Nov.10,1881 BK L,p.507
MAJOR J.SCOTT to Olevia Johnson Mar.3,1915 BK O,p.234
SAMUEL SCOTT to Vivia Deloach Feb.27,1902 BK N,p.379
IDA SCOTT to J.S.Cobb Nov.15,1894 BK N,p.51
MAMIE SCOTT to Henry Davis Dec.27,1906 BK N. p.577
MARY ANN SCOTT to Jesse Holliman Jan.28,1838 BK F,p.217

CONCORDIA PARISH LOUISANA MARRIAGES

ANN SCOTT to William G. Bruce   Nov.2,1850
GEORGE W. SCOTT to Frances A.Fink   May 29,1847
JOHN F.SCOTT to Nettie Faulkenberry   July 8,1890
JOHN W.SCOTT to Sarah Magoun   Jan.15,1859
LORENA SCOTT to J.R.Steele   Jan.17,1883
MINOR J. SCOTT to Annie Brady   June 3,1896
NANCY B. SCOTT to William S. Steele   July 25,1851
NEOMA SCOTT to J.E.Foreman   Feb.13,1878
PARYLEE SCOTT to L.(Levi) B. Jackson   Aug.26,1869
PRISCILLA SCOTT to John W. Butler   July 8,1868
SAMUEL B. SCOTT to Mrs. Susannah Bruce   Apr.19,1851
WILLIAM A. SCOTT to Mary E.Rountree   Dec.8,1865

Mary Brannan to John Silvya(Sylver) Aug.7,1820 BK A,p.70
Judy Brannan (Also Jude) to James D.Adams May 16,1821 BK A,p.88
Thomas Brannan to Patsy White Aug.27,1823 BK B,p.212
Tamzan Brannan to David Allen Feb.19,1824 BK B,p.209
Margaret Brannan to Patrick C.Hamilton Nov.1,1929 BK E,p.107
Elizabeth Brannan to William Miller Feb.19,1829 BK E.p.107
Carmalita Brannan to Nelson Brown Dec.21,1845
Rachel Brannan to Wm.S.Newman Feb.4,1846
Nancy Brannan to Alexander Newman Jan.5,1847 BK H,p.136
Thomas Brannan to Jane (Jeter) Ford Jan.11,1852 BK I,p.133
Catherine A.Brannan to Josiah A.Knight May 17,1855 BK I,p.300
David Brannan to Nancy Harvey June 29,1861 BK K,p.330
Douglas C.Brannan to Fannie Button May 27,1869 BK L,p.97
Mary L.(Lucendia)Brannan to Wm.A.K.Cooper Dec.16,1874 BK L,p.286
Davis A.Brannan to Mary E.Netterville Apr.11,1878 BK L,p.405
B.W.(Ben) Brannan to Lydia E.Netterville Oct.6,1886 BK M,p.115
M.M. Brannan to W.E. Davidson Dec.8,1892 BK M,p.346
Anita R.Brannan to A.M. McGehee Mar.20,1902 BK N,p.381
Ola Brannan to Henry A.Williams Dec.16,1908 BK O.p.47
Edna Brannan to J.A.Massey Oct.26,1915 BK O,p.248
Davis (A) Brannan to Sallye Petty Aug.8,1912 BK O,p.146
Blanche E.Brannan to Levi P.Caston Aug.4,1922 BK O,p.480
Anita Brannan to Edward Carey Corley Aug.22,1923 BK O,p.525

EAST FELICIANA PARISH LOUISANA

Thomas Brannan to Mary Hammons Aug.19,1837
Thomas R.Brannan to Mary Smith Aug.22,1846
Joel Brannan to Agnes Sweeny Jan.13,1870
Rhonda Jane Brannan to Joseph Bogan Nov.21,1849

JETER / GETER

WILKINSON COUNTY MARRIAGE BOOKS 1802-1824

1808 William Jeter to Elizabeth Morgan Sept.13&22 Bond 264,Cert
     266
1813 Argulus Jeter to Polly(Mary)Phipps Apr.22,BK A,pg.259

1817 Sterling Geter to Phebe Phipps Mar.20,BK A.pg.3

     (In Feliciana Parish,La.,John Jeter m.Charlotte Lambert
     March 15,1820.They would later move to Wilk.Co.Ms.)

1827 Sally Jeter to J.Kincaid(both Jeter and Geter spellings)
     Feb.7,BK E pg.8.
1827 Sarah Jeter to J.Hammond Dec.5,BK C,pg.45
1828 William Jeter to Heneritta Quine Feb.26,BK E.pg.12
1838 Sterling Jeter to Narcissa Swayze Nov.8,BK F,pg.260
1839 Nancy Jeter to Caleb Swayze May 2,BK F,pg.260
1841 Elizabeth Geter to Henry Scott Mar.4,1841 BK G,pg.266
1844 Jane Jeter to Ferdinand C.Ford (Fred) Feb.8,BK G,pg.266
1844 Lucinda Jeter to   ? Womack (no date)
1852 Jane Jeter Ford to Thomas Brannon Jan.11,BK I,pg 133

     (In 1848,Sterling L.Jeter m.Martha N.Noland in East
     Feliciana Parish,La)Sterling L.was the son of John and
     Charlotte Jeter.
     (In 1849,Caroline Jeter m.Henry D.Robinson in East
     Feliciana Parish,La.
     (In 1851,William Jeter m.Anna Jane Cobb in East Feliciana
     Parish,La.)

1852 Rachael Jeter to J.Aswell Jan.28,BK I,pg.134
1852 Davis S.Jeter to Mary Jler (1st m.)
1855 Andrew J. Jeter to Elizabeth H.Miller Jan.10,BK I,pg.290
1856 David S.Jeter to Sarah Ann Jler Jan.1,BK I,pg.327 (2nd m.)
1857 Theresa Jeter to William J. Netterville Feb.18,BK K,pg.52
1864 Sterling Geter to Mrs. Sarah Ann Rogers Richardson
Dec.1,BK K,pg.315(Sarah m.1st to Jno.Richardson Jan.2,1851)

     (Mary E.Jeter to John J.Ostein in East Feliciana Parish,La.
     1865)

1872 S.(Sterling) Rufus Geter to L.Cage Dec.24,BK L.pg.219
1874 David E.Jeter to Mary(Polly) E.Wilson Dec.10,BK L,pg.28
1874 David L. Jeter to Catherine (Marie) Spangler Dec.3,BK L.
     pg.28
1875 Dulcie Geter to William L.Hayes Jan.28,BK L,pg.300
1886 William H.(Herman) Geter to Hattie J.Curtin Nov.25,BK M
     pg.123

123

1889 Argles P.Geter to Ella Archie May 23,MB M.pg.222
1890 Bessie(Elizabeth Jane) Geter to J.W.Curtain Oct.7,MB M.
     pg.270
1898 (Fredrick) Hays Geter to Amanda Rabb Nov.3,MB N.pg.240
1905 H.(Henry Parham)P.Geter to Katie A.Carter June 30,MB N.
     pg.508
1905 Jennie Geter to G.A.Raworth June 14, MB N.pg.505
     (dau.of S.Rufus and Laura Cage Geter)
1907 Nellie Geter to A.K.Farrar June 3,MB N.pg.593
     (dau.of S.Rufus and Laura Cage Geter)
1912 Edna May Geter to Charlie Hag(Haag) Dec.30,MB O,pg.159
1915 H.P.Geter to Eunice McGraw Feb.11,MB O,pg.230
1916 Leo Geter to Emlie Leak June 11,1916 MB O.pg.266
1919 Hays P.Geter to Lettie Ogden July 29,MB O.pg.364
1921 Hays F.Geter to Tenedalle Nettle June 21,1MB O.pg.442
1922 Mable D.Geter to Leonard E.Nettles Jan.24,MB O,pg.461

                WILKINSON COUNTY MISSISSIPPI LAND DEED BOOKS

1814 BK A.pg.357   Henry Phipps to Argulas Geter ,100 acres
1829 BK F.pg.   John W.Jeter and Wm.Jeter pd.$263 for 14 yr.
                    Negro boy named Pete Jeter.
1833 BK G.pg.734   Argless Jeter gave minor dau.Martha Matilda
                    Jeter,one 6 yr.old girl,Harriett.
1833 BK F.pg.245 and 257, John W.Jeter
1837 BK Q.pg.205   Sterling Jeter,Thos.Mayes,Benj.Turberville
                    $1,000 to Chas.Lynch .Sterling elected
                    constable
1840 BK M.pg.150   Argles to wife,Mary(Polly Phipps),children
                        Sterling Jeter,Nancy Jeeter,Jane.WILL
1840 BK N.pg.679   David S.Jeter to R.Clampet
1840 BK Q,pg.364,463,94
1840 BK Q.pg.286   David S.Jeter and wife Mary M. rec.$1,000 from
                    Jones Platt for track of land (42.86 acres)
                    SW 1/4 of SE 1/4,Sec.1,t 2,r 2W.Cert.#7626N.
1852 BK P.pg.430   Argless Geter gives Agenia(Ugenia) O.Ford,said
                    daughter,a boy called Ned,aged 3 mo.old.
1853 BK Q.pg.205   David S.Jeter to mother Charlotte Geter,slaves
                    Sip,40,Duncan 18,later to go to his father,John
                    Jeter.
1852 BK Q.pg.94   David S.Jeter and Mary his wife for $50 by
                    Elizabeth C.Proper ,3 1/2 acres for a lot in
                    town of Woodville.

1853 BK Q.pg.205   Sterling Jeter gave to mother Charlotte Geter,a
                    man 55 yrs. old called Dick,Benford 21,Allen
                    20,Rachel 50,girl Sidney 17,after her death to
                    go to my father,John Jeter.
1857 BK R.pg.185   Arglass W.Jeter pd.$1500 to Sterling for
                    Sterling's share of their father's estate who
                    is still living

STATE OF LOUISIANA, } *Know all men by these presents, That we* John Jeter

and William Hickburn

are held and firmly bound unto Wm C Wade

Parish Judge of the parish of Feliciana, and his assigns, in the full sum of five

Hundred dollars, lawful money of the United States, to which

payment well and truly to be made, we bind ourselves, our heirs, executors, administrators

and assigns firmly by these presents. Signed and sealed with our seals, this fifteenth

day of March A. D. 1820

WHEREAS the above bounden John Jeter

has this day obtained, from

the Parish Judge of the parish of Feliciana, a *Licence* to celebrate a marriage between him

the said John Jeter

and Miss Charlotte Lambert

NOW the condition of the above obligation is such, That if there exists no legal

impediment to the celebration of said marriage, this obligation to be void and of no effect,

otherwise to remain in full force and virtue.

WITNESS,

John Jeter

Wm Hickman

1858 BK R.pg.348   David Jeter pd.$375 to Wm.K.Prater for 1/4
                   land.(Refer to BK R.pg.302 for this land.

1859 BK R.pg.369 &374 David S.Jeter and Sarah A.Jler his wife,
                   $10.00 by Daniel L.Flynn for his share of
                   land in T3,R2W,NW L/4,Sec.44 for 160 acres.
                   (Kept others from knowing how much was actually
                   paid for land)

BK R.pg.205   Charlotte Jeter--Sterling L Jeter....???

know all Men by these presants that I
David Lambert A silsun of Louisana of the
parish of felisana by the ne quest of
John Jeter have givin My Consent that he
the said Jeter should Marey My Daugter
Charlotte Lambert — given under my hand and seel
this — 14th day of March — 1820

                              David Lambert — sener

BARRETT
  Danielle Lauren 58
  James Michael 47
  Jeneva 58
  Joe Nell 47
  Joel Glendon (Glen) 47
  Joshua Ryan 15
  Kenneth Joel 47
  Michael Glen 47
  Michael Glen (Mickie) 47
  Myrtte Michele 47
  Ricky 58
  Sam 58
  Virgie 47
  William c. 47
BASSET
  Angelia Kaye 46
  Bobbie 46
  Clyde Vester 46
  Ronald Emory 46
BEARD
  Charlie N. 78
  Donnie Eliza 60
BEAUMANM
  Fred 68
  Margaret Christine 25
BEETZ
  Charlie 30
  Henry Ford 30
  Opal Mary 30
BELKNAP
  Teddie Lou 112
  Wray 112
BELL
  Bobby Eugene 43
  J.B. 44
  Jan 29
  James Harold 53
  Jason Bryan 44
  Jean Lorraine 29
  John 2
  Larry Neil 29
  Mary Elizabeth 29
  Michael Glenn 43
  Misty Llynn 54
  Monica Jane 44
  Rayner 29
  Ruth Madison 114
  Robert Miles 53
  Stacey Nichole 55
  Susan 29

BELL (cont.)
  Thelbert 43
  Theresa Lei 43
  William 5
BERGERON
  Madeleine 68
  Renee 25
  Willard 25
BERNAHAN
  John 24
BERRY
  Calvin 96
BEST
  Dorothy 113
  Wm.F. 114
BIAS
  Minerva 102
BIGGS
  Nancy Collette 113
BILLINGS
  Josh 100
  Ruth 100
BIOR
  Laura 109
BIRD
  Willie Bell 119
BIRDWELL
  Archie David 116
  Doris 116
BISHOP
  George 45
  Mary 45
  Shelton Ray 45
  Shelly Denise 45
  Stacy Larae 45
BLACKWELL
  Lela Joice 53
BLAIR
  Renise 110
BLAKENEY
  Irna 71
  R.H. 81
BLOODWORTH
  Linda Dianne 14
BLOUNT
  Adeline Burley 17
  Gay 38
BOGGS
  Margaret Ruth 111
  Rossie LaFaye 111

BOND
- Walter Arlis 112
- Zo Nelda 112

BONE
- Martha Jane 54

BONG
- Na Bong 54

BORDELON
- Berly 29

BOST
- Adelene 112
- Alma 108
- Becky 113
- Carlene 113
- Clifton Otis 112
- Della 112
- Donald Lee 113
- Gwendolyn 112
- John David 113
- Kathleen 113
- Linda 113
- O.A. 113
- Otis Alfred 112
- Randy Lee 113
- Richard 113
- Ricky 113
- Robert 108,112
- Shad Andrew 113
- Shelia 113
- Shelly Collette 113
- Teresa 113

BOTELER
- Christopher Kyle 99
- Paul 99

BOWLIN
- Azalia 43
- Harold
- William L. 43

BOYD
- Anj 29
- Arch 24
- Robt. 24
- J.W 83
- Janet 64
- James 24
- John 24,112
- John David 112
- John W. 26-2,26-3, 112
- Lislie Nicole 64
- Mary 26-2
- Mary C. 26-3
- Mary G. 26-2,26-3,
- Melissa (K or D) 13
- Melissa (K or R) 14

BOYD (cont.)
- Nancy 26-3
- Nancy J. 26-2
- Ralph E. 64
- Ralph E. Sr. 64
- Wm. 83
- Robert 26

BRACHLEY
- Jessie F. 72

BRADLEY
- Don Damon 30
- Donya DeShay 30
- Eugene 40

BRADSHAW
- Carl Daniel 63
- Carl Eugene 63
- James Ray 63

BRADY
- Annie 35
- Lynsey Lucille 67
- Thomas Carroll 67

BRALEY
- Angela Sue 72
- Jessie F. 72
- John F. 72

BRANNAN
- B.W. (Benjamin) 7
- C.A. 92
- Davis 92,93
- Davis Arglass 94
- Jane 93
- Lucenda 92,93
- Mary 92
- Violet 92
- Virginia E. 92

BRANNON
- A.(G.or J) 92
- Anita 94
- Anthony 93
- Benjamin 93
- Benjamin J. 93
- Benjamin W. 93
- C.A. 93
- David 94
- David A. 93
- Doug. C. 92
- Douglas 93
- Edna E. 93
- Ford 92
- Harriet C. 92

BRANNON (cont)
    John A. 92
    Lucinda 94
    Mary Lucenda 93
    Thomas 92
    Thos. 92
    Viola E. 94
    Violet 93
    Virginia E. 93
    W.W. 92
BREEDLOVE
    Emily Ann 48
    Glen Dale 48
    Glen Dewitt 48
    Judy Ann 48
    Patricia Elaine 48
    Richard Lamar 48
    Rivers Lee 48
    Robert Miles 53
    Stacey Nichole 54
    Thomas Watkins 48
    Timothy Paul 48
    Todd Leighton 48
    Tye Michael 48
BRENNAN
    Lena Mae 58
BRENTZ
    Andra Allen 18
    Brandy Ann 18
    Hendrix E. Jr. 18
BROUSSARD
    Alex P. 13
    Alma 14
    Charley C. 14
    Cornelia Adelle 117
    Donelly 14
    Elaine 14
    Howard 14
    J.P. 14
    Jesse 13
    Julia 13
    Lizzie Herron 14
    Louis Frank 116
    Louis Fulda 13
    Louis V. 13
    Louis Victor 117
    Louise 14
    Mattie B. 13
    Ola Olevia 13,116
    Orelia M. Sr. 14
    Orelia M. Jr. 14

BROUSSARD (cont.)
    Orelia M.III 14
    Pauline 13
    Shirley 14
BROOKS
    Janie Marie 52
    M.L. 67
    Nora Claire 67
BROWDER
    James Aubrey 48
    Tamara Michelle 48
    William Michael 48
BROWN
    Annie 13,109
    Annie May 60
    Denise 67
    Ida 13
    Jack Willie 13
    Jake Walker 65
    John 7
    Kitty 26-4
    Martha Jane Wiggins 17
    Minie 26-4
    Robert P. 26-4
    Ruby 119
    Stella 17
    Sonny 98
    Theodore 119
    William Cowser 38
BRUCE
    Aeolian 77,78
    Aeolian E. 77
    Aeolian N. 32
    Ann Scott 32
    Benjamin L. 32
    Charles N. 32,77
    Charles Ney 78
    John N. 75
    Mary Ann 75
    Olie May 78
    Robert J.W. 75
    Sarah Ellen 33
    Susannah Turner 75
    W.w. 76
    Walter J. 77
    William G. 75,77
    William J. 33
    Wm.(Billy) 32
    Wm.B. 80
    Wm.C. 32
    Wm.G. 39,40,79

BRUNDAGE
    Frank Leslie 69
    Leslie Elizabeth 69
    William Gregory 26
    William (Greg) Gregory 26
BRUNSON
    Martha Jane 115
BRYAN
    Ida 31
    Johnnie Ruth 116
    Johnny 116
    Mabel Jones 116
BRYANT
    Ida Isabel 95
    Lewis H. 92
    Pocahontas 112
BUCHANAN
    Adm.R. 23
BUICE
    Lawrence 112
    Linda Kay 112
    Ronnie 112
BUNCH
    Elizabeth 95
    Isaac 67
    Mary Elizabeth 67
BUNDDRICK
    Pearl 26-4
    W.V. 26-4
BURLEY
    Adeline 17
    Betty 39,40,79
    Calvin Scott 81
    Charlie 16,80
    Cyrus B. 16,80
    Cyrus Jr. 81
    Donald 17
    Etta Olivia 81
    Hansell 17
    Hansell Enos 36
    Joel 81
    Marion 80
    Ovid 80
    Walter 80
    Walter Ernest 36
    Walter S. 16
    William(Billy) 17
    William Franklin 36
    William Frank Sr. 17
    Willie 80

BUICE
    Lawrence 112
    Linda Kay 112
    Ronnie 112
BURNETT
    Donna Lynn 113
    Frances 40
BURRIS
    Jesse Stallings 78
BURROW
    Lois 110
BURT
    Peggy 41
BUSBY
    Deborah Denise
    Gary Dewayne 45
    James Gregory 46
    John Patirick 46
    Kenneth Laverne 45
    Kenneth Richard 45
    Margie Lannelle 45
    Matthew Spenser 46
    Sampson Mcune 45
    Thurmon Lejune 46
    Venable Carroll Moore 45
    Venable Carroll III Moore 45
BUSH
    Jeanette 56
    Joseph Larkin 114
    Linda Lou 114
    Margeratte Jeanette 56
BUTLER
    John W. 37
BYES
    Joseph 101
BYRD
    Carolyn Christine 118
    James 118

-C-

CAGE
    Geraldine 71
    Laura M. 93
CAGLE
    Elby George 51
    Patsy Jean 51
CAIN
    Carolyn 45
    Marcellous 45

131

CALHOUN
    Margie 13,116
    Jessie 116
    Robert Dabney 39
CALLICOATTE
    Elizabeth 39
    F.Monroe 40
    Fannie 40
    George W.Sr. 39
    Ida 40
    John 39
    Laura 40
    Martha(Mattie) 40
    Sally A. 79
    Sarah 39
CALPER
    John 76
    Mary Ann 76
CAMPBELL
    Addie Bruce 78
    Alva 38
    Annie 78
    Annie(Olie) 78
    Annie Rourke 78
    Emily Virginia 78
    C.C. 12
    Howard Preston 78
    Jonathan Cross Jr.MD 78
    Jonathan Cross Sr. 78
    Jonathon Cross III 78
    Jo Beth 116
    Kathleen Edna 78
    Lois 80
    Maj.Seab Washington 78
    Patrick Howard 78
    Seab W. 78
    Seaborn Woods 78
    William H. 101
CARACCI
    Carrie Marie 19
CARLILE
    Audrey Denise 110
    Jim C. 110
CARMAN
    Jeminia 26-3
    John 1,7,23,24,26-3
    Martha A. 82
    Samuel C. 82
    Sarah 7,81,82,85
CARMON
    E.G. 83
    J.W. 83

CARMON (cont.)
    Jane 83
    Jesse 83
    John 81,83
    John A.C. 83
    Martha 83
    Martha A. 83
    Ruth A. 83
    Samuel 83
    Samuel C. 83,84
    Samuel J.(S or I) 83
    Sarah 83
    Susannah 83
    William 83
    Wm. 83
CARPENTER
    David Dale 64
    Harry Scott 64
    Prentice Hollis 64
    Prentice Hollis(Bucky) 64
CARTER
    Amanda 104
    Ardis 95
    Bernice 96
    Casey 106
    Casey Chriswell 115
    Dorothy Loraine 96
    Estella 115
    Gertie 107
    Isaac 96
    Isaac Abraham 96
    Isaac W. 70
    John 96
    Judson 96
    Judy 70
    Julius M. 70
    Kate A. 98
    Lee 96
    Lewis 96
    Lewis Christopher 104,114
    Louis 106
    Lydia Rebecca 70
    Manda(Amanda) 106
    Mary 96,99,106,119
    Mary Amanda 70
    Mary Elizabeth 96
    Mittie Lee 70
    Mona Doris 96,99
    Mona Laverne 96
    Sarah Amanda 114
    Vernan 115

CARTER (cont)
    W.Vernan 96
    William James 96
    William Vernan 96,99
CARVER
    Virginia 98
CASEY
    Gwendolyn L. 41
CASH
    Eva 42
CATCHINGS
    Ann 100
CAVIN
    Helen Olivia 36
CETER
    Duncan C. 93
CHANDLER
    Glenn 61
    Nancy Suzanne 59
    Tom 59
    Willa Dean 59
CHILDRESS
    Amy Dawn 115
    Donna Avent 115
CHRISTIAN
    Carol 54
    Ned Eden 54
CLAPP
    Christinia Renee 110
    Connie Ray Sr. 110
    Donnie Ray Jr. 110
    Tillman 110
CLARK
    Clifford 13
    Harlin E. 46
    Janet Sue 46
    Leona 82
    William A. 82
CLARKE
    Claude 118
    Gloria 118
CLEARY
    Clyde 119
COBB
    Cliff 95
    J.S. 74,92,95
COCHRUM
    J.T. 115
    Mary Larlene 115
COLE
    Clarinda 116

COMER
    Benj. 35
    M. 35
    Nancy Adaline Lanehart 35
COMPLING
    Frances Lucy 52
CONWAY
    Louise 26
    Robert 26
COODY
    Buford 45
    Carolyn 45
    Valie 45
COOK
    Eleanor 88
    Merryman 88
COONER
    Deanna 110
COOPER
    Wm.A.K. 93
COPELAND
    Berlie 112
    H.E. 57
    Helen 112
    Herbert 112
    James 112
    James Westly 112
    Myrtle 112
    Nancy 50
    Oather 112
    Other(OL) Lee 112
    Ramona Wilson 57
    Sybil 112
    Willie 112
    Wm.Edward 112
CORK
    Samuel 7
CORLEY
    Edward Cary 94
CORTELYOU
    John 100
COVENTON
    Sharon D. 60
COX
    Lena Ellen 43
CRAINE
    Dorothy Laverne 96
    Roger 96

CRANE
Edith Idell 14
Edna Effie 14
James Crayton 13
Julie 29
Lynn 29
Olevia 16
Ollie 13
Samuel Pinkney Sr. 13
Sammy 29
CRAPP
Nellie 117
CRAWFORD
Carmen Gayle 58
Jack William(Trey) 58
Jack William II 58
Kimberlie Lea 59
Roger Kelley 59
Russell Travis 59
Samuel L. 82
CROSS
Albertina Cora 16
Ann 13
Annie Rebecca 16
Augusta Elizabeth 36
Bolliver 21
Charles Bruce 36
Elizabeth 85
Elizabeth Scott 4,13
Ella 17
Eugene Prentiss 17
Eula 36
Gladys Phoebe 17,36
Hansell Flynn 13,36
Hansell Pinkney 36
Harvey Estell 36
Harriet 16
Hattie Olie 78
Herman Obid 36
Howard 30
Howard Pugh 36
Hugh Ira 16
James Daniel 19
James Elliott 19
James Flynn 36
Jesse Boatner 17
John 7,10,82
John Allen 17
John Allen Jr. 17
John P. 4,11,12,17,23,25,
    27, 82,85

CROSS (cont)
John Pressbury 13,35
John Warren 16
Jonathan Peal 17
Jonathan Simms 17,78
Joseph Estell 36
Lena Mae 37
Levi 17
Levi Scott Jr. 17
Lilliam Beatrice 36
Lola Corinne 17
Lola Pauline 36
Marion Wilburn 16
Marion William Sr. 36
Marsaline Gillis 35
Martha 13
Mary Belle 36
Mary Ethel 16
Mary Jane 19
Mattie J. 17
Merle 30
Milton Scott 36
Myrtle 36
Nancy 16
Noah Webster 37
Olie 17
Omer 17
Ora 37
Pamela Joy 36
Phala 17
Pheebe 35
Ramoth 4,17
Ruth Valentine 19
Samuel 6,13,20,32
Shane 29
Sidney Bell 36
Susannah 21
Theresa Bell 36
Theresa Scott 20
Tinnie Marie 36
Trace 29
Ula Scott 36
Una Netterville 36
Vela 17
Velma Lorena 17
Warren Presberry 16
Warren Swingler Jr. 29
William A. 20
William Adkins 12,35,36
William Adkins Jr. 36
William Winston 36

CROSSBY
    Sarah 87
CROUCH
    Velma Smith 116
CRUMP
    Cleo 117
CRUZE
    Elizabeth 87
    William 87
CRYE
    Annie 51
    Mattie Odell 51
    Rich Turner 51
CUDMORE
    Walter Eugene 40
CUPP
    Charles Carlton 16
    Charles Stephens 16
    Janis Carol 16
    La Deanne 16
    Norma June 16
    Virginia Lynn 16
CURRY
    Stewart B. 8
CURTIN
    Grover C. 96
    Hattie J. 95
    J. W. 96
    Leona 96
CURTIS
    Barbara 45

-D-

DALE
    Geo W. 38
    Ruth Maude 29
DALEY
    Dan 99
DALY
    Dan 99
    Elaine 18
DAVENPORT
    Amy Renee 65
    Ricky Paul Jr. 64
    Ricky Paul Sr. 64
DAVIDSON
    Y. 90

DAVIS
    Addie 70,106
    Arglass William 71
    Bertice 94
    Bertice Elizabeth 70
    Brenda Kay 70
    Burgess Rosa 71
    Corrine 110
    Eddie 95
    Eddie Gerald 70
    Eddie Inman 70
    H.R. 94
    Henry 95
    Hugh 93
    Janet 70
    Jo Ann 70
    Kara Pauline 70
    Kimberly Danielle 71
    Larry 70
    Laurnce 70
    Lawrence William 70
    Lucinda 93
    Mamie 70
    Mary (Mamie) 106
    Mary 94
    Pete 70
    Ralph 71
    Richard Allen 70
    Susan Alyne 71
    Timthy 20
    Walter Ernest 71
    Walter Ernest Jr. 71
    William Henry 70,71
    William H. 106
DAWSON
    Lewis William 71
    Mary Jane 72,95
    Mary Virginia 36
    Nancy Sarah Ann 17
DAY
    Elizabeth (Becky) 64
DEACON
    Dylon Scott 48
    Millie 48
    Perry 48
    Sanford 48
DEAN
    Darious A 72
    Nellie Ruth 72

DELOACH
Lucrecia Jane 60
Vivi Ione (Intro)
Annis (Dooley) (Intro)
Wiley 39
DENTON
Bertha Covine 53
DES PORTES
Ulysse G. 15
DE VILLE
Claude D. 51
Donna 51
DICKEY
Brandt 108
Charles 108
Laura Ellen 108
Lydia Carol 108
DICKINSON
Henry C. 21
DILLARD
Dennis 56
Eubert 56
Justin Lee 56
DIXON
Robbie Lee 56
DOBBINS
Nancy 113
Sidney Byrom 113
DODGEN
Gary Kim 57
Tiffany Alana 57
William 57
DOLL
Caroline 99
DONALD
Miriam 67
DONNELLY
Amanda Beth 119
Larry William 119
Michael Van 119
Nancy 94,101,107
Sarah 102
William 101,107
DOSSETT
Clarence E. 68
Marilyn Sue 68
DOUGHERLY
Ann Mary 114
DOWNS
Nancy 92
DRAINE
Tony 3

DUNKLY
John 6
DUFON
Connie Ann 53
DUGGER
Benjamin Franklin 58
Lila (Loe) Nell 58
DUCAN
Gladys D. 72
Jewel Edna 67
Samuel Rainey 67
DUNLAP
W.M. 26-2,26-3
DYE
John F. 28
Sarah A. 28
DYKES
Nellie Leona 71
DYLAN
Scott 4

-E-

EDWARDS
Lillie Mae 57
Lois Gillman 49
Marjorie Lee 36
Ola Mae 14
EICKHOFF
Mr. 9
ELIOT
Lottie 111
ELLIS
David Paul 29
Hayden 78
Henry David 117
Lori Ann 29
Mamie Susan 117
Stephen Phillip 29
Thomas 89
ELLSBERRY
Nancy 101,107
Elmo 105
EMMONS
Britney Renee 53
Claudia Elizabeth 52
Robert Warren 53
Warren Robert 53
ENGLES
Captain 94

ENIS
    Carolyn Diane 65
ENLOW
    Althea Melba 18
    Benjamin Franklin 17
    Brenda Joyce 19
    Clinton Lemuel 18
    Darwin Shay Jr. 19
    Ethel Augusta 19
    Harley N. 19
    James C. 18
    James McCormick 18
    James Michael 19
    Jason McCormick 19
    Jesse McCormick 17
    Kermes Dawson 18
    Lillian Scott 18
    Malcolm D. 19
    Malcolm D. Jr. 19
    Malcolm D. Sr. 19
    Ramoth Cross 4
    Ramoth Rosalie 19
    Thelma 18
ESCHETE
    Jacqueline 47
    James Earl 47
EYLER
    Megan Rochelle 49
    Stephany 49
    Steve 49
EVERETT
    Amanda 105
    Brady Lynn 114
    Brady Odell 114
    Charlie 105,107
    Christi Leigh 114
    David Lynn 114
    Dr. T.J. 104,107
    Euall 105,107
    Kacie Lee 114
    Levi Bart 114
    Scott Brady 114
    Stephn Kyle 114
    Stephen Lee 114
    Thomas 105
    W.T. 104
    William 105
    William T. 104
    Wm.T. 107

-F-

FAIRFIELD
    Mary Jane 51
FARMER
    Roy Edward Sr. 63
FARRAR
    A.K. 114
    Ann M. 114
    Ann w. 104
    Ben (Speedy) F. 114
    Benj. F. 104
    Benjamin Franklin 114
    Cordell 115
    Cordell Wayne 115
    David Lee 114
    Derrll Gene 115
    Ella C. 104
    Henry E. 104,114
    Kevin Scott 115
    Mary Ella 114
    Mary H. 104,114
    Parnell 115
    Randall Wayne 115
    Shelia Annet 115
    Susan Diane 114
    T.H. 104
    Thornton H. 104,114
FAULKENBERRY
    Nettie 11,12
FAULKNER
    Barbara 70
FELTER
    Alice 103
    Benjamin A. 103
    Elison 103
    Elison A. 103,108
    June S. 103
    Nancy 103
    Prudy 108
    Rosa E. 103
    Susan 103
    W.A. 103,108
FERRELL
    Alice Merrena 17
FINK
    Frances A. 11
    Frances H. 10
FINKLEA
    Carol 57
    Colleen Beth 57
    Helen 57

FLAVIA
    ?   10
FLINN
    Daniel L. 31
FLOWERS
    John   63
    Mary Wilna   63
FLOYD
    Hattie Harper   62
    Hattie E.Harper   94
    Louisa   62
    W.T.   62
FOLK
    Ben P.   47
    Jack Hayne   47
FORD
    Elizabeth   101
    Ella C.   114
    Eugene   92,93
    Ferdinand C.   92
    Jeanne Mae   116
    O.T   93
    Oliver   92
    Oliver T.   93
    Robert   102
FORTENBERRY
    Rosalie   68
FOREMAN
    Daisy   12
    Felix   12
    Henry H.   24
    James   12
    Mary S.(Elizabeth N.) 12
    Maude   12
    Minerva   12
    Moody Atkins   12
FOSTER
    Nellie Dorris   50
FOX
    Ida Mable   53
FRANK
    Lawrence James   72
    Marie Louise   72
FRANKS
    Dr.   16
    Matilda Cummings   16
    Susan Rachel   16
FREEMAN
    Avis Mae   48
    Ferdanand Columbus   48
    Louine   51

FROST
    Jennie   3
FRYE
    Estelle   72
FURR
    Dennis   2

-G-

GALTRY
    Charlotte   101
GALLIEN
    Gay   51
    Joseph A.   51
GARDILL
    Ray   99
GARRET
    Delilah   87
GASSAWAY
    Christopher Chad   108
    Clyde Ray   108
    Hershal Ray   108
    Michael Timothy   108
    O.L.   108
GELSTON
    Dorothy   25
GEORGE
    Will   108
GERMAN
    Belinda Kay   60
    Christina Marie   60
    Morris Lee   60
GELSTON
    Dorothy   25
    John   25
    Nellie Elizabeth   25
GEMAR
    Alfred Lloyd   4
    Alfred Lloyd Jr.   4
    Anna Belle   4
    Carol Marie   4
    Craig Arnold   4
    Jerrod Scott   4
    John Alfred   4
    Johnny DeLand   4
    Sam Cotton   4
GETER
    Adrian   99
    Alec Boyd   96

138

GETER (cont)
    Alec Boyd Jr   96
    Alma   95
    Ann Marie   95
    Arglass P.   95
    Arglass William (Doc)98
    Barbara   98
    Bobby   100
    Carye   99
    Cecil   98
    Clifford Aubrey   98
    Clinton   98
    Curtis   99
    David Brandon   99
    Dennis Aubrey   98
    Dolly   12,97
    Donald   98
    Dulcie   98
    Dulcie R.   100
    Edna   98
    Edna Mae   95
    Elizabeth Jane (Bessie)   96
    Ella Susan   99
    Frances   93
    Freddie   98
    Gordon (Bud)   99
    Gordon Joseph   99
    Gordon Louis (Bubba)   99
    Hazel   97
    Henry Lee   96
    Henry Parham   96,98,99
    Henry Parham III   96,99
    Henry Pickney   97
    Henry Pickney Jr.   97
    Herman   95
    Jane   97
    Jerry Leo   95
    Jimmy V.   99
    John   99
    Judith Lynn   99
    Katherine   96
    Katherine (Tootsie)   99
    Kathleen   99
    Kay   99
    Kerry Ann   99
    Leo Arglass   95
    Leo Arglass Jr.   95
    Leroy   97
    Lev Magaruder   98
    Louis   98
    Luther   100
    Lydia Ann   98

GETER (cont)
    Mabel   97
    Marion   95
    Mary   97
    Mary Ella   96
    Mary Ellen   100
    Mary S.   93
    Nellie   93,114
    Phyllis Leisa(Sissie)   99
    Robert   96
    Rodney   99
    Ronald   98
    Roudolph Wayne   98
    Rufus   7,93
    Sarah   100
    Shirley   98
    Virginia   95
    Virginia(Jenny)E.   93
    Whitney   95
    Whitney Jr.   95
    William   93
    William Boyd   96
    William Herman   95
    William Lee   93
    William Parham   96,99
GIBBS
    Arthur Lee   109
    Christopher   109
    James Marvin   18
    James R.   109
    John Clinton   18
    John Louis   18
    Kristi Ann   18
    Mark R.   109
GIBSON
    James   102
    Jeminia   26-1
    Jeminia Jane   26-1,26-3
    Mary   26-2, 102
    Mary Ann Bruce   75
    Mary Ann Frances   26-3
    Mary Frances   26-1
    Minor   26-1,26-2,26-3
    Minor Jr.   26-1,26-2
    Rendon M.   75
    Sarah   26-3
    Sarah Ann Elizabeth   26-3
    Stephen   26-1
GILLIS
    Janie   112

GIRLINGHOUSE
    Ethel 28
    Ethel Debelle 18
    Lettie Banks 18
    Lloyd Ray 18
    Thelma Enlow 4,17
GLASSCOCK
    Benjamin Farris 16
    Fred Gillard 16
    Joseph Craig 16
    Julia Ferrell 14
    Linnie Elizabeth 16
    Thomas J. 12
    Thomas Jonathan Jr. 16
    Thomas Jonathan Sr. 16
    Walter Warren 16
    William Edward 16
GLASSL
    Amye Gail 50
    Ferdinand J. 50
GLENN
    Eileen 110
    Ethel 26-4
    Gail 110
    Thomas 110
GODDE
    Fannie Mae 2
GODWIN
    Ina 26-4
    Mr. 26-4
GOETSCH
    Barbara 41
GONSOULIN
    Joette Denise 95
    Joseph Charles 95
GONZALES
    Maggie 111
GOUSETT
    Raymond 72
GRAHAM
    Redina Nettles 98
GRAVES
    Adella 112
    Margart Adella 108
GREEN
    Bruce 116
    Gile 118
    Justin Terrell 116
    Mamie Inez 118
    Richard Kyle 116
    Shannan Lynn 116
    William (Billy) 116

GRIFFITH
    Minnie 44
GRUSENDORF
    Debbie 111
    Earl 111
GUERIN
    Henry Howard 119
    Lillian Ellen 119
    Martha Jeanette 119
GUNN
    Oma 115

-H-

HACKETT
    George 9
HAGOOD
    George B. 2
    J.A. 83
HAAG
    Charlie 95
HAGUE
    Edward Dallas 8
    Frances Ann 8
HAIGOOD
    Lewis 24
    Nancy 29
HALE
    Lorena Scott 37
    Scott 37
HALFORD
    Joe T. 111
    Louise 111
HALSTEAD
    Marjorie Eloise 72
HALL
    Julia Broussard 13
HALLORAN
    Martin B. Jr. 118
    Sarah Johnelle 118
HANNA
    James Sr. 2
HARKEY
    Margaret 62
    Minnie Louisa(Weeze) 62
    Swep 62
HARPER
    Arnold Joe 53
    Hattie Floyd 62

HARPER (cont)
    James 62
    Jessica Nichole 53
    Mack Johnny 53
    Mr. 81
    W.N. 62
HARVEY
    James R. 26-4
HARRINGTON
    Brandon Dewayne 52
    Raymond 52
    Rockey Dewayne 52
HARRIS
    Amy Elizabeth 110
    Jonathon Boyd 110
HARRISON
    Annie 83,84
    Augustus W. 83,84
    Benjamin 24
    Gussie Lee 84
    J.W. 25
HASLIP
    Babe 103
    Eveline 103
    John (N ? W) 103
    Martha 103
    Mattie 103
    Minerva 101
    Rebecca 101
    Rebecca 101
    S.W.(Samuel) 103
    William 111
HAWKINS
    Arleen Gail 109
    Claude Brown 109
    John 109
    Kate 100
    Klein 71
    Lillian 100
    Marion Klein 71
    William L. 100
HAYGOOD
    Lewis 23
HAZELIP
    Miss M. 102
HAZLIP
    Eveline 101
    John 101
    Lilla 102
    Martha 102

HAZLIP (cont)
    Mary 102
    Samuel 102
    Sarah W. 102
    Wm.F. 102
    Wm.J. 102
HAZELTINE
    Robert 56
HEMINGTON
    Sarah 31
HENSARLING
    Brian 99
    John David 99
    Robin 99
    Ron 99
HENNIGAN
    Geneva 28
HENNINGTON
    Sarah 27,28
HERMAN
    Donna Louise 55
    Harry 54
    Jerrey Melvin 54
    Jonathan Wade 55
    Lisa Michelle 54
    Melvin Jordon 54
    Shanna Marie 55
HERRON
    Alvin 115
    Laura Gayle 115
    Lucy 115
HICKS
    Mattie Ruth 49
    Leon 49
HICKMAN
    Chris 64
    Tiffany Leigh 64
HIGDON
    Betty 62
HILLMAN
    Jacqueline Nan 49
    William Ary(WA) Sr. 49
    William Ary II 49
    William Ary III 49
HINES
    Mary 48
    Mary Linda 48
    William 48
HODGE
    Amanda Dianne 46
    Amy Michelle 46

HODGE (cont)
    Charles Henry (CH) 45
    Charles Henry Jr. 46
    Charles Henry III 46
    Donald Roy 46
    Dorothy Ann 45
    Elizabeth Joan 46
    Gloria Nell 45
    Jacqueline Marie 47
    James Madison 45
    Janice Elaine 46
    Jessica Lynn 46
    Lacey Jo 47
    Patricia Louise 46
    Regan Mae 46
    Ronald Troy 47
HOGAN
    Eula Eva 48, 51
    Lenner 108
HOLLAND
    Ann 18
HOLLEY
    James Allen 50
    Judy Aline Sanford 50
HOLLY
    Chas.A. 81
    Nanthaniel B. 81
HOLLEMAN
    Edmund 88
HOLLIMAN
    Jesse 28
    Nancy 28
HOLLINSWORTH
    Allen A. 71
    Billie 71
HOLLOWAY
    Mary 71
HOLMES
    Alice 103
    Allyson Denise 111
    Amanda 102,104
    Amanda Elizabeth 107
    Amy Michele 111
    Angela Dawn 120
    Ashley Michelle 112
    Bobby Eugene 111
    Brittany Danielle 112
    Carolyn Marie 109
    Chester 105,108
    Christopher Neal 111

HOLMES (cont)
    Daniel Kyle 112
    Darold Suford (Pete) 108
    Darrell Glen 112
    Dave 106
    David Eugene 119,120
    Davis 105
    Davis R. 113
    Deborah Jean 119
    Don Allen 111
    Donna Kay 108
    Dub Allen 111
    Earl Everette 110
    Edwin (ED) Lee 111
    Elizabeth 103,104,116,120
    Emeline 103
    Eudoria 102
    Eugenia 102
    Everett L. 108
    Everette 105
    Fannie 108
    Francis (Frank) 104,119
    Frank J. 105
    Gary Eugene 111
    Gerald W. 110
    Gerald Wayne 110
    Gregory Louis 112
    Harold Buford (Jack) 108
    Hazel Mary 109
    Hellen 105
    Hellen Lou 112
    Holly Amanda 111
    James Andrew 111
    James Rodney 110
    Jefferey Spencer 111
    Jill Elaine 111
    Jimmy Don 111
    Jimmy Weldon 112
    Joe Allen 111
    Joe Ann 111
    Joel David 111
    Joshua Edward 120
    Karie 105
    Kathleen Ann 109
    Kimberly Kay 112
    Leon 105,120
    Lizzie 106
    Lonnie 108
    Lula 106
    Lula E. 105

HOLMES (cont)
Lynda Jean 109
Marcus Gonzales 111
Maria 103
Maria L. 103
Marilyn Jean 110
Mary 94,120
Mary M. 96,104,114
Mary Katherine 16,116
Mearl Alma 110
Menia 102
Michael Lee 111
Michael Wallace 111
Minerva 101
Moselle 119
Nancy 102,104
Nancy Gail 108
Nannie 105
Nannie M. 108
P.G. 102,104
Pamela Jane 110
Patricia Diane 119
Phillip Ulas 110
Phoenix (Phineas) G. 45,
    94,101,107
Prudy 104
R.S.C. 101
Rayborn (Ray) James 110
Rebecca 45,101
Robert Keith 111
Robert William 109
Rufus 103
Sandy Jo 112
Sarah 102
Sarah Rebecca 94,107
Sardinia S. 101
Sharon Rae 111
Theodore 102,103
Thomas 101
Thomas W. 101,107
Thos.W. 102
Timothy Michael 110
Tony Lay 109
Valerie Denise 110
Wayne (Red) Sterling 109
William 26-1,105,112,112
William Charles 111
William F. 108
William Robert (Bill) 119
Wm.A. 103
Wm.F. 102,104
Wm.H. 103

HOLT
Bama 30
HONEYCUTT
Artie Lee 111
HORNSBY
Wm.F. 102
HOWKINS
John Smallbrook II 69
John Smallbrook III 69
HOWLET
Ancridge 86
Seth 86
HOY
Isabel 26-2,26-3
HUGER
Alice Beekman 69
HUDE
Jack Jr. 98
Jack III 98
HUGLEY
Benjamin Matthew 60
Brea McCall 60
Bridget Michell 60
HUI
Na Bong 54
HURST
Jo Ann 111
HUTKA
Bernice Agnes 120
Brenda Kay 120
Johnnie Edward 120
HUTTON
FLORENCE MAE 117
HYERS
Beth Suzanne 60
Chester 60

-I-

IDOM
Calvin 118
Steve Calvin 118
ILENE
Walker 46
INGRAM
Benjamin Drew 99
Mike 99
INMAN
Brandon 71
Carmine Renee 71

IRBY
        Ethel   119
        J.D.   115

                    -J-

JACKSON
        Charley Dean   37
        John Sr.   52
        John Van Jr.   52
        Levi B.   37
        Mildren   24
        Patricia Diana   38
        Rebecca Ann   52
JAMAR
        Beorge Walter   57
JAMES
        Scott   31
        William   52
JAYNES
        Dalton Craig   116
        Dalton Henry   116
        L.Z.   109
        Jennings   48
JENSEN
        Brandon Gerald   71
        Herbert Haynes   70
        Herbert Nelson   Jr.   71
        Herbert Nelson Sr.   70
        Janet Lynn   71
        Joseph Allen (Jody) 71
        Kenneth Blakeny   71
        Nelson   52
        Nicole Teresa   71
        Robert Blakeney   71
        Robert Nelson   71
        Sarah   52
JERNIGAN
        Amanda Celia   22
        Frank 1,2,4,30,83
        Frank Blakely   22
        Levi Franklin   22
        Margaret Ann   22
        Mary Jones   22
        sara Francs   22
        William Blakely   22
        William Lewis   22

JETER
        Amy Conway   69
        Arglass   45
        Argless   92
        Argless W.   92
        Argulus   91
        Arguluss   87
        Cornelius   87,88
        Davis   91,100
        Edna Frances   68
        Eliazer   87,88
        Elizabeth 45,92,94,107
        Eugenia (Ugenia) 100
        Glenda Kay   68
        Hal   87,88
        Jane   92
        J.W.(Jimmy)   68
        James Powel   69
        Jill Scott   69
        John W.   91
        John William   86
        Joseph   87
        Jill Scott   69
        June   91
        Lucinda   94
        Margaret   86,88
        Martha Matilda   95
        Mary   92
        Nancy   91
        Sterling   91
        Sterling Rufus   93
        William   86,91
        William Watt   68
JETER/GETER
        Argless William   95
JEETER
        Argles   89,90
        Davis   90
        Elizabeth   90
        June   90
        Lucinda   90
        Mary   89
        Nancy   90
        Sterling   90
JOHNSON
        Belvia Olevia   65,95
        Connie Lynn   63
        David Adolphus   65
        David Bryan   119
        David Bryan Jr.   119
        Dolly   54

JOHNSON (cont)
    Harley Vivian   119
    Jennine Denise   73
    John   63
    Joseph Densel   73
    Joseph Densel Jr.   73
    Joseph Fountain   73
    Justin Scott   119
    Loena Ray   63
    Mary Jewel   56
    Rose Marie   52
    Theo Burrel   119
    Truman   52
    Vivian Ann   119
JONES
    Henry   6
    Katie Beatrice   78
    Larry   26-4
    Mabel   116
    Patsy Louise   108
    Sherry Lynn   60
    Thelma Callie Mae   110
    Thurman   108
    William   60
JUDD
    Ben Burris   55
    William Ben   55
JUNKIN
    Wanda Carol   48
    Willie Wesley   48

-K-

KAUGL
    Irene   52
KEENE
    Ben   38
KELLEBIEN
    J.E.   7
KELLER
    Carrie   36
KEMP
    Benjamin   56
    Paul Zane   56
KENNEDY
    Aline   62
    Charles Woodrow   62
    Karen Leigh   62
    Kathryn Lynn   62
    Woodrow   62

KETHLEY
    Viola   68
KILCREASE
    Jn   87
    Minor   88
    Peggy   88
KILSEY
    Sarah A.   95

KINCAID
    Col. William   7
KING
    Dacvid   62
    Donnie Donald W.   62
    Giles   62
    Swept   62
KLINE
    Letha   67
KNIERIM
    Jay Robert   30
KNOWLES
    Daniel L.   51
    Karen Ruth   51
KOCH
    Edward   70
    Elizabeth Leann   70
    Leslie Hope   70
    Ollie   27
KUGA
    Elizabeth Joan Rubic   56
    Paula Faith   56
KOHN
    Darrel G.   37

-L-

LABOON
    Annie   54
LAMBERT
    Charlotte   91
LAMBRIGHT
    Curtis   19
    Tiffany   19
LAND
    S.L.   95
LANDCASTER
    Mary Elizabeth   67
LANDON
    Hugh   9

LANEHART
Addie 78
A.W. 92
Jess I. 17
Jesse 13
Nan 14
LANIAS
Bertha 28
LARRY
Jones 26-4
LAVIN
Tom (MD) 99
LAWDEN
Rev.J.C. 62
Lawrence
Ernest 46
Kelly Louise 46
Linda Sue 46
LEAK
Dave 70
David Frederick 116
Fredrick Andrea 70
Fredrick Andrew 116
Lelia Ellen 70
Janet Lynn 116
Mary Ruth 116
LEAKE
Bernice 98
emilie 95
Irene 118
Theodore 99
Vera 63
LEE
Bryon 56
Erick Jason 56
Ronald James 56
Sean Michael 56
LEHMANN
Karl 12
LEHSTEN
David M. 109
John 109
Katherine Lynn 109
Lisa M. 109
Mathew Wayne 109
Lilla 102
LEITNER
C.E. 82
LERMA
Doris 58

LESTER
Jeff 40
Jeff Jr. 40
Laura 40
Willie 40
LEWIS
Claudia Jane 43
LINAM
Wanda Rae 41
LIPE
Claude Eugene 72
Lonnie Eugene 72
Sarah Leanna 72
Virginia(Virgie) 72
LIVINGSTON
Pauline 70
LOMONACO
Pauline 70
LONG
Susie Lee 48
LOPEZ
Arthur 58
Ashley Love 58
Marcus 58
LOVELACE
Doris 112
Hosie 112

-M-

MACALUSA
Rose Mary 19
Vincent 19
MADDOX
Michael 57
Lottie 109
MAGOUN
Althea 30
C.S. (MD) 80
Elliott 30
Sarah B. 80
MAHANEY
G.J. 99
Martha 99
Michael Geter 99
Rachel 99
MANGUM
Fannie 46

MANN
    Rhonda 46
MARR
    Bob 60
    Nancy 60
MARTELLO
    Rose 65
MARTIN
    Bethani Jo 109
    Debra Micheale 44
    Elizabeth 73
    Fannie Lou 53
    Gary Lynn 44
    Jerrell 109
    James David 44
    James Ellia 44
    James Ellis 44
    Jo Anne 44
    Joe Ellis 44
    John 87,88
    Shanda Nicole 109
    William Harold 109
MASHBURN
    Exie Ylene 53
MASON
    Ray 29
MASSEY
    J.A. 93
    Shirll 46
MATTHEW
    Ann 119
MATTHEWS
    Frances 62
MAXEY
    Delores Lee 41
MAXIE
    Melissa Jane 117
    Rebecca Lyn 117
    William Frank 117
    Wm.Warren Jr. 117
    Wm.Warren Sr. 117
MAXWELL
    Edna Smith 14
    Ruth 54
MAYERS
    Ann Marie 72
    Ronald Glen 72
McCALEB
    Sidney B. 114
McCALIP
    Fred Willard 68
    Gladys Merle 68

McCARSTLE
    Anna Catherine 65
    Donnis Rae 65
    Eugene Clayton 65
    Fred Clifton 65
    Fred Clifton Jr. 65
    Fred Clifton III 65
McGARTHY
    Margaret 109
McCARVER
    Lillie Mae 108
    Patsy Louise 108
McCASKELL
    Jana 70
    Kenneth 70
    Robert 70
McCLELLAND
    Dora 107
    Mettie 107
    Otis Ocar 107
McCOY
    Ella J. 67
McCURLEY
    Kathryn 117
McDANIEL
    John Wayne 66
    Lynsey anne 66
McDANIELS
    Gerold Howard 62
    John Deland 62
    Laura Harkey 63
    Mary Frances 63
McDONALD
    Arthur K. 28
    Lula 108
    Mary Lucille 36
McGee
    Jessie E. (Judge) 38
McGEEHEE
    Golda 63
McGOO
    Laverne 58
McGRAW
    Arthur 26-2
    Beverly Ann 63
    David Burnell 62
    Doris Melissa 63
    Emily 62
    Emily Scott 62
    Eunice 96,98
    Ginger Lee 63

MCGRAW (cont)
    Harry Burnell 62
    Harry H. 62
    Harry McDonald 62
    Janet Suzanne 62
    Linda Laverne 62
    Mary Margart 62
    Nancy Lynn 62
    Shirley La Verne 63
    Thomas (Dick) Earl 63
    Thomas Earl Jr. 63
    William Harry 62
McGREW
    Judy Byington Byrd 118
McGUFFIE
    George 28
    Orville 28
McINTOCH
    Jimmy 65
    Rolilyn Brown 65
McKEITHEN
    Lillian M. 72
McKEY
    Ruth 70
    Tessie 71
    Troy Lee 71
McKLEMURRY
    Alvester 98
McLEOD
    Tommy 118
McMILLEON
    Barry Gene 54
McMULLEN
    Janet 56
McNEELY
    James P. 92
    John Ford 92
    Mary ann 92
    Murdock D. 92
MERRELL
    Judy Case 18
MERRITT
    Delcy Ray 98
MERCK
    Elby Dale 29
    Elton 29
MEEKS
    Jennifer Paige 108
    Justin 108
    Randy 108
    Sarah 108

MELTON
    Maybelle 110
MERTZ
    Henry 99
    Henry Jr. 99
    Mellisa 99
    Tracy 99
MICKLER
    Lany 24
MIDDLEBROOK
    Debra Lee 62
    Vernan 62
MILES
    Edward James 53
    Elizabeth Denise 54
    Joyce Annette 54
    Kenneth Edward 53
    Kenneth Edward Jr. 53
    Nickie Michelle 54
    Peggy 109
    Shelia Ann 53
MILLS
    Samuel 87
MILLER
    Crystal Vernice 52
    Deloras 49
    Hattie 26-3
    Naomi 84
MILLING
    Andrew Y. 82
MITCHELL
    Effie 67
MITCHAEL
    Christie Lea 109
    Gayle Lynn 109
    Stan 109
MOAK
    Mary Katherine Geter 98
MOORE
    Alice Virginia 48
    Bertha 49
    Betty Jane 118
    Brenda Sue 53
    Denise 110
    Dyer 108
    Evelyn Diane Cain 45
    Henry Grady 53
    Jane 83
    Sadie Irene 108
    Tobie Delton 118

MORGAN
    Buster   110
    Clifton H.   46
    Elizabeth   91
    Ida Bernice   112
    James Stewart   46
    John Stacy   50
    Kasey Leigh   46
    Kelly Lynn   46
    Kimberly   50
    Lindsey Elizabeth   46
    Lulu   110
    Randy   110
    Reuben   110
    Ricky   110
    Stacy   50
    Staci Leigh   50
    Trobia Moreno   46
MORRIS
    Carolyn   42
    Chalmers   118
    Danny Lloyd   54
    Ellen   108
    Garvie Lloyd   54
    Julia   70
    Lloyd   54
    Nellie   118
    Sandy Dewayne   54
    Sonya Danielle   54
    Tiffany Nicole   54
    Zelda Mae   42
MORSE
    Charles Shubert   42
    Charles Shubert Jr.   42
MOSLEY
    Wm.Bryan Jr.   112
    Wm.Bryan Sr.   112
MOSELEY
    Geo.   88
    George   87
    Nancy   87
    Pricilla   88
    Salley   88
    Sally   88
MOTL
    Laura Clara   58
MULLINS
    Albert   53
    Bertha Louann   53
    Jackie Lynn   53
    James Albert   53
    Jimmy Ray   53

MUNDLE
    Samuel   26-2
MUNN
    Milton Lee Sr.   54
    Milton Lee Jr.   54
MURRAY
    Ginger   57
    Margaret ann Geter   98
MUSE
    Fannie   45
MUSHATO
    John   24
MONTOGOMERY
    Charles   1
    Hugh   1
MOON
    Clara   19

--N--

NELSON
    John   46
    Pamela   46
NETTERVILLE
    Geraldine   98
    Isaac Abraham   96
    Lydia   93
    Mary E.   94
    Martha Jane   96
    R.e.   94
NETTLES
    Bonnie   97
    Brenda   97
    Eva Mae   97
    Frances   97
    Glen Boyce   98
    J.B.   97
    Jennings   97
    Jim   98
    Keith   98
    Limda   97
    Malva   98
    Michelle Denise   98
    Robbin G.   98
    Rodgers   97

NEWMAN
Alexander 92
Cleo 108
Helen 108
Martha 92
Nancy 92
NELSON
David L. 36
NEUMAN
Gloria 53
NEWELLAND
Margaret Jane 69
NICHOLS
Stanton G. 58
NIX
Delia Mae 114
NIXON
Anna Francine 30
Howard Doyle 30
NORCROSS
Aubrey 49
Charles 49
Pam 49
Stella 49

NORTHCOTT
Bailey Preston 37
Rachel Scott 37
NOSSER
John M. 67
Mary Louise 67
NOVACIC
Marsha Ann 113

-O-

O'CONNOR
Mary E. 109
Michael J. 109
O'DELL
Mary 120
OGDEN
Littie 97
OLIN
Dorothy 67
Gary Sherman 67
James Andrew 67
Lawrence 67

OLIVEAUX
Lottie Lee 53
ORGAN
Joyce Winfred 43
OWENS
Capt. 50
Elsie 50
Jesse 50
Johnnie Martha 55
Saml 50

-P-

PADGETT
Carolyn Ann Jamar 57
Christopher Blake 57
Lawrence Joe 57
Shelli Lynn 57
PAGE
Billy Gene Sr. 53
Melissa Jean 53
Pamela 46
PARHAM
Catherine Audrey 95
Peterson G. 95
PARISH
Fred 51
Geraldine 51
Pamela Eileen 51
PARK
Emma Henrietta 21
PARKER
Brady 60
Brian 60
Delbert Wayne 58
Richard 60
Teresa Paulette 30
PARKINS
Eva Maude 116
John David 116
John Henry Sr. 116
Raymond Daniel 116
Raymond J. 116
PARNELL
Eliza 82
PARSON
Marie 110
Mary Alice 112

PARTRIDGE
    Martha Susan   117
PARROTT
    Celia Miriam   22
PAUL
    Brenda Kay   29
    Carl Ussery   29
    Carla Ruth   29
    James Kenneth   54
    Jerry Wayne   54
PEACOCK
    Margaret   60
PEARSON
    Alex   72
    Alex Vincent   72
    Jessica Lynn   72
    Walter Vincent   72
PEEPLES
    Archie Eugene   56
    Cynthia Dawn   56
    Donnie   56
    Katherine Tammatha   56
    Patricia Ann   56
    Richard O'Neal   56
    Robert Eugene   56
    Samuel Lee   56
    Teri Lynn   56
    Virenia (Nia) Gwendolyn   56
PERRYMAN
    Truit   117
    PETTY
    Sallye   94
PETERS
    Goldena Mae   41
PETTY
    Clyde Ray   43
    Raymond Edward Jr.   43
PHIPPS
    Henry   89,91
    James   89
    Phoebe   91
    Polly (Mary)   45, 89,91
PICKNEY
    Henry   97
PIEPER
    Edmond   111
    Joyce Allyne   111
PLAYER
    Joshua   6

PLYMELL
    Beth   115
    Paula Kay   115
PORTER
    Ronald Lee   56
POER
    Lavinea Scott   79
    Robert   44
PORCHER
    Isaac   2
POWELL
    Carrie   16
    Clara Bell   16
    James Douglas   16
    Jeannie   16
    Jonathan Almeryne   16
    Olivia   16
    Samuel Davis   16
    Scott   16
    Truman   91
    Wade Hampton   16
    Wiley S.   16
PRESCOTT
    Bradley Eugene   40
    Fredrick Stephen MD   40
    Valerie Elizabeth   40
PRICE
    Beatrice   57
    Vera Jacquelyn   57
    Vernon   57
PRINCE
    Ambolean   78
PROCTER
    Samuel   5
PRYOR
    Curtis Eugene   42

                    -Q-

QUIGLEY
    Robert   24,26,26-2

                    -R-

RABB
    Mary   101

RAINFORD
    Jim   19
RAMSEY
    Mary Lois   115
    Raymond   115
RAWARTH
    G.A.   90
    George   90
    Helen   90
    Laura   90
RAWLS
    Hattie Dell   48
REECE
    Edith   96

REED
    Alvin Cecil   118
    Catherine Irene   118
    Kelley Michelle   47
    Kevin Shawn   47
    Khristine Dawn   47
    Khristine Dawn   47
    Monroe F.Jr.   47
    Monroe F. Sr.   47
REEVES
    Rachel Scott McGee   20
    W.D.   38
REYNOLDS
    Mittie   1
RHODEN
    Elizabeth   49
    Everette   49
    Willie Mae   49
    Richard   49
RICE
    Sarah Barbara   118
RICH
    Anita Joyce   52
    Raymmond Laroy   52
RICHARDS
    Jessie   115
RICHARDSON
    Artelissa   24,25
    Crystal Arleen   16
    Harriett Jeminia   25
    James E.   25
    Jesse C.   25
    John   25
    Margaret E.   25
    Rebecca   25
    Wm.   25

RICHEY
    John   2
RICHISON
    Artelissa   23
RILEY
    Brenda Kay   119
    Johnny J.   119
RIMER
    Margaret Matilda   26-3
ROBERSON
    Scott Harrington   16
    Vearl Virginia   16
    Wiley Clinton   16
ROBERTS
    Erline   98
    Geoffrey Hayden   72
    Hale E.   72
    Hale Edward Jr.   72
    Hamilton Scott   72
    N.C.   83
    Nathan   82
    Paula Frances   72
ROBERTSON
    Creighton   84
    Edward   84
    Evelyn   99
    Henry   25
    John   1,2,3
    Leroy   84
    Ruth   29
ROBINSON
    Debra La Shey   63
    James M.   24
    John W.   21
    Leroy   63
    Ronald Dowrin   63
    Sallie   21
RODGERS
    Jimmy   96
    Lester   55
    Mildred   97
    Oleta   68
ROGERS
    Jake Leroy   19
RODDY
    Mary Ann   103,108
ROLLINS
    Donna Sue   48
    John Elbert   48
    William Elbert   48
    William Elbert Sr.   48

152

SCOTT (cont)

Deborah Ann 60
Deborah Lynn 49
Donald Wayne 67
Doris 62
Dorris 106
Drew Eric 60
Edna Earl 54
Edward 60
Edward Ivy 51
Edward Timothy 51
Eliza 26,26-2,102
Elizabeth 1,5,6,13,31,62
       104
Ella 37
Ella Mae 68
Ellen 37
Ellen Marie 43
Emily Louise 43
Emma Elizabeth 43
Ethel 44
Ethel Alberta 44
Fay Louis 41
Frances Ellenor 43
Francis Marion 40
Francis Marion Jr. 79,80
Francis Marion Sr. 79
Garry Lynn 41
George 1,2,3,6,7,23,26,
       26-1,26-2,26-3,
       26-4,85
George E. 26-1
George Elisha 26-3,26-4
George Elisha Jr. 26-3
George W. 5,10,11,12,25
       27,31
George Wendell 50
Gladys 45,106
Grantham Leonidas 65
Gregory Keith 60
Gwendlyn Irene 60
H.W. 102
Harry 94,106
Harry Lemel Jr. 67
Hattie Edith 65
Hattie Harper Floyd 106
Hazel 79
Helen 16,45
Helen Ann 80
Helen Vivian 48

SCOTT (cont)

Henry (Harry) 104
Henry 5,6,7,27,28,31,
       85,92.
Henry H. 104
Henry W. 39,45,107
Henry William 32,41,45,79
       ,82,94
Herbert E. 106
Herbert Ivy 51
Howard 105,106
Howard Glenn 68
Howard William 67,95
I.O. 41
Ida Bryan 74
Ida Isabel 91
Isabel Hoy 26-4
Iola 43
Irvin Kent 41
Irvin Marion 40
James 5,23,28,85
James D. 26-2
James Daniel 26-3
James Edwin 42
Jamie Louise 26-4
Jemina 26-2,23,
Jeminia 23,26-1,26-2,26-3
Jennifer Renee 51
Jessica Ann 51
Jo Tiffany 51
John 7,23,32,48,51,106
John F. 11,12,25
John Howard Sr. 49
John Howard Jr. 49
John Leroy 67
John Minor 2
John Sr. 2
John W. 5,6,7,10,11,23,
       24,25,28
John Y. 26-2,26-3
Josiah 35
Juanita Elizabeth 67
Karen Yvonne 72
Kelly Denise 60
Larry 26-4
Larry Davis 65
Lawrence Walter 72
Lavinia 35
Lavinia Elizabeth 44
Lesia Annette 23

SCOTT (cont)

Levisa 28
Lillian Bessie 44
Linda Ann 72
Lizzie 106
Lorrie Olivia 65
Lorena 37
Lydia 26-2,26-3
Lydia Marie 60
Mabel Clair 44
Mabel Elizabeth 38
Marion 26-3
Marion Eugene 26-4
Marion Blanche 49
Mary C. 26-2
Minnie 26-3
M.E.(Major) 104
Major 5,6,8,24,31,105
Major A. 11,79,
Major E. 74,91,95
Major James 95
Marilyn Sue 72
Major (Minor) 23
Margaret 1
Martha Ann 81
Mary (Mamie) 70,95,105
Mary Ann 23
Marion Blanche 49
Melinda Gail 52
Michael Ray 81
Miriam Claire 67
Michael Wayne 50
Monroe 24
Mittie 56,106
Nancy 26,26-2,26-3
Nancy B. 28
Naomi 38
Nellie 80
Nellie Magoun 81
Nolan 106
Nolan Arglass 67
Opal Pauline 49
Pamela Ruth 43
Parylee 37
Patricia Gail 72
Patricia Joyce 68
Patricia Nell 52
Pricilla 37
Rachel Kate 38
Rainey Nosser 67
Raymon DeWayne 51

SCOTT (cont)

Raymond Michael 51
Rev.Harry Lemel 67
Ronnie Edward 81
Ronnie Edward Jr. 81
Rosa Lee 67
Roy Thomas 42
Sallie 104,106
Sallie Vera 63
Sam 1,106
Samuel 4,5,94
Samuel B. 39,75,77,79
Samuel C. 40
Samuel Major 26-2
Sammie Pettit Sr. 60
Sammie Pettit Jr. 60
Sarah 31,42.26-2,26-3
Sarah 31,42
Sarah Ann 28,51
Sarah Estelle 43
Sarah R. 105
Sherry Mae 73
Shirley Ann 53
Steve 26-4
Steven Baker 41
Steven Ray 41
Sue Ann 42
Susan Lynne 66
Susan Rachel 42
Susannah 39,26-2,26-3
Tamekka Deshawn 60
Ted 26-4
Terri Faith 41
Thelmarie 31
Theresa 35
Thomas DeWayne 64
Thomas Francis 32,39,40,79
Thomas J. 64,94,102,
Thomas Jr. 44
Thomas Lee 42
Thursa Mae 67
Tom 63,106
Tonya Elizabeth 40
Valerie Diane 65
Virginia Arleen 42
Virginia Lois 53
Viva 106
Walter 105,106
Walter T. 95

SCOTT (cont)
    Walter Thompson Jr. 72
    Walter Thompson Sr. 72
    Wendy Ann 51
    Whitney Dee 64
    William 1,5,26-1,18,35,
        40,44,78, 94
    William Sr.28,
    William Jr. 27,31
    William Anthony 60
    William Derwood 43
    William E. 26-2,26-3
    William Keith 66
    William Paul Sr. 50
    William Paul Jr. 50
    Willie Ray 65
    Winfield 42
    Winfield Hunter 40
    Wm A. 35
    Zacharias W. 37
SCRUGGS
    A.S. 83
    Thomas 81
SEAL
    Jans W. 24
SELF
    Clyde Roy 49
    Erica Lynn 49
    Jarred Michael 49
    Jennefer Elizabeth 49
    John Tilden 49
    Rita Kay 50
    (T.C.)Pete 49
    Jacob Timothy 50
SESSER
    Andrew Brandon 68
    David Leo 68
    Henry Marten 67
    Jewel Leo 67
    Jim Nolan 68
    Jonathan Michael 68
    Kathryn Clare 68
    Larry Dale 68
    Letha Elizabeth 68
    Lori Jennine 68
    Madeleine Nicole 68
    Nolan Terry 68
    Royce scott 68
    Ryan Scott 68
    William Brent 68

SESSIONS
    J.K. 92
    Jas.M. 92
SEVAW
    Jenny 30
SEVIER
    Lucy 47
SHANE
    Marion 80
    Ovid 80
    Ruth 80
    Willie 80
SHARP
    Chrystal Faith 41
    Michael K. 41
SHEDD
    Annie Lee 4
SHEPPARD
    Lisa 111
SHIELDS
    Gabriel B. 11
SHILLINGS
    Bonnie 108
SHOWLESB
    Mary Ella 17
SIGMON
    Ethel 63
    Ethel Jacquline 63
    Jacks(Bo) 63
SIMS
    Capt. John 6
SIMMONS
    Charlene 71
    Charles 71
    Clyde F. 64
    Craig Randall 64
    Deborah Kathleen 64
    Elizabeth Arleen 64
    Harold Champion 58
    Jennifer Ann 99
    Jonathan Gordon 99
    Percy Edwin 64
    Percy Randall 64
    R.E. III 99
    R.E. Roddy 99
    Teresa 71
    Terry Lynn 63
    Vra May 58
SKAGGS
    Shirley Ann 60

STEELE
    Annie Elizabeth 37
    Annie McClure 37
    Bessie Belle 27
    Beulah 38
    Dottie 100
    Frederick P. 37
    Joseph 37
    Joseph Robert 37
    Lorena 38
    Lorena Scott 20
    Lorena Rawlings 38
    Naomi 37
    Phoebe 38
    Phoebe Belle 13
    Wm.Gaston 38
STOKES
    Brandi Nicole 49
    Buddy 49
    Melissa Michelle 49
STORK
    Daniel Ray 52
    Lester Alexander 52
    Steve Lester 52
STORY
    ? 96
STOUT
    Margarita May 62
    Swepson Fleetwood 62
STROTHER
    John 90
STUEG
    Louise 117
STURGEON
    Alonzo 105
    Alonzo Hackett 117
    Alonzo Holmes 118
    Alonzo Holmes Jr. 118
    Bess 116
    Blanche 27,70,104,105,
    Blanche Estelle 116
    Catherine Yvette 118
    Cecil Reed 118
    Charles Ellis 118
    Charles Ellis Jr. 118
    Ceddie Holmes 117
    Elizabeth 104,113
    Elizabeth Holmes 70
    Elmo 105
    Eugene 33,104,105
    Eugene T. 13

STURGEON (cont)
    Eugene Thomas 116
    Frank Stewart 117
    Frank Stewart Jr. 117
    Grace 117
    Hartsel 104
    Hartsell 105
    Hartsell Laura 117
    Hiram 116
    Hiram Evans 118
    Horace 104,105
    Horace B. 117
    India Anne 117
    James Anthony 118
    James Ira 116
    John 104
    John M. 13
    John (S) 105
    John Alvy 117
    John Henry 117
    John Millard 116
    John Millard III 116
    John Millard Jr. 116
    John Robert 118
    John T. 116
    Kate 105,117
    Linda 13,
    Linda June 116
    Lizzie 105
    Louis Virgil 118
    Louis Virgil Jr. 118
    Margie Calhoun 34
    Mary 105
    Mary Nell 117
    Marie Eugene 118
    Millard 34
    Patrick Scott 118
    Starla Elizabeth 118
    Susan Elise 118
    Valencia Lynn 118
STYLES
    Agnes Effie Wilson 58
    Jason 58
    John Henry Jr. 58
    John Henry Sr. 58
    Sammie Lorie 58
    Samuel Washington 58
    Tammy Lauri 58
    Toni Laura 58
SUGGS
    Miriam Elizabeth 112
    Troy 112

SUMMERS
    Beuna Vista 56
SUMRALL
    Gerry Paul 56
    Mary Elizabeth 68
    Paul L. 68
    Pauline 68
SWARTZ
    Fredrick 37
    John 37
    Joseph Robert Steele 37
    Shannon Lee 37
SWATTS
    Elizabeth 11
    Harry 24
    Henry 11,23,25
    Henry W. 11,25
    John 25
    Milletant 23
SWAYZE
    Caleb 91,92
    Caleb C. 95
    James 91
    Mary Jane 91,92
    Narcissa 91
SWINDELL
    Chapman Lee 59
    Corey William 59
    Michael Joe 59
    Nichalos Lee 59
SWINDLE
    Ella 117
SWINNY
    Mrs. Wm.Barton 98
SYLVESTER
    Elzy 64
SYMANK
    Ervin E. 111
    Marla Kay 111

-T-

TAYLOR
    Ida Lou 57
    Janie 57
    Johanna 65
    Margt. 25
    Mary 23

TAYLOR (cont)
    Rena 80
    Richard Leigh 57
    Sam 14
    Timothy Leigh 14
    Zachary (General) 40
TAYLORS
    Col.Thomas 3
TAZEWELL
    Rachel 107
TEMPLE
    Herman 98
TERRY
    Walter S. 110
THETFORD
    Felizx Nelson 115
    Robert Nelson 115
    Sandra Ann 115
THOMAS
    Albert 110
    Alice A. 37
    Barbara Mae 111
    Mary 109
    Rebecca J. 110
THOMPSON
    Dolly Dewana 19
    John B. 23,24
    John Wayne 19
    Richard 19
THORNBURG
    Edward C. 44
    Mary 44
    Ramon B. 44
THORNHILL
    Donald Malvin 54
    Tony Lee 54
THORNTON
    Sadie Mae 54
TIMMS
    Charles 21
    Samuel 21
    Sarah Young 21
TINNIE
    Mary 36
TOMSON
    Nancy Lou 52
    Nettie 52
    Ralph 52
TOWER
    Arvel Grace 47
    Nettie 52
    Ralph 52

TRACY
    Dorothy 63
TRAPP
    Edgar 26-4
TREVILLION
    Dorsey 96
TRISLER
    "Cutie" 30
    Alex 30
    Betty Ruth 29
    Brooks 29
    Cade 29
    Carrie 28
    Cosby 30
    Cynthia Ann 30
    Faith Lea 30
    Hardy 28
    Harvey 28
    Henry 28
    Henry Clay 28
    James 30
    James Scott Jr. 28
    Jenny 28
    Joe 28
    Leona 30
    Lorena 30
    Marvyn Maude 29
    Mary 3
    Mary Virginia 30
    Matilda Scott 28
    Millard 30
    Myra 30
    Noah 30
    Phoebe Bell 30
    Roger 29
    Roswell 28
    Sammy Millard 29
    Samuel Albert 29
    Samuel Albert Jr. 29
    Tom 28
    Walter 38
TROHA
    John 48
TUMEY
    Winnie Alta 71
TURNBULL
    Jennifer Hope 120
    John Elliot 119
    Timothy Land 120

TURNER
    Amanda 113
    Amy 113
    Boyd 113
    Henry Clinton 75
    James Madison 75
    Juanita 113
    Lanell Dale 109
    Rhonda 113
    Ronnie 113

                -V-

VANDERVEER
    Donald 43
VANDREAX
    David 6
VASQUEZ
    Phyllis 99
VAUGHN
    Cradock 86
    Partheny 86
    Vivian 43
VELTER
    Thomas 98
VENTRESS
    James Alexander 100
    L.T. 100
VERALIN
    Angie 117
    Ronnie 117
    Ronnie David 117
VINCINELLI
    Delchesia Louisa 72
VINES
    Mildred 98

                -W-

WADE
    Amber Nicole 53
    David 44
    Helen Diane 44
    Ivan William 53
    Jeffery Alan 53
    Jeffery Alan Jr. 53

WAGENSCHEIN
     Kimberly 112
     Paul 112
WAHL
     Else (Vogel) 18
     Ursula 18
WAHLSTROM
     Ed 47
     Wanda Lee 47
WALDEN
     Cora Bell 44
WALKER
     Alfred 63
     Bridget Lynette 63
     Glenda 111
     James Alford 63
     Lisa Michael 63
     Mary Virginia 28
     Sarah 111
     Mrs. B.C. 92
     Margaret Annell 111
WALSH
     T.A. 93
     T.W. 93
WALLING 54
     James Brandon 54
     James Kendall 54
     Mabel 54
     Oliver 54
WARREN
     Florence Dormae 113
WEISS
     Billy Gene 113
     Jamie R. 113
WELCH
     George 23,25
     Jenny 28
     Margaret E. 25
     Mary 25
     Polly 23,25
WEST
     Beryl Keith 114
     Cindy Lee 114
WESTBERRY
     Ernestine 98
WESTCOTT
     Bonnie Michele 67
     Eddie Dwight 67
     John B. 67
     Mary Bonnie 67
     Scott Dwight 67

WESTERFELD
     Ray 111
     Stacie Renee 111
     Terry 111
WESTERFIELD
     Billie Carl 109
     Carl 109
     Ginger Kay 109
     Lane 109
     Rosemary Pollard 109
WHEAT
     Herman 44
     Jesse Marion 44
     Patricia Ann 44
WHEELER
     Doris 118
WHITAKER
     Capt.Willis 3
     Lacy Ann 96
     Mona Lynn 96
     Warren Wood 96
WHITE
     Alice Joycelyn 65
     Dorothy Nell 117
     Jones 65
     Louis C. 18
     Patsy 92
     Pauline Broussard 13
     Virginia Elizabeth 70
WHITEHORSE
     Indian Chief(Landcaster) 67
WHITLINGTON
     Marguerite 73
WHITTLEY
     Niddie Mae 63
WIESE
     Ernest Ray 57
     Fredrick Sigmund 57
     Megan Noel 57
     Sidney Ray 157
     Summer Kathleen 57
     Vivian Louise 57
WILBURN
     Lena Mildren 56
WILEY
     Charlotte Smith 14
WILHELM
     Virginia 110
WILKINSON
     Francis Elizabeth 68
     Jim 68
     Mary Jane 72

WILLIAMS
    Augustine 3
    Debbie
    Dollie Pearl 110
    Frank Fuller 110
    Gwindle 112
    John 29
    John W. 29
    Kathleen 71
    Lynda Ann 29
    Renee 18
    Roger 18
WILLIAMSON
    Barry Glenn 71
    Barry Glenn Jr. 71
    Doyle 71
WILLINGHAM
    Alisa Kathleen 115
    Alvin 115
    Ann Larlene 115
    J.D. 115
    Jeffery 115
    Kathleen 115
    William 2
    Wm. 3
WILLIS
    H.R. 43
WILSON
    Ada Mabel 38
    Agnes Effie 58
    Amber Renee 57
    Carolyn Smith 57
    Catherine Elizabeth Dale 38
    Christopher Allen 64
    Edna Marie 58
    Ernest Rudolph 73
    Ellie Nora 116
    Frances Vandilla 36
    Joseph Rudolph 73
    Katherine Louise 56
    Luther Rudolph 73
    Lydia Catherine 36
    Mittie Scott 45
    Monica 57
    O'Levia Neil 57
    Ramona 57
    Robert Samuel 57
    Roger Bernard 58
    Roger O'Neal 56
    Sandy 64

WILSON (cont)
    Scott Allen 58
    Sherry Theresa 58
    Thomas Jefferson 38
    Virgie Lee 57
WINBURN
    Demcy 2
WINSTEAD
    Mildred 54
WINN
    Minor 3
WIRT
    Debra Ann 51
    Morgan Edward 51
WIRICK
    Zacheriah 7
WISE
    Katie 65
WIXCON
    Nina Mae 67
WOLF
    David 37
WOLFE
    Junie 47
WON
    Hong Jong 54
WOOD
    Clyde 100
    David H., 102
    Douglas 102,103
    Dorothy Gayle 100
    Nancy 101
    Tom 100
    Tom Jr. 100
    Wiley 101
    Wiley M. 102
    William N. 102
WOODARD
    Jos. 6
WOODWARD
    Elizabeth 2
    Elizabeth Simpton 2
    Thomas 2
WOOLEY
    Derek 30
    Robert 30
WRIGHT
    Charlie Buck 60
    Christina 70
    Cliff 70
    Evan Miller 117

WRIGHT (cont)
    Howard 117
    John 70
    Langston Preston 38
    Mark 70
    Pearl 60
    Raymond Lawrence 38
    Robert Jeffery 49
    Virgil Golson 117
    William Benjamin 49
YOUNG
    Ann Tweed 21
    Archie Andrew 21
    Archie Mathews 21
    Evelyn 50
    John Andrew 21
    John Leslie Dixon 21
    Joseph Stanton 21
    Lillie Estell 21
    Margaret Presbury 21
    Mark 50
    Rose Alice 22
    Sara Evelyn 22

www.ingramcontent.com/pod-product-compliance
Lightning Source LLC
Chambersburg PA
CBHW080411270326
41929CB00018B/2977